HIT THE BEACH

HIT THE BEACH

THE DRAMA OF AMPHIBIOUS WARFARE

SIMON FOSTER

CASSELL

First published by Arms and Armour Press 1995
This Cassell Military Classics edition 1998

Reprinted 1998

Cassell plc
Wellington House, 125 Strand, London WC2R 0BB

British Library Cataloguing-in-Publication Data: a catalogue
record for this book is available from the British Library

ISBN 0-304-35056-7

Edited and designed by Roger Chesneau DAG Publications Ltd

Cartography by Peter Burton

Printed and bound in Great Britain by
Cox & Wyman Ltd., Reading, Berks.

Contents

MAPS

ABBREVIATIONS

AEW	Airborne Early Warning (radar)
AOA	Amphibious Operating Area; later renamed Transport Area (TA)
ARA	*Armada Republica Argentina* (Argentine Navy)
BMA	Base Maintenance Area
CAP	Combat air patrol
CBG	Carrier Battle Group
CBU	Cluster Bomb Unit
CLFFI	Commander Land Forces Falkland Islands
FAA	1. Fleet Air Arm; 2. *Fuerza Aérea Argentina* (Argentine Air Force)
LPD	Landing Platform Dock (designation of the two British assault ships *Fearless* and *Intrepid*)
LSL	Landing Ship Logistics
MEZ	Maritime Exclusion Zone
SSN	Nuclear powered fleet submarine
STUFT	Ships taken up from trade
TEZ	Total Exclusion Zone
TRALA	Tug Repair and Logistic Area

Introduction

THIS book looks at the conduct of four amphibious campaigns: the capture of Quebec in 1759, the Dardanelles offensive of 1915–16, the American landings at Inchon in 1950 and the Falkland Islands war of 1982.

An amphibious assault is recognized as one of the most dangerous of military operations—a recognition which goes back as far as the days of the Ancient Greeks. Today amphibious warfare is more important than ever. Now that the stand-off between the two super-powers is over, the world seems a much more dangerous place, with nasty, small-scale wars fought on ethnic or religious grounds raging all over the world. 'Amphibiosity', as one practitioner terms it, gives a country the means to intervene to restore the situation, to win back territory or to rescue dependent civilians or hostages; in peacetime 'amphibiosity' gives that country the capacity to offer disaster relief.

To be able to land and deploy forces on an enemy shore represents a formidable undertaking and exercise of power. Yet amphibious forces are extremely benign. During a crisis they can be kept out of sight and require no right of passage to reach their operating area. With modern replenishment techniques, they can be kept at sea for months, projecting power in a low-key fashion. If tension increases they can be moved nearer the shore, and if the situation cools they can be withdrawn again. With the end of the Cold War 'amphibiosity' has become more important than ever and this has been recognized by most of the world's larger navies—though whether budget allocations will reflect this is a different matter.

Of the four campaigns discussed in this book, three were successful and one a failure. The lessons of the campaigns are of considerable relevance today. The reasons for Wolfe's success on the Plains of Abraham are similar to those which gave victory to MacArthur at Inchon and to Thompson at San Carlos; the opposite of these reasons explains why Hamilton failed so disastrously at the Dardanelles. He who forgets history is condemned to repeat it.

The author is grateful to the many people who helped in the research and writing of this book. In particular he is grateful to the staff of the Department of Documents at the Imperial War Museum in London and to those who served in the Falklands who were gracious enough to answer his enquiries. Many did not wish to be named, so these wishes have been respected.

Simon Foster

CHAPTER ONE

The Golden Age

*A Military Naval Littoral War, when wisely prepared and discreetly
conducted, is a terrible Sort of War. Happy for that People who are
Sovereigns of the Sea to put it into execution! For it comes like
thunder and lightning to some unprepared part of the
world.*—Thomas More Molyneux, 1759

AMPHIBIOUS operations are often thought of as an aspect of warfare
developed during the twentieth century. Yet during the Seven Years'
War and the American War of Independence in the eighteenth century, the
British Army and the Royal Navy mastered the techniques of amphibious
warfare and thus were able to exploit the military advantages of naval
power. During the Seven Years' War (1756–63) the operations conducted
against Louisburg, Quebec, Guadeloupe, Belle Isle, Martinique and Ha-
vana rested on Britain's ability to move men and equipment by sea and land
them where required; similarly, during the American War of Independence
(1776–83) the invasions of New York, Rhode Island, South Carolina, Saint
Lucia and Pennsylvania would have been impossible but for the Royal
Navy's knowledge of the techniques of amphibious warfare.

This expertise was developed as a result of Britain's having a small army
which was conducting operations over a large area through which movement across country was both time-consuming and difficult. It would have
echoes nearly two hundred years later: if beachmasters who landed at
Quebec in 1759 (though they were not then known as such) could have
exchanged places with those on 'Gold' Beach in Normandy on 6 June 1944
they would have found much that they recognized in the way of organization.

During this period the British learned that planning and preparation were
of vital importance. Troops and equipment had to be assembled, embarked
and arranged so that during the passage to the landing site the organization
of the Army was maintained. Once at the landing site, command procedures
had to be implemented to move the troops, in correct order, from ship to
shore. Finally, the Navy had the task of keeping the Army supplied once the

latter was ashore: even an eighteenth century army needed large quantities of gunpowder, shot, ball ammunition, fodder for horses and pack animals and food, all of which had to come by sea.

During the passage to the landing site a sophisticated visual signalling code was established which allowed every ship in the force to indicate the cargo or the unit of troops embarked. Thus in the fleet taking troops to Saint Lucia in 1778 all transports carrying ordnance flew blue vanes from their mainmasts while the transports carrying the soldiers of the 28th Foot flew white flags with two red balls from their foremasts. Ships carrying the commanding officers of regiments or officers of the staff were further distinguished. The Army's communications were maintained by a special set of flag signals which the commander-in-chief could use to communicate with his subordinates or staff officers embarked in other ships without interfering with the naval signals required for the manoeuvring of the fleet.

During the passage the division of responsibility was clearly delineated between the Navy and Army commanders. The Navy commander was responsible for the command of all ships involved in the operation be they commissioned men-of-war or transports. He set out the order of sailing and allocated escorts for the merchant ships. Transports and victualling ships were divided up into groups and placed under the command of a naval officer known as the Agent for Transports. The Agent issued sealed orders to the Master of each vessel in his group which contained general orders and specific instructions to be followed in case of separation. However, in some cases Army officers were also assigned to merchant ships where the cargo was of any importance. If the invasion force had to pass through shoal or narrow waters, the Navy commander was responsible for sending out survey boats to establish a safe channel, as Captain James Cook did in the St Lawrence River before the invasion of Quebec. All these measures were intended to ensure that the invasion fleet arrived safely at its destination.

Once at the landing site, the troops had to be moved ashore. But where did the Navy's responsibility end and the Army's begin? A clear chain of command had to be established to ensure that at a given and agreed point in the operation command moved smoothly from the sailors to the soldiers. In this respect much had been learned from the disaster of the raid on Rochefort in 1757, where command boundaries had not been established before the landing. At the subsequent court martial of the general officer commanding, General Sir John Mordaunt, Admiral Sir Edward Hawke stated that he

> . . . always looked upon it to be his duty as Admiral, to convey the Troops to the road of Basque, and there, if possible, to find out a Landing-place for them, and in case of their landing to give them all the Assistance in his Power for

that Purpose, but with respect to the question, 'Whither they should land or not' . . . he consequently thought, it was the Part of the Generals to determine that Question by themselves . . . he thought it was [a] matter of judgement which merely related to them and that the Sea had nothing to do with it.[1]

Hawke was oversimplifying his case: the decision not to land at Rochefort was made by Mordaunt on the basis of advice tendered by the commanding officers of the warships. Apparently much was learned from the Rochefort expedition, however, for in the Seven Years' and American Wars, once the landing place had been selected,

. . . the whole command of them is given to a Sea Officer who conducts them to the place of landing . . . the Marine officer has little to do until the men are out of the Boats for then is the Time for him to show his Judgement.[2]

In other words, the Army only assumed command when the soldiers clambered out of their boats on the beaches.

Once the ships had arrived off the landing site, the anchorage had to be protected. Warships and transports at anchor were very vulnerable to forms of attack such as fireships and more ingenious engines of destruction such as the *Turtle* submersible commanded by Ezra Lee during the American war. Warships were stationed around the anchorage while small boats armed with soldiers patrolled around the anchored vessels. The next requirement was for the beaches to be surveyed along with the territory lying immediately behind the beach. On the night before the landing on the Île d'Orléans in the St Lawrence River, General James Wolfe sent forty rangers to reconnoitre the island. At the same time staff conferences were held between the Army and Navy commanders so that the operational plan could be fully explained to junior officers: no one would be in any doubt about his part in the plan. These aspects of an operation—protecting the anchorage, reconnaissance, briefing all officers involved—may seem to be common sense, but many an operation has foundered because of a neglect of these principles.

On board the transports infantry prepared by inspecting their arms and equipment. Each man would be issued with sixty rounds of ammunition, two flints and two or three days' rations together with a canteen filled with a mixture of rum and water. Bedding and other non-essential items were left on the transports to be landed later. Each soldier was also issued with an oiled cloth to wrap around the flintlock of his musket to keep it dry. Owing to the complicated nature of loading a musket and the need for firepower on the beach should the landing be opposed, infantry would load their weapons before disembarking and carry them slung over the shoulder with the barrel uppermost so that the ball did not fall out. The cartridge belt and bayonet were also slung over the shoulder to prevent their getting wet.

It was the usual practice for the naval commander to appoint a senior captain or commodore to take charge of the actual landing. Thus at Quebec Admiral Sir Charles Saunders appointed Captain James Chads (sometimes spelt 'Shads') to conduct the landing at Wolfe's Cove. It was his task to supervise the disembarkation of the troops from the transports into small craft, to form these craft up into what would now be described as assault waves and to convey the force ashore.

Where possible, the first wave of infantry went ashore in flat-bottomed craft. The need for such landing craft was realized after the Rochefort raid and two such vessels were developed. The first was 36 feet long, had a beam of 10 feet 2 inches and was rowed by twenty oarsmen; the second was slightly smaller at 30 feet in length and was rowed by sixteen oarsmen. Except for the number of oarsmen, the two types were essentially alike: both had bluff bows, were clinker built and were steered by a detachable rudder. Each craft also carried a mast, a sail and a 40-pound grapple. The numbers of flat-bottomed craft were supplemented by longboats, cutters and barges belonging to the men-of-war and the transports, although the flat-bottomed boats were greatly preferred. It has been the perennial cry of officers engaged in amphibious landings that they never have sufficient landing craft at their disposal, and General Wolfe at Quebec was no exception.

The flat-bottomed boats were embarked in the warships and transports and special booms and other rigging were sometimes required to hoist them out into the water. Each boat would be commanded by a Lieutenant or experienced Warrant or Petty Officer and manned by experienced seamen from the warships and transports. It was not unknown, however, for the soldiers to have to row themselves ashore.[3] On receipt of a signal from the officer commanding the landing, the boats would pull to their allocated transports to embark troops. Each transport disembarking troops flew a distinguishing flag while doing so, which was lowered as soon as the boats pulled away. Thus the force commander could see at a glance how well the disembarkation was proceeding. Each boat carried between forty and sixty soldiers drawn from the same rank and file, thus allowing the unit to deploy quickly into fighting order once ashore. The soldiers sat facing each other on thwarts which ran lengthways down the centre line of the boat. All were under strict orders to keep silent, remain seated and not fire their muskets.

After being loaded with troops the boats proceeded to an assembly point where they were organized into formation for the landing. The landing formation was dictated by the Army's order of battle. The boats were assembled into echelons, the boats within each echelon formed into two or three parallel lines. To make the task easier, each boat had its number in the formation painted on the bow. The first echelon was always the assault battalion—grenadiers and light infantry in British service. Once the first echelon was ashore, the remainder of the infantry would follow, with the cavalry, artillery and supply elements landed later. The timing of the landing of these echelons was crucial: as each one landed another would reach the shore. Thus the momentum of the assault would be maintained.

During the approach to the landing site the boats would be covered by gunfire from the escorting warships. Naval gunfire support was very effective on account of the great number of heavy cannon available. At the conclusion of the New York campaign in 1776 the British were so impressed by naval gunfire support that they rebuilt and converted a merchant ship to take sixteen 24-pounders for the sole purpose of conducting shore bombardment.

The process of the landing would be familiar to anyone with a knowledge of contemporary landing operations. As the boats neared the shore, the bombardment ceased and just before the boats entered the surf the grapple was thrown out astern to act as a kedge. As the boats took the ground, seamen jumped out to hold the bows steady while the troops clambered out over the sides and bow and waded ashore to assemble. Once empty, the boats returned to those transports flying flags (indicating the presence of troops on board) and repeated the operation until the whole landing force was ashore.

Once the troops had been landed the Navy's work was not over, for they had to be supplied. As General Sir John Ligonier noted in 1757,

A safe and well secured Communication between the Camp and Sea, from whence you are to receive your Supplies of all Kinds, is absolutely necessary; the whole depends on it.[4]

Any landing was logistically dependent on the Navy. Naval vessels and small craft also gave the British Army great tactical mobility. Wolfe could never have moved around the St Lawrence River with such ease were it not for the small craft of the Royal Navy. The Navy helped not only by providing ships: at Quebec and countless other places sailors formed working parties and went ashore to support the Army.

The use of sea power gave the British Army great mobility and striking power during its wars in America in the late eighteenth century. The Controller of the Navy during this period, Sir Charles Middleton, was so moved by the amphibious operations undertaken in America that he proposed the maintenance of a permanent amphibious force in England which, he argued, would pose a strategic threat to the whole North Atlantic basin—a remarkable proposal for a country dedicated to the maintenance of nothing but the barest naval and military establishment in peacetime.[5]

There can be no question, however, that Britain's naval supremacy and the Navy's adoption and mastery of amphibious techniques gave the British Army an importance and striking power wholly disproportionate to the size of the military force involved. The eighteenth century was the 'golden age' of amphibious warfare in the Royal Navy. Seldom since then has knowledge of amphibious techniques been so widely disseminated and their importance acknowledged and appreciated.

The most striking example of this amphibious proficiency was the capture of Quebec in September 1759 during the Seven Years' War. Quebec was the capital of French Canada and stands 300 miles up the St Lawrence River on the north bank. The city was founded in 1608 by Samuel de Champlain, captured by the British in 1629 but returned to France in 1632 under the terms of the Treaty of St Germain-en-Laye. Further British attempts to capture it were made in 1690, and in 1711 when Admiral Sir Hovenden Walker's fleet was wrecked in the Gulf of St Lawrence.

The expedition against Quebec was ordered in January 1759 and sailed from England on 16 February. Its dispatch followed the successful capture of Louisburg in 1758. Louisburg, on Cape Breton Island at the mouth of the St Lawrence, had been taken by the British employing a force of 12,000 men supported by twenty-two ships of the line, fifteen frigates and dozens of transports. Louisburg commands the entrance to the St Laurence River and Quebec was the next French stronghold.

The military commander was Major-General James Wolfe, who at the age of 32 was a veteran of four battles. Royal patronage had eased his path to promotion but it would be unwise to dismiss Wolfe as a mere product of patronage. He was a serious student of the profession of arms and was well regarded as a regimental commander, where his belief in training produced some of the best soldiers in the Army. However, this was his first independent command and it was known that he possessed a streak of recklessness. The naval commander was Vice-Admiral Sir Charles Saunders, a much steadier pair of hands, who had been one of Anson's lieutenants in his celebrated circumnavigation of the globe in 1740–44. An officer of great courage and determination who had commanded HMS *Yarmouth* with distinction at the Second Battle of Finisterre in 1747, Saunders had been Commander-in-Chief of the Mediterranean Fleet when he was offered the new appointment.

The expedition got off to a bad start when a French squadron evaded the British blockade at the mouth of the St Lawrence. The French squadron had brought reinforcements, food and the Marquis de Bougainville, one of the most gifted French staff officers. Moreover, de Bougainville brought news of British intentions and thus the French commander, the Marquis de Montcalm, was able to make his dispositions accordingly.

This was a serious blow, for Wolfe had hoped to take Quebec by *coup de main*. However, he had not reckoned on the support which Saunders was about to offer him. Saunders proposed to take his whole fleet—twenty-two ships-of-the-line, four frigates, three fireships, three bomb ketches, three sloops and 119 transports and victualling vessels—up the St Lawrence to support Wolfe in his attack on the city. Such a voyage had never been attempted and involved the negotiation of the dangerous Traverse Passage below Quebec. The arrangements worked perfectly. Under the command of Admiral Phillip Durrell, marker boats were placed on either side of the channel and pilots were provided for such ships as required them. By 26 June the last transport had passed through the Traverse and on 27 June Wolfe seized the Île d'Orléans up river from Quebec and disembarked his army there.

However, a reconnaissance of the city showed that his task would be very difficult. Quebec stands on a promontory marking the confluence of the St Charles and St Lawrence rivers. Wolfe proposed to deploy his army across the promontory with his right on the St Lawrence and his left on the St Charles. Thus he could make the most use of naval support in investing the city. However, Montcalm had so disposed his forces as to make such a plan impossible to execute.

Over the next two months Wolfe made several attempts to capture the city, but on each occasion Montcalm's rigid defensive strategy proved impossible to break. Not only did Montcalm enjoy the luxury of good defensive positions, he also possessed superior numbers, some 14,000 French regular and colonial troops. As the summer wore on into autumn and with winter looming, it seemed as if the expedition were a failure. Wolfe was under continual pressure from Saunders to move, for with the coming of winter the latter's ships could not remain iced up in the St Lawrence: they would have to head for the open sea.

The last attack was abandoned because of bad weather on 9 September. However, the effect of the repeated attempts on Quebec had been to draw Montcalm's defences out on his flanks, thereby creating a gap in the centre. Wolfe instantly perceived this as the fatal weakness in the French position. On 9 September, the same day the attack was abandoned, Wolfe conducted a reconnaissance above Quebec and discovered that at a place called the Anse de Foulon there was a path up the cliff leading to the Plains of Abraham and that the area was held by no more than a hundred men. On returning to his flagship Wolfe boldly announced that he would land at the Anse de Foulon and take Montcalm by surprise.

Wolfe's subordinates had been preparing their own plan for another, more conventional attack on the city and were extremely worried by his plan, in particular that he was ordering a night landing involving a hazardous trip down river in boats. The brigadiers went so far as to prepare a remonstrance—to which Wolfe paid scant heed. The operational plan was for an advance force of 400 light infantry to land at the Anse de Foulon during the night of 12/13 September, overpower the guards and secure the beach. They would be followed by 1,300 infantry commanded by Colonel Robert Monckton—all that could be carried in one lift—and a further 1,000 men would arrive by river as soon as boats became available. Meanwhile Colonels Carleton and Burton were to march another 1,000 men to a point on the river opposite the Anse de Foulon, from where they would be ferried across the river. Thus by the morning of the 13th Wolfe hoped to have 5,000 men deployed in front of the city. Behind the infantry would come transports bringing artillery and ordnance to conduct a siege.

In the evening of 12 September Vice-Admiral Saunders prepared a demonstration off Beaufort below Quebec while other forces made a feint up river. Meanwhile the actual landing force embarked, and at 2.00 a.m. on the 13th the boats were cast off and headed for the Anse de Foulon. Fortunately the French were expecting a convoy of supply boats and the landing force was able to pass for them, thus avoiding raising the alarm. The command of the landing force was given to Captain James Chads, who performed the masterly feat of navigating the force for fifteen miles down river on a racing tide and in the dark to arrive punctually at his objective. Wolfe appreciated the difficulty of his task and had given his regimental commanders strict instructions that 'No officer must attempt to make the least alteration or interfere with Captain Chads' particular province.'[6]

The light infantry, 400 men under Colonel Howe, were the first to disembark and headed up the cliff to overpower the guards and secure the landing site. By this time the frigates and transports with the main landing force were arriving. The French batteries at Samos and Sillery were now alerted to what was afoot and opened a desultory fire. However, they were quickly taken from the rear by the light infantry and the landing proceeded apace. Once the second wave was ashore the boats hastened across the river to collect Burton's Corps, which had come overland from Levis. Thus by the morning of 13 September Wolfe had deployed over 5,000 men on to the Plains of Abraham without interference from the French.

On hearing of the landing Montcalm decided to attack immediately without waiting for reinforcements from the Marquis de Bougainville, his subordinate commander, up river. This was unfortunate, for the pick of his infantry were with Bougainville and the need to leave forces to counter the threat posed by Saunders' manoeuvrings below Beaufort meant that the number of men he was able to deploy against Wolfe was literally halved. In truth Montcalm had no choice: he did not know how many men Wolfe had landed but he knew that the number would only grow with time.

This decision was disastrous, for Montcalm's forces hurtled out of the city and approached the British infantry standing rigid in their ranks. Wolfe's training now paid off: the British stood stock still and reserved their fire until the French line had closed to within thirty yards. Then,

Our troops received their fire and reserved their own, advancing till they were so near as to run in upon them and push them with their bayonets, by which, in a very little time, the French gave way, and fled to the town in utmost disorder.[7]

On the beach below the Plains of Abraham the sailors who were dragging the 24-pounder naval guns up the cliff heard three crashing volleys from the British line, followed by the cheers and cries of despair as the French line broke. However, the triumph was marred by the news that Wolfe had been killed: his body was brought back to HMS *Lowestoft* at 11.00 a.m. On the French side Montcalm, too, had been fatally wounded.

The battle was enough. The British invested the city and the 24-pounders were established in batteries to commence a siege. By the end of the week following the landing over 100 guns and mortars were established on the heights while Saunders' ships battered the city from below. The threat was more than the half-starved garrison of Quebec could endure, and on 27 September the French offered to surrender. The Articles of Capitulation were signed the next day.

The assault on Quebec had been a brilliantly conducted operation which had succeeded in its immediate objective. However, in the wider context of the war in North America it was only half a victory. The British had been unable to link up with Amhurst's forces advancing from the south, and the presence of a French squadron up river meant that the garrison at Quebec would not be secure throughout the winter.

Nevertheless, the operation ranks as near perfect and deserves a place alongside Normandy, Inchon and other amphibious triumphs. The key to the success had undoubtedly been the close co-operation between the Navy and the Army. In his report to the Admiralty Saunders had written: '. . . during this tedious campaign, there has continued a perfect good understanding between the army and Navy.'[8] Would that such sentiments could be expressed of some more contemporary amphibious operations! The Army fully reciprocated the Navy's sentiments. Brigadier-General George Townshend, who had succeeded Wolfe in command, wrote

> I should not do justice to the Admirals and the naval service if I neglected this occasion of acknowledging how much we are indebted for our success to the constant assistance and support received from them, and the perfect harmony and correspondence which has prevailed throughout all our operations.[9]

Though Wolfe's intuitive flair had rescued the expedition from the impasse reached during the summer, it was Admiral Saunders who was the real hero of the affair. His decision to support Wolfe by taking his fleet up the St Lawrence gave the latter an unprecedented degree of strategic mobility. As Sir Julian Corbett concluded in his seminal study of the campaign,

> Though he lacked the genius of Wolfe, his hand throughout was the surer of the two, and dazzling as was the final stroke by which Wolfe snatched victory from failure, the steadier flame of Saunders' exploit is destined to burn beside it without loss of radiance for all time.[10]

In the pantheon of heroes of amphibious warfare, Saunders ranks equally with such skilled practitioners of our own time as Bertram Ramsay, Kelly Turner, James Doyle and Douglas MacArthur.

Notes to Chapter 1

1. *The Proceedings of a General Court Martial . . . Upon the Trial of Lieutenant General Sir John Mordaunt, by virtue of His Majesty's Warrent* (London,1758), pp.114–15.
2. MacIntire, John, *A Military Treatise on the Discipline of the Marine Forces, when at Sea, Together with Short Instructions for Detachments Sent to Attack on Shore* (London, 1763), p.225.
3. Mordaunt Court Martial, p.48.
4. *Ibid.*, p.75.
5. Laughton, J. K. (ed.), *Letters and Papers of Charles Lord Barbham*, Vol. 38, Navy Records Society (1910), pp.45–7.
6. Corbett, Sir Julian, *England in the Seven Years' War 1756–59*, Vol. 1, Greenhill Books (1992), p.467.

7. PRO ADM 1/482, Despatch of Vice-Admiral Sir Charles Saunders to the Secretary of the Admiralty, 21 September 1759.

8. *Ibid*.

9. Corbett, *op. cit.*, p.472.

10. *Ibid.*, p.476

CHAPTER TWO

A Bad Start

There was no co-ordination of effort. There was no connected plan of action. There was no sense of the importance of time.—David Lloyd George

SELDOM in history has a campaign begun with such high hopes but ended in such disaster as the Dardanelles campaign of 1915–16. As the official historian, Brigadier-General C. F. Aspinall-Oglander, wrote in the conclusion to his account,

> The drama of the Dardanelles campaign, by reason of the beauty of the setting, the grandeur of its theme and the unhappiness of its ending, will always rank among the world's classic tragedies.[1]

While the various European powers mobilized for war in August 1914, Turkey remained neutral. However, the seizure by the Royal Navy of two capital ships completing in British shipyards caused a wave of anti-British feeling. The Germans made much of this by 'giving' the Turks the battlecruiser *Goeben* and the cruiser *Breslau*, which had recently sought sanctuary in Turkish waters. An Anglo-French squadron blockaded the Dardanelles in retaliation and the British Naval Mission, which was assisting the Turkish Navy, was withdrawn. German influence grew, and it could only be a matter of time before Turkey entered the war on the side of the Central Powers.

In early October the Turks closed the Dardanelles to Allied shipping while the *Goeben* bombarded several Russian ports on the Black Sea. This act of aggression led to war with Russia, and on 3 November the Allied fleet off the Dardanelles bombarded the forts at the entrance to the Narrows, the stretch of water leading from the Aegean to the Sea of Marmara. Within a few days a state of war existed between Turkey and the *Entente*. Even before Turkey entered the war, however, Britain had taken steps to protect her interests in the Middle East. Troops from India had been dispatched to guard the oilfields in the Persian Gulf, and in November 1914 fighting broke out in Mesopotamia. British and Indian troops also arrived in Egypt to guard the Suez Canal, the vital link to India and the Far East.

Forcing the Dardanelles had long been an aim in Britain's various difficulties with the Ottoman Empire throughout the nineteenth century. With a new campaign in the offing, the idea was seized upon by Winston Churchill, First Lord of the Admiralty. His Cabinet colleagues were less impressed—their attention was focused on the struggle in France and across the North Sea—but by the close of 1914 the lack of progress in France caused the thoughts of some to turn east to the Mediterranean.

It was the Russians who provided the impetus towards a decision: although they drove back a Turkish offensive in the Caucasus mountains in January 1915, they were sufficiently alarmed to seek British assistance. Churchill's proposals now seemed the best way of helping the Russians by drawing Turkish forces away from the Caucasus. However, the plan was not just a matter of diverting forces away from the Caucasus: the operation involved the age-old ideal of taking Constantinople—a dream which went back to the Crusades. In more practical terms, if the Navy could penetrate the Dardanelles into the Sea of Marmara, the effect would be incalculable: Turkey could well be forced out of the war.

Initially the project was purely a naval attack, Vice-Admiral Sackville Carden, the naval commander of the Eastern Mediterranean Squadron, having called for the gradual destruction of the forts guarding the entrance to the Dardanelles. The idea was well received in London and on 15 January 1915 Carden was told that he could proceed. To assist in the task he was sent the new battleship HMS *Queen Elizabeth*, which had just completed at Devonport Dockyard and which could calibrate her new and powerful 15-inch main armament on the forts. But in early February the War Council decided that some military participation might be necessary if the naval assault proved insufficient. Subsequently Field Marshal Kitchener, the Secretary of State for War, offered, then withdrew, then offered again the services of the 29th Division for the expedition. This was the last division of regular infantry left in the United Kingdom, and throughout the campaign the 29th would retain its character as a Regular Army unit based on fierce regimental loyalty and a strong sense of competition.

The 29th would be the first to land at Helles on 25 April; it would see action at Suvla; and it would then return to Helles to cover the final evacuation. It was commanded by Major-General Sir Aylmer Hunter-Weston, an officer who had seen service in France and who was considered brave and determined. The Division duly sailed for the Dardanelles, where it was to be joined by the Australian and New Zealand Army Corps (ANZAC,) under the command of Lieutenant-General Sir William Birdwood, which was en route for France but was retained in Egypt. The Anzacs were very much an unknown quantity. Physically they were the largest and most impressive troops available. Private George Peake of the 1/8th Lancashire Fusiliers described them as 'the biggest set of men I'd seen in all my life. I don't think I saw one that was under six feet, all big stout fellows.' The antipodean climate made the Anzacs particularly well suited to operations in the Mediterranean. However, their relaxed attitude to military practice, their general indiscipline in camp and their fluent use of those aspects of the King's English not found in the dictionary did not endear them to military authority.

Subsequently the 42nd East Lancashire Division, a division of Territorials who had volunteered for overseas service, was allocated to the campaign together with the Royal Naval Division (RND), a hybrid unit consisting of sailors not required for sea service, reservists and the surplus manpower from some northern infantry battalions. With its officers and men dressed in Army uniform but wearing naval badges of rank and adhering to naval customs and traditions, the RND soon acquired a distinctive character and reputation all of its own.

The entire force was designated the Mediterranean Expeditionary Force (MEF), and command was entrusted to General Sir Ian Hamilton. Hamilton was an extremely distinguished officer who by August 1914 had probably seen more action (Afghanistan, the North-West Frontier, Sudan and the First and Second Boer Wars) than any other officer of his generation. Additionally, he was known as a refined and cultured social figure and was widely respected in literary and artistic circles in London.

The role of the MEF was uncertain. Kitchener saw it merely as a garrison and warned Hamilton in the strongest terms that the 29th Division was only on loan from France. Undoubtedly everyone expected the Navy's assault on the Narrows to be successful. This was certainly the frame of mind in which Hamilton and his staff arrived at Mudros on 17 March 1915 to witness the Navy's final attempt to penetrate the Dardanelles.

The Navy's attempts to force the Narrows began on 19 February and made slow progress. The forts at Sedd-el-Bahr and Kum Kale, guarding the entrance to the Dardanelles, were neutralized, but inside the Straits the fleet encountered considerable difficulties. The minesweepers found it heavy going against the current, while the forts were standing up well to the naval gunfire. Moreover, the Turks were making increasing use of mobile artillery batteries, which were very difficult to locate and engage.

The Navy made its most significant attempt on the Narrows on 18 March. By then Carden had been replaced by Vice-Admiral John de Roebeck. Old pre-dreadnought battleships were to destroy the forts first, in order to make the work of the minesweepers easier. The operation began well but in the afternoon disaster struck when the French battleship *Bouvet* and the British battleships *Ocean* and *Irresistible* were sunk and French *Gaulois* damaged. De Roebeck had to admit defeat.

In the aftermath of this repulse an important conference took place on board HMS *Queen Elizabeth*. De Roebeck admitted that the Navy could not proceed with the operation without support from the Army. But it was not simply a matter of landing the troops on the peninsula. Kitchener had made it clear to Hamilton that no landing could take place until all the MEF was concentrated in one place. In fact the MEF was spread out all over the Mediterranean. The RND was at Mudros on the island of Lemnos and the 29th Division was still en route from the United Kingdom, while the 42nd Division and the ANZAC Corps were still in Egypt. Worse still, the transports were not tactically loaded. Everything would have to be unloaded and re-stowed. Mudros was nothing other than a secure anchorage, so the whole force would have to return to Egypt. Hamilton advised Kitchener that the earliest he could mount an assault was 11 April. So the transports sailed away and the MEF sorted itself out in Egypt while the bazaars ran riot with rumour and speculation about what was afoot. In fact the reorganization of the MEF was a considerable logistic feat, accomplished in a very short period of time.

Meanwhile Hamilton's staff wrestled with the problem of mounting a complicated amphibious operation. In broad outline Hamilton had already decided to land at the southern end of the Gallipoli peninsula so as to keep in close contact with the fleet, but although he had a general outline in mind the specifics were far from clear. The Asian shore had already been ruled out by Kitchener: a landing here had much to commend it—the area was lightly defended and the troops would have a march over easy country to take them to the rear of the forts on the Asian side, whose fixed batteries could only fire seawards—but the only two sites, Besika Bay and Yukyeri Bay, were twenty-five miles from the Narrows.

The Gallipoli peninsula is 45 miles long and twelve miles wide at its broadest point. It offered four landing sites, the Bulair area in the Gulf of Saros, Suvla Bay, Gaba Tepe and Cape Helles. Any further intrusion into the Straits was impractical because of fire from the forts on the Asian side. Hamilton rejected Bulair because reconnaissance indicated that Turkish defences there were too strong. Additionally, Bulair was rejected on account of its difficult terrain and vulnerability to counter-attack from both directions should Turkish forces in Thrace intervene. Likewise Suvla Bay was rejected because too little was known of the coastal and topographical aspects of the area. Hamilton decided to make his main landing at Cape Helles, with an equally strong landing at Gaba Tepe some thirteen miles to the north.

The most important aspect of an amphibious operation is surprise, but any doubts about British intentions toward the Dardanelles had disappeared completely by the end of March 1915. However, although the Turks knew that an operation was imminent, they did not know when and where the British proposed to strike and thus Hamilton retained some tactical surprise. Two factors determined the choice of Cape Helles as the landing area: first, the main purpose of the operation was to allow the minesweepers to complete their task and be of direct assistance to the Navy; second, the landing had to be within the capabilities of the soldiers involved, and of the sailors putting them ashore.

Hamilton's staff settled on Cape Helles, with the overall aim of capturing the Kilid Bahr Plateau. From this point the MEF could dominate the European side beneath them and the Asiatic coast across the Dardanelles and thus allow the naval attack to be resumed. The possible landing sites were reduced to four, Suvla Bay, Gaba Tepe, the southern tip of Cape Helles and Sedd-el-Bahr. Suvla was rejected for the reasons already described and the fact that it was too far from the Kilid Bahr Plateau. To the south lay Gaba Tepe, where there were several good beaches which were, however, known to be fortified; moreover, any landing here would result in a beach-head vulnerable to attack from all sides except the rear. The most favourable option was Helles: here, although the beaches were known to be defended, the shape of the peninsula would allow maximum support from the fleet. If a landing at Helles could be linked to one at Gaba Tepe along the southern slopes of the Sari Bair Ridge, both sides of the Kilid Bahr Plateau would be threatened, together with Turkish communications. Moreover, the simultaneous execution of two landings would increase the degree of surprise and keep the Turks guessing as to which was the main thrust.

This was the essence of the plan presented to Hamilton by his staff on 23 March. The landings at Cape Helles would be made by the 29th Division on three beaches, named 'X', 'W' and 'V'. 'X' Beach was on the west coast, just under a mile north of Tekke Burnu. It could be hardly be described as a beach: there was but a small strip of sand, but there was a good path up to the cliffs and it was known that the area was lightly held. 'W' Beach lay between Tekke Burnu and Cape Helles and 'V' Beach lay slightly to the east. 'V' Beach was a natural amphitheatre bounded by Cape Helles on the left and the ruined fort of Sedd-el-Bahr. In a late addition to the plan it was decided to land a battalion-size force at the eastern end of Morto Bay at a point called 'S' Beach. The British were familiar with all these beaches and believed that naval gunfire would eliminate the barbed wire entanglements and trench systems established by the Turks, although all the evidence gathered in previous bombardments suggested that in fact the defences stood up very well; Hamilton himself watched HMS *Triumph* bombarding Cape Helles and noted shells bursting on the wire to no visible effect.

The troops of the first and second waves would embark in warships anchored a mile or so from the beaches. The infantry would disembark into ships' boats, towed by tugs in groups (called 'tows'). When only a short distance from the beach, the tugs would cast off and the boats would row for the shore. As soon as the beaches and the high ground were secure, the main force would arrive in transports and be ferried ashore in the same fashion.

In an effort to speed up the disembarkation of infantry, Commander Edward Unwin RN, commanding officer of the destroyer HMS *Hussar*, proposed the conversion of a collier to carry two thousand infantrymen. The ship would be run ashore on 'V' Beach and the troops would then emerge from ports cut in her sides, move along specially constructed gangways down a bridge of lighters connected to the shore by a steam hopper and then step on to the beach. In this fashion the size of the first wave could effectively be doubled. Despite some opposition, Rear-Admiral Rosslyn Wemyss secured the scheme's adoption and Unwin was ordered to turn his plan into reality. For the role of this modern Trojan Horse the *River Clyde*, a ten-year-old collier, was selected.

In order to give the landings at 'V' Beach some cover, a detachment of French troops was to land on the Asiatic shore at Kum Kale while a second diversionary operation, at Besika Bay, was also to be mounted by the French. Right at the end of the planning stage Hamilton further amended the plan by deciding to land a force of 2,000 men on the west coast of the peninsula at point called 'Y' Beach, about a mile west of Krithia. Hunter-Weston did not welcome this addition but made no objections.

The beaches around Cape Helles were sufficient for only one of Hamilton's three divisions, so the Anzac Division was ordered to land north of Gaba Tepe in an area thought to be lightly defended. There was a tendency among the staff at GHQ to regard the Australians and New Zealanders as enthusiastic but undisciplined and thus they were allocated what was considered to be the easiest part of the operation. Hamilton's third division, the Royal Naval Division, was not to land with the other two but instead was to take part in a feint off Bulair to draw any Turkish reinforcements away from the peninsula and confuse their command about the true direction of the offensive.

Hamilton's plan was elegant in its simplicity. The 29th Division would land at Helles, advance north and occupy the Achi Baba Ridge. Meanwhile the Anzacs would secure the Sari Bair heights and push across the peninsula and take Mal Tepe, a commanding position north-west of Maidos. Thus the defenders at Kilid Bahr would be cut off from north and south. Hamilton believed that the Army assault would be matched by a renewed attempt by the Navy on the Narrows. The Turks would thereby find themselves pressed from two sides—'a double thrust at their heart'.[2]

This was the basic misunderstanding between the military and naval staffs which lay at the heart of the failure of the operation. Hamilton believed that as soon as his troops had landed the Navy would renew its assault. It was clear that the Navy intended to wait until the Army had taken the peninsula and neutralized the forts before making any moves up the Narrows. In 1924 Hamilton had written the word 'correct' in the margin of a book on Gallipoli by an American historian, who commented that

> Certainly General Hamilton did not suspect that naval co-operation would be limited and to a large extent his plans the following month were based on the assumption of a combined attack with the Fleet.[3]

As a result of this misunderstanding Hamilton's plans were of a short term nature. In 1924 Hamilton wrote:

> In my mind the crux was to get my army ashore... Once ashore I could hardly think that in the long run Great Britain and France would not defeat Turkey ... the problem as it presented itself to us was how to get the troops ashore.[4]

Accordingly, no emphasis was given to the orders issued to the 29th Division on the critical importance of moving inland quickly after landing; the orders were, indeed, mind-bogglingly complex. However, the plans dwelt mainly on trivialities. Serious issues such as ship-to-shore co-operation were barely addressed by the staff. Most importantly, no thought was given to what was to be done if the assault was held up: how would the troops be maintained ashore in an area that possessed little or no fresh water and where there were no suitable natural harbours?

In theory the British possessed plenty of advantages in connection with the landings. The Royal Navy held undisputed command of the seas: there was no series maritime threat to the conduct of the landings or to the maintenance of the troops once ashore. Although German U-boats would score significant successes off Gallipoli (the sinking of HMS *Majestic* on 27 May 1915 by *U21* being one), they were no more than a nuisance and they could not interfere with the conduct of the campaign. The strength of the Navy meant that sufficient warships, particularly pre-dreadnought battleships, were available for escort and bombardment duties without weakening the Grand Fleet in the North Sea. Moreover, the British possessed virtually unlimited shipping to transport and supply the troops and bases near to the theatre of operations where supplies could be built up.

However, in some respects the British were poorly prepared for the operation. For example, the arrangements for command were inadequate. Although Hamilton and de Roebeck enjoyed good relations, there was not the 'good and perfect understanding' between their staffs which had characterized Army–Navy relations on the St Lawrence River in 1759. How could there be? Hamilton's staff were in Alexandria and de Roebeck's were at Imbros. As many of the questions under discussion involved logistics and naval resources, this was an important handicap. Moreover, Hamilton did not even have a full staff. He had gone out to the Mediterranean in such a hurry that the 'A&Q'⁵ departments, responsible for supplies, had not even been appointed. No wonder questions of logistics received such short shrift.

Furthermore, at this stage no one thought to consider whether the MEF was of sufficient strength to take on its new, more wide-ranging role: the force had been organized as a garrison, but now it was to make an opposed landing on a hostile shore. It was clearly inadequate for the task it was set and lacked a good deal of specialist equipment. In particular, ammunition scales were far too low, with only 500 rounds per rifle in the 29th Division and 430 in the RND. There was also a lack of artillery ammunition—623 rounds per gun for the 29th Division's 18-pounders—and it was of the wrong type. Most artillery ammunition was shrapnel, which was quite useless against fortified positions. The War Office remained complacent in the face of these shortages and Hamilton did not press the point, feeling that once he had been given the job he ought to get on with it. Had he had his 'A&Q' branches with his staff, he might have been made to concern himself with these mundane but important details.

On 4 April the MEF re-embarked on their transports and for the next fortnight a steady stream of ships left Egypt for the Aegean. GHQ arrived back at Mudros on 10 April and the first task was to acquaint de Roebeck and his staff with the plan. On 13 April the first formal orders were issued to the units involved.

The naval force which was supporting the landings now consisted of eighteen pre-dreadnought battleships, twelve cruisers and twenty-nine destroyers. For the support of the landings the fleet was divided into seven squadrons, of which the most powerful were the 1st (Rear-Admiral Wemyss) and 2nd (Rear-Admiral Cecil Thursby), supporting the landings at Helles and Gaba Tepe respectively. Within these squadrons the ships were further subdivided into 'covering ships', which were to provide fire support before and during the landings, and 'attendant ships', which were to land the troops and then provide logistical support.

Meanwhile, on the other side of the hill, the result of the failure of the British attack of 18 March was to stimulate greater activity among the defenders. It is difficult to overestimate the psychological effect the events of that day had on the Turks. In 1915 the supremacy of the Royal Navy was an article of faith throughout the world, yet here in the Dardanelles the Turks, whose country was so often decried as the 'Sick Man of Europe', had beaten it off. Although the Turkish Government may have been corrupt and inefficient, there was no doubt about the bravery or determination of its soldiers.

The determination of the Turks was stiffened still further with the appointment on 25 March of Marshal Liman von Sanders, a German officer, to command the Turkish 5th Army in the Dardanelles. German artillery, engineer and pioneer officers were appointed to Turkish units as 'advisers', and events began to benefit from a much needed central control. Von Sanders set about improving the defences with a will. Beaches were barricaded with barbed wire both above and below high-water mark, roads were constructed to aid mobility on the peninsula using non-Muslim labour battalions of the Turkish Army. Most importantly, von Sanders altered the Turkish defensive plan for the area. Instead of trying to hold everywhere at once, he maintained a small screen of troops around the coast while concentrating the bulk of his forces inland. To the north were the 5th and 7th Divisions at Bulair, the 3rd and 11th Divisions were on the Asiatic shore and the 9th Division was at Cape Helles; the army reserve was the 19th Division at Maidos. The 9th Division's zone was further divided into a northern sector running from just south of Suvla Bay to Gaba Tepe and a southern sector running from Semerly Tepe to Cape Helles. Of the three regiments (each of three battalions) in the 9th Division, the 27th was assigned to the northern sector, the 26th to the southern sector and the 25th to reserve.

The arrival of von Sanders and his emphasis on mobility invigorated the Turks. Despite persistent gunfire from the British fleet, every night von Sanders had the Turks building stronger and deeper positions facing the sea and laying mile after mile of barbed wire. The results of these labours were visible every morning to the watching British. 'If only the English will leave me alone for eight days . . . ' von Sanders is reported to have said. In the event he got three weeks.

The growing Turkish defences did not appear to bother Hamilton or his staff. This is one of the most damning indictments of Hamilton's conduct of the campaign. The roots of this failure lie in the belief that the Turks would provide no serious opposition, a belief supported by the performance of the Turkish Army in the years before the outbreak of the First World War. However, Kitchener had provided more up-to-date intelligence on the Turks. Less than a week before the landing he telegraphed Hamilton with the news that Turkish troops in Mesopotamia in the recent fighting there had shown 'determination and good discipline'.

On 19 April the final conference was held aboard the *Queen Elizabeth*. The one outstanding item to be settled was the time of the landing. There was much discussion, but in the end it was decided to land the Anzac Corps at Gaba Tepe before first light while at Helles the landing would take place after dawn and be preceded by a bombardment. It was decided to land on 23 April, but bad weather forced a forty-eight-hour postponement. Indeed, it was not until the 23rd that the wind dropped and the transports and warships began to put to sea. The atmosphere was heady and emotional: it was as if the expedition were a modern crusade to liberate Constantinople. However, not all the men were enthusiastic. Captain Guy Geddes of the 1st Royal Munster Fusiliers, embarked in the *River Clyde*, reported that

> What struck me most forcibly was the demeanour of own men, from whom not a sound, and this from light hearted, devil may care men from the south of Ireland. Even they were filled with a sense of something impending which was quite beyond their ken.[6]

By the evening of 25 May the worst fears of the Munsters would have been amply confirmed.

Notes to Chapter 2

1. Aspinall-Oglander, Brigadier-General C. F., *History of the Great War: Military Operations, Gallipoli*, Vol. II (1932), p.479.
2. James, Robert Rhodes, *Gallipoli*, Batsford (1965), p.84.
3. *Ibid*.
4. *Ibid*., p.89.
5. Adjutant and Quartermaster.
6. Imperial War Museum, Department of Documents, Papers of Colonel Guy Geddes: TS account of the landings.

CHAPTER THREE

The Landings

*These by the Dardanelles laid down their shining youth,
In battle and won fair renown for their native land.*
—Anon, Fifth Century BC

THE Covering Force of the Anzac Corps, consisting of the 3rd Australian Brigade under Colonel Ewen Sinclair-McLagan, was to land to the north of Gaba Tepe in two waves before dawn on 25 April and advance inland quickly to a point called Gun Ridge, maintaining as wide a front as possible. The 11th Battalion was on the left, the 10th in the centre and the 9th on the right, with the 12th Battalion in reserve.

At 0100 on 25 April the battleship HMS *Triumph* arrived off Gaba Tepe, followed by the three battleships *Queen*, *Prince of Wales* and *London* carrying the first wave of 1,500 troops. The troops disembarked into the ships' boats, and just before 0300 the 'tows' steaming behind the battleships moved slowly towards the peninsula. At 0330 the battleships halted when two and a half miles away from the shore and the tows proceeded on their own.

The first signs of dawn were just beginning to show when the tows were cast off and the forty-eight boats began the pull for the shore. For over three hours the Australian and New Zealand soldiers had been sitting in cramped conditions in the open boats. They were cold and stiff: the strain was enormous. It seemed impossible that they would not be spotted by the defenders on the shore.

Even at this early stage things began to go awry. The darkness meant that it was impossible for the tows to station themselves 150 yards apart as laid down in the orders: they would have lost sight of one another. Instead they bunched up and were only fifty yards apart. This had the effect of contracting the front from 1,600 to 600 yards. Of even greater significance was the fact that, due to navigational and human error, the troops were landed a mile to the north of the specified landing point.[1] All forty-eight boats landed around Ari Burnu, with none landing south of Hell Spit. This was to have far-reaching consequences.

The troops on 'Anzac' Beach were from the 9th Australian Battalion: they managed to land and remove their packs as ordered before fierce rifle and machine-gun fire broke out from the defenders. As the remainder of the first waves came ashore, the destroyers *Ribble*, *Usk*, *Chelmer*, *Scourge*, *Foxhound*, *Colne* and *Beagle* began landing the men of the second wave. As visibility improved it became clear that something had gone horribly wrong. Instead of confronting the southern face of Plugge's Plateau and MacLagan's Ridge, the Australians found themselves beneath the more hostile northern face of the plateau and the cruel northern escarpment of Razor Edge. The men of the 10th and 9th Battalions had become mixed and companies landed on the beach in considerable confusion.

Yet, despite the chaos, it had been so firmly drilled into the Australians that they were to keep moving that small parties of men, admirably led, were making rapid progress, and within a few minutes of landing a small group of Australians had reached the top of Plugge's Plateau. From there they could see the extent of the confusion. An obstacle known as 400 Plateau lay to their right instead of their left, while below them the incoming boats were confronted with almost sheer sandstone cliffs. One soldier asked of his officer, 'What are we to do next?' and received the reply, 'I don't know I'm sure—everything is in a terrible muddle.'

Nevertheless, progress continued to be made, though often at great cost. Lieutenant-Commander Ralph Wilkinson was watching from the destroyer HMS *Ribble*:

The Australians were fine. I felt proud that I was a Briton. They pulled in singing a song, 'Australia will be there'. A good many lost their rifles in their eagerness to jump out of the boats and I could see them scaling the cliffs and waving their sword bayonets, and hear them 'cooeeing' like mad. Unfortunately their discipline was poor as they in parties of threes and fours pursued Turks inland until they themselves were scuppered by the enemy's reinforcements.[2]

By 0600 the Australians were in possession of First Ridge, parties were moving over Second Ridge and on the left the Turks were thrown back in disorder across Baby 700. The number of Australians ashore was now in excess of 4,000 and the number of Turks was not more than 700. Near a monstrous cliff called The Sphinx a small group of attackers hauled themselves over the top, forcing the defenders to flee, and by 0700 an Australian officer had reached the top of Scrubby Knoll and was able to look down on the gleaming waters of the Narrows. It seemed that the objective lay within easy reach.

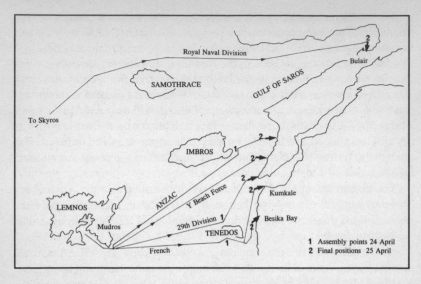

The Dardanelles: Development of Landing Forces, 23–25 April 1915

The fighting on 'Anzac' Beach now became extremely confused. As the main body of the Anzac Corps landed, the confusion on the beach multiplied accordingly. The beachmasters did not land until 1000, by which time Anzac Cove was an administrative shambles. New arrivals coming ashore were sent to Shrapnel Cove to re-form and then arbitrarily dispatched to the fighting on various sectors of the beach-head. Maps were useless and orders based on those maps valueless. A group of New Zealand troops took over an hour to move a hundred yards because the map they were using did not show an impassable obstacle in their way. No one had any precise knowledge of what was happening. By 1400 over 12,000 troops had landed and were opposed by under 4,000 Turks, yet this advantage was wiped out by the nature of the ground, the confusion caused by landing in the wrong place and the disintegration of unit formations. By 1700 the Anzacs were being driven back towards the sea and fighting for their lives.

It was at this stage, when everything seemed to be progressing in broad agreement with the plan, that fate intervened. General Mustafa Kemal, commanding the Turkish 19th Division at Boghali, had been woken in the early morning by gunfire coming from the general direction of Gaba Tepe. He ordered his division to be readied while conferring with his corps commander, General Essed Pasha of the Turkish III Corps at Gallipoli.

Born in 1881, Kemal had been educated in the military schools of the Ottoman Army. Although he was an original member of the Young Turks, he lost sympathy with their aims and his career suffered accordingly. Despite extensive experience in the field in Libya and in the Balkans, in February 1915 he was serving in Sofia as the Turkish military attaché. Kemal was an able but not outstanding commander, but now his moment had come. He judged that the landing at Gaba Tepe was more than a feint and, despite Essed Pasha's order to investigate it with a battalion of his division, had his whole division on the road and marching 'to the sound of the guns'. The Turks found the going rough, for even they were unfamiliar with this part of the peninsula. Kemal went on ahead with members of his staff, and they had just reached the slopes of Chunuk Bair when they encountered Turkish troops fleeing before a party of advancing Australians. Kemal rallied them, brought up the first battalion, the 57th, and drove the Australians back.

This was the critical moment. While driving the Australians back, Kemal grasped the key to the defence of the peninsula. It was not the number of men nor the number of guns that mattered: it was a question of who held the high ground. If the British gained the high ground they could direct their artillery with impunity; if the Turks held the hills, they would overlook the enemy and constantly force him to attack. The hills called Chunuk Bair and Sari Bair were the key to the southern half of the peninsula: whoever held them, held Gallipoli. During the progress of the campaign over 50,000 men would die on the slopes of Chunuk Bair.

Kemal now acted like a man possessed. The remainder of his division was committed against the Australians in to a grim series of struggles. There was no front line on 'Anzac'. Parties from both sides would suddenly find themselves attacked and grim hand-to-hand fights would ensue. Points were won, lost and won again by both sides. Sometimes it seemed that units were fighting on their own, for they lost touch not only with their headquarters but also with units to the right and left of them. It was sheer chaos. On the Turkish side Kemal was everywhere, threatening and encouraging, leading by example. 'I don't order you to attack, I order you to die' was one of the orders he issued to units under his command.

By 1600 the Turks had gained the upper hand in the confused fighting and the Australians began to fall back, abandoning the positions they had reached following the landings. However, this was not the cause of the crisis. The error in the landing of the Australians was now having even more pronounced effects. Birdwood had hoped to have seized a strip of coast at least a mile in length; instead his Corps was occupying a small beach 1,000

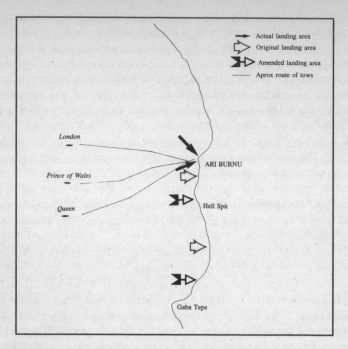

Actual landing area
Original landing area
Amended landing area
Aprox route of tows

London
Prince of Wales
Queen

ARI BURNU
Hell Spit
Gaba Tepe

The Dardanelles: 'Anzac', 25 April 1915

yards long and 30 yards wide while the whole position was less than two miles wide and three quarters of a mile deep. The congestion of men, animals, guns, equipment and stores on the beach was unimaginable. Regimental, brigade and divisional headquarters were perched on top of one another, surrounded by hospitals, signal units, prisoner-of-war cages and all the other impedimenta of a modern army.

On the front line, or what passed for the front line, the soldiers were continually overlooked by the Turks who now held the high ground. They had no artillery support and could expect none, for there were no firm targets for naval gunfire to engage. By nightfall the situation was becoming critical and an atmosphere of doubt and discouragement began to settle on the beach-head. Desperate calls were coming in from every part for ammunition, reinforcements, artillery fire and casualty evacuation. It was in these confused circumstances that Generals Bridges and Godley, the two divisional commanders, sent a message to Birdwood on board HMS *Queen*, asking him to come ashore. When Birdwood reached headquarters he was appalled to hear that both his subordinate commanders recommended evacuation. From Russell's Top and Walker's Ridge in the north, the Anzac line ran across the head of Monash Valley, then south-west along MacLaurin's Hill to the seaward side of 400 Plateau, then along Bolton's Ridge to the sea. It was at the head of Monash Valley that the situation was most critical. Here the Australians were overlooked by the Turks and the names the soldiers gave to their positions here—Bloody Angle, Dead Man's Ridge, The Valley of Despair—testify to the ferocity of the fighting. The Anzacs were exhausted and in the appalling terrain there was no hope of making any advance. However, Birdwood was persuaded that it was the only option. Accordingly, he dictated a signal to Hamilton:

> Both my divisional generals have represented to me that they fear their men are thoroughly demoralized by shrapnel fire to which they have been subjected all day after exhausting and gallant work in the morning . . . If troops are subjected to shellfire again tomorrow morning, there is likely to be a fiasco, as I have no fresh troops with which to replace those in the firing line. I know my representation is most serious but if we are to re-embark it must be at once.[3]

Hamilton was having none of it. Heartened by the fact that the submarine *AE2* had broken through into the Sea of Marmara and that she would wreak havoc on Turkish shipping, he told Birdwood that his men would have to stay. He added that Birdwood could expect relief from the 29th Division advancing from the south very soon. The postscript to his order has gone down in history: 'You have got through the difficult business, now you have only to dig, dig, dig, until you are safe.'[4]

Officers and men alike on the hills around Sari and Chunuk Bair began to dig, so that the seaward slopes resembled a honeycomb. In the event, the counter-attack never came. Kemal's division had suffered over 2,000 casualties and could do no more than hold its ground. At 'Anzac' the first phase was over. Surprise had been lost and there remained little more than a grim and costly battle of attrition. However, the gallantry and raw courage of the Australian and New Zealand troops had laid the foundation for a glorious military tradition and the emergence of a national identity for a new nation.

Just after the Anzacs went ashore, the battleships and destroyers carrying the first wave of the 29th Division stood in towards Cape Helles. The experience of the British troops at Helles was varied. On some beaches the troops simply waded ashore; on others Turkish resistance was fierce and the deeds done on those beaches are the stuff of legend. The day began with the naval bombardment by the battleships *Cornwallis*, *Swiftsure* and *Albion*. Helles was held by no more 1,000 Turkish troops of the 3rd Battalion, 26th Regiment. These troops had been harassed by naval bombardment on the previous day and also by aircraft of the RNAS. They had had little sleep and had no artillery and only four machine guns, all of which were at Sedd-el-Bahr.

When the naval barrage ended the boats began to head for the shore. To the north of the main landing site around Helles the Plymouth Battalion of Marines, one company of the 2nd Battalion the South Wales Borderers and the 1st Battalion the King's Own Scottish Borderers had landed completely unopposed at 'Y' Beach. By 0600 they were well established: scouting parties were proceeding inland, and when Hamilton steamed past in the *Queen Elizabeth* the only activity visible was the reflection of the sun on cans of water being carried up the zig-zag path from the beach.

Further south at 'X' Beach two companies of the 2nd Battalion the Royal Fusiliers had been covered by a bombardment by HMS *Implacable* and had scaled the cliffs without casualties, capturing a patrol of twelve rather stunned and shocked Turkish soldiers. *Implacable*'s bombardment was unique, for on the initiative of her gunnery officer, Lieutenant-Commander John Scott RN, she did not cease firing when the tows started their approach; instead, she carried on firing 12-inch shell at the bluffs above the beach, over the heads of those in the boats. The effect on the troops of seeing the gunfire demolishing the cliff face was remarkable:

> They were simply enthralled by the sight of the cliff face being literally blown away by the ship's guns, and the spectacle of the ship steaming in firing was magnificent . . . I have often felt that if the other landings had been similarly conducted there have been a different tale to tell.[5]

To their right the remaining three companies of the 2nd Battalion the South Wales Borderers had landed successfully on 'S' Beach.

The flank landings on 'Y', 'X' and 'S' Beaches had succeeded because they were unexpected. Yet the plan for 'W' and 'V' Beaches dispensed with the factor of surprise, relying instead on the crushing weight of the naval bombardment to compensate for it. But the bombardment failed to neutralize the defences as anticipated. Poor fire control and target indication was one reason; another was because the huge clouds of dust thrown up by the explosions of the shells made spotting extremely difficult. A third reason was that just before the troops went ashore the bombardment lifted to Turkish positions behind the beaches: at the very moment when naval gunfire should have been keeping the defenders down, it was engaged

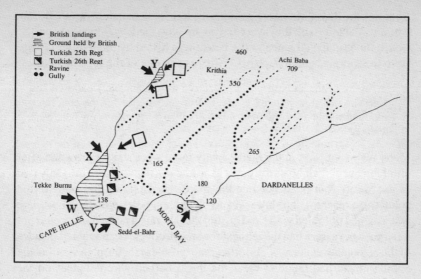

The Dardanelles: Helles, 25 April 1915

elsewhere. Thus the defenders re-occupied their trenches and readied their weapons.

'W' and 'V' Beaches were more substantial and appeared ideal for the rapid disembarkation of large numbers of troops. However, they were also easy to defend. The steep cliffs not only overlooked the beaches but surrounded them. It is not surprising that these two landings were the least successful and most costly. Moreover, the failure of staff to appreciate this and insist on a frontal assault rather than an outflanking movement from 'Y', 'X' and 'S' Beaches shows a distinct lack of imagination and a failure to appreciate the realities of assaulting these beaches. After all, it was not as if Hamilton and his staff lacked the time for preparation.

The defenders at 'W' Beach had not been dislodged by the bombardment: on the contrary, the Turks believed that their fate was sealed and were prepared to sell their lives dearly. They were well provided with ammunition, their barbed wire and trenches were intact and before them they saw the tows carrying men of the 1st Battalion the Lancashire Fusiliers.

Shortly after 0600 the 'W' Beach tows started their run in to the beach. The boats were cast off when fifty yards from the shore and almost immediately came under heavy fire. The complicated landing plan broke down immediately. In theory the Lancashire Fusiliers were to move off on either side of the beach, secure Hill 138 and then link up with the 1st

Battalion the Royal Munster Fusiliers, the left-flank battalion on 'V' Beach, while on the left flank they were to link up with the Royal Fusiliers on 'X' Beach. Instead the advance to the beach was halted by the murderous fire from the shore. Captain Richard Willis was in one of the leading boats:

> The timing of the ambush was perfect: we were completely exposed and helpless in our slow-moving boats, just target practice for the concealed Turks, and within a few minutes only half of the thirty men in my boat were left alive.[6]

Many men were shot in the boats; many more were shot or drowned after climbing out of their boats too early in an attempt to avoid the fire. Only two of the twenty-four boats reached the shore. The first task for many of the soldiers on reaching the shore was to clean their rifles which had become waterlogged or fouled with sand during the landing, a task which would not have been necessary had the request for breech covers been granted (shades of the eighteenth century!). The other main problem for the men was that the bombardment had failed to clear the thick, barbed wire defences on the beach. The Fusiliers were unable to get through this wire and many were killed while they waited. Small parties of determined men did manage to cut through, but not in sufficient numbers to take the beach.

It was at this stage that Brigadier Hare, the brigade commander, spotted a suitable landing site on the left of the beach under Tekke Burnu which offered some shelter from the Turkish fire. Accordingly, the second wave was directed to land there and succeeded in storming the Turkish defences from the left flank. But it had been a grim business: the Lancashire Fusiliers had lost six officers and 183 men killed, four officers and 279 men wounded and 61 men missing—a total of 533 casualties. A epic could written about the deeds of that one battalion on 25 April, but its heroism can be measured in the decorations awarded to the Lancashire Fusiliers—six Victoria Crosses, two Distinguished Service Orders, two Military Crosses and one Distinguished Conduct Medal.

In fact the Lancashire Fusiliers nearly succeeded in taking their objective, Hill 138. The Turkish commander was already hard pressed from 'X' and 'V' Beaches. He had no reserves to commit to 'W' Beach. The way to Hill 138 lay virtually unopposed. However, the confusion on the beach meant that this opportunity could not be exploited. The brigade commander was severely wounded and his successor was killed shortly afterwards. Compasses, binoculars and maps had been ruined by immersion in the sea and the heavy casualties and bewilderment at the ferocity of the defence all combined to hold up the advance. At 1130 men of the Essex Regiment from

'W' Beach linked up with the Royal Fusiliers on 'X' Beach. Yet the determination of the defenders, outflanked and outnumbered (by 10 to 1), prevented these advantages from being exploited.

The events on 'V' Beach were even worse. 'V' Beach was intended to be the scene of the largest and most important of the landings, yet after the expansion of the landings on the flanks it involved only one company more than was present on 'Y' Beach. Three-quarters of the 1st Battalion the Royal Dublin Fusiliers were to land on the beach from tows. Thirty minutes later the Munster Fusiliers, half of the 2nd Battalion the Hampshire Regiment and the remainder of the Dublin Fusiliers were to storm ashore from the *River Clyde*. The objective was to seize the village of Sedd-el-Bahr and then join up with the Lancashire Fusiliers to form a continuous perimeter across to 'X' Beach on one side and to Morto Bay on the other.

The *River Clyde* grounded at 0620—slightly late as she had been delayed by the strong current—at the same time as the tows carrying the 1st Battalion the Royal Dublin Fusiliers. There was a complete absence of any activity from the shore, so much so that one officer was moved to write, 'We shall land unopposed.'[7] In fact the Turks, three platoons and four machine guns, were disposed in excellent defensive positions, waited until the troops came ashore and then opened fire. The Dublin Fusiliers were devastated in their boats and as they came ashore. Less than half the battalion reached the beach and many men were wounded. The only shelter lay in a bank of sand about sixty feet from the water's edge which provided cover. For those on 'V' Beach the protection of the bank made the difference between life and death.

Meanwhile, in the *River Clyde*, Commander Unwin's plans had gone awry. He had hoped that the impact of the ship grounding would cause the steam hopper to shoot forward between the ship's bows and the shore; instead, the hopper veered off to the left and went aground in the wrong place. Unwin decided to connect the *River Clyde* to a spit of rocks running out from the shore, using two lighters which had been towed alongside the hopper. Assisted by Able Seaman William Williams and Midshipman George Drewry RNR, Unwin hauled the lighters into position and held them there while the troops began to disembark. However, it was not long before Williams was hit and had to relinquish the rope holding the lighter. The lighters were swept away and veered off to the left.

Casualties among the Munsters and Hampshires leaving the *River Clyde* were very high. The soldiers poured out of the sally-ports cut into the ship's side and down the gangways. Having decimated the Dublin Fusiliers, the Turkish fire concentrated exclusively on the two columns of men coming out of the *River Clyde*. Captain Guy Geddes of the Munster Fusiliers recalled that

> We got it like anything: man after man behind me was shot down but they never wavered. Lieutenant Watts who was wounded in five places and lying on the gangway cheered the men on with cries of 'Follow the Captain'. Captain French of the Dublins told me afterwards that he counted the first forty-eight men to follow me, and that they all fell. I think no finer episode could be found of the men's bravery and discipline than this . . . of leaving the safety of the *River Clyde* to go to what was practically certain death.[8]

Only a handful of men managed to reach the beach and the protective cover and the sandbank, where they joined the remnants of the Dublin Fusiliers. It was at this stage in the battle, with the flank landings successful but the two main landings in severe trouble, that the command organization broke down.

The 29th Division's commander, Lieutenant-General Sir Aylmer Hunter-Weston, was observing the landings on 'W' Beach from the cruiser HMS *Euryalus*. He was not told, nor did he make any efforts to determine, the situation at 'V' Beach apart from receiving reports that all was going well. Accordingly he ordered the main force to land at 0830. The main force was commanded by Brigadier-General H. Napier. As his boat neared the shore, those on the *River Clyde* tried to warn him off, but Napier was not to be dissuaded. He and many others were killed in their boats.

Hamilton, de Roebeck and Keyes watched the scenes from HMS *Queen Elizabeth*. With the aid of binoculars, the commanders could see the dead lying on the beach and across the Turkish wire and could discern that there had been no progress. Accordingly the *Queen Elizabeth* laid down another bombardment with her 15-inch guns, but to no avail. As soon as the shelling stopped and the soldiers made another attempt on the wire, the Turkish troops opened fire again.

Hamilton had no control over the ships in the operation and was trying to exercise command from a warship which had her own operations to perform. His principle formation commander, Hunter-Weston, was on another ship, while the majority of his staff were still on Lemnos. The suggestion was made that the troops assigned to land at 'V' Beach to should be diverted to 'Y' Beach, where the landings were unopposed. Hamilton, adopting a very detached view of events, was reluctant to put the plan to Hunter-Weston on the grounds that the commander-in-chief should not interfere with the operational commander. When the suggestion was eventually made, at 0915, Hunter-Weston declined on the grounds that to alter the disembarkation plan would cause more chaos than anything else.

Accordingly the Worcestershire Regiment and the Essex Regiment were switched from 'V' to 'W' Beaches, where their arrival compounded the confusion.

Colonel Owen Wolley Dodd was ordered to take command at 'W' Beach following Hare's death and that of his successor. Dodd realized that Hill 138 had to be captured if a juncture between 'V' and 'W' Beaches were to be effected. Just after 1400 the hill was taken by the Essex Regiment, but any further advance was prevented by Turkish positions and wire, which did not feature on the British maps. Behind Hill 138 was another hill, known to the Turks as Guezji Baba, which was also not on the British maps and which was even more stoutly fortified than Hill 138. Both hills were linked by a trench running along a raised shoulder of ground, and it was clear that Guezji Baba would also have to be taken. The Worcestershire Regiment launched an attack from two sides and, forcing their way through the wire, drove the Turks off the hill: by 1600 the hill was taken. The Worcesters then pushed on and by nightfall were overlooking 'V' Beach. However, they could advance no further. As dusk fell on the peninsula both sides dug in and consolidated their positions. At 'V' Beach the coming of darkness meant that the remaining men on the *River Clyde* could get ashore, although once the moon rose they were exposed to random sniper and machine-gun fire.

The most perplexing events were happening to the north on 'Y' Beach, where the troops had spent a quiet morning with no activity other than sending out patrols which reached the village of Krithia unopposed. There was confusion among the two battalion commanders as to their objectives and as to which was the senior. No attempt was made to dig in and reinforce the position, so that when Turkish counter-attacks began to develop in the afternoon and evening the British were poorly deployed to meet them. By nightfall 'Y' Beach was in a state of siege with a fierce and unco-ordinated battle raging in the darkness. Poor staffwork and communications prevented reinforcements from being dispatched, though they were available. In the confusion that night the troops began falling back on the beach and in the morning of the 26th they were taken off by the Navy without any formal order to evacuate having been issued by either Hunter-Weston or Hamilton. It would be two weeks before 'Y' Beach was back in British hands. A great opportunity to outflank the strongly held positions at Helles was lost and the damage to the campaign was irreparable.

At night on 25 April the situation was as follows. At 'Y' Beach the Marines and KOSB were fending off Turkish counter-attacks. 'X' and 'W' Beaches had been linked, but the troops were doing their best to dig in. At 'V' Beach the survivors were lying in the *River Clyde* or behind the sandbank, while at 'S' Beach the South Wales Borderers were also digging in. The French had landed at Kum Kale with mixed results. It was hardly the bold attack on the peninsula which Hamilton had hoped for.

It was not until the evening of 26 April that forces from 'W' Beach joined those from 'V' Beach after the village of Sedd-el-Bahr and Hill 141 had been taken. The British troops were now strung out in a single perimeter along the base of the peninsula. The situation favoured an advance to link up with 'S' Beach, but instead Hunter-Weston ordered the 29th Division to dig in: 'There must be no retiring. Every man must die at his post rather than retire.'

Despite the gallantry of the troops of the 29th Division on the beaches—fifteen Victoria Crosses were awarded for deeds of valour performed at Helles in the first thirty-six hours of the campaign—the landings had failed to achieve their intended result. As Hamilton noted,

> The result of the operation has been a failure, as my object remains unachieved. Our troops have done all that flesh and blood can do against semi-permanent works and are not able to carry them. More and more munitions will be needed to do so.[9]

Notes to Chapter 3

1. See Steel and Hart, *Defeat at Gallipoli*, MacMillan (1994), pp.54–9, for an explanation of how this occurred.
2. Imperial War Museum, Department of Documents, Papers of Captain R Wilkinson RN: TS copy of letter dated 3 April–8 June 1915.
3. Moorhead, Alan, *Gallipoli*, Hamish Hamilton (London,1956), pp.153–4.
4. *Ibid.*, p.155.
5. Commander S. E. Norfolk to Captain H. Lockyer, 3 September 1936. Imperial War Museum, Department of Documents, Papers of Captain H. Lockyer RN.
6. Willis, Major R. R., 'The Landing at Gallipoli', *Gallipoli Gazette* (1934), p.72.
7. James, Robert Rhodes, *Gallipoli*, Batsford (London, 1965), p.121.
8. Imperial War Museum, Department of Documents, Colonel G. Geddes: TS account, p.3.
9. James, *op. cit.*, p.157.

CHAPTER FOUR

Stalemate

We have landed and dug another graveyard.—Ashmead Bartlett, correspondent of *The Times*, describing the Suvla Bay landings

THE immediate development after the landings was a race by both sides to build up their positions. This was a race the Turks won, owing to their having direct communications with their interior. The severe casualties suffered by the British on 25 April and Hamilton's admission that nothing more could be accomplished without further troopsled to his being reinforced on a massive scale. From Egypt he received the 42nd East Lancashire Division (a Territorial unit) and the 29th Indian Brigade, less two battalions composed of Muslim Punjabis who remained in Egypt for fear they would be unreliable if pitted against their co-religionists (their place was taken by Gurkha troops).

The Turks had reinforced their positions with the 7th Division, part of the 11th Division and part of the 5th. These reinforcements of fresh troops succeeded in halting attacks launched on 28 April...the first Battle of Krithia—to take Achi Baba, the objective of the original assault. The attacks failed and Achi Baba remained four miles away in Turkish hands until the end of the campaign, brooding over the British and French lines as a constant reminder of their failure.

During the nights of 1/2 and 3/4 May the Turks went on the offensive but their attacks were beaten back. Hamilton resumed the offensive on 6 May. He joined an Australian and a New Zealand brigade from 'Anzac' with a brigade from the Royal Naval Division to form a composite division which was inserted into the line at Helles. Achi Baba was the objective, but the Turkish line held firm. The Second Battle of Krithia lasted for three days, from 6 to 8 May. As on previous occasions the British and French made little headway. The Turks counter-attacked on 9/10 May, and on the 11th the 29th Division was finally relieved by the 42nd Division, while the two Anzac brigades were returned to their parent corps.

The struggle at Helles now settled down into a grim battle of attrition, with the British VIII Corps, consisting of the 29th, 42nd and Royal Naval

Divisions, holding the left of the peninsula and the French holding the right. The prerequisites of trench warfare—grenades, trench mortars and vast supplies of artillery and munitions—were sorely lacking. The same was true at 'Anzac', but the troops at Helles had to contend with Turkish shelling from the Asiatic shore, which had a wearying effect.

At 'Anzac' reinforcements arrived during the night of 28/29 April in the shape of four battalions of the Royal Naval Division and dismounted troopers from the 1st Australian Light Horse Brigade. However, Birdwood had to abandon his plans for a general offensive on 30 April simply because the 1st Australian Division was below strength on account of battle casualties. On 2 May a local offensive began well in Monash Gully but was abandoned when naval gunfire fell short into the advancing troops. Apart from the usual routine of trench warfare, life then became fairly quiet at 'Anzac', firstly because of the transfer of two brigades to Helles but secondly, and more importantly, because the soldiers were working so hard at simply existing on that hostile shore that there was little time for much else. Hamilton noted that nearly half his front-line troops were engaged in logistic and maintenance duties.

The Turks had suffered over 14,000 casualties at 'Anzac' since 25 April but the threat posed by the Anzac position meant that there could be no slackening off: a small Anzac advance would be enough to cut off the Turkish troops at Helles. After a personal visit to the peninsula in May, Enver Pasha ordered a fresh assault using the newly arrived 2nd Division. On 18 May the Turks began an artillery bombardment of the positions at 'Anzac', and this was followed the next day by infantry assaults. The Turks had massed some 30,000 men with the single aim of driving the Australian and New Zealand troops into the sea. Fortunately the Royal Naval Air Service had sighted the Turkish troops disembarking at Maidos and the Anzacs were ready to repulse the attack. The slaughter was terrible. The Anzacs lost some 500 men in beating back the attacks but over 10,000 Turks perished between 0400 and 1200.

Formal negotiations between Liman von Sanders and Hamilton resulted in a nine-hour truce on 20 May for the burial of the dead. At last the adversaries could come face to face with one another. Private Henry Barnes was in the 4th Australian Brigade:

> I wasn't one of those burying the dead but I sat on the parapet and after a while walked over and offered bully beef to one Turk. He smiled and seemed very pleased and offered me a whole string of dates. Jacko, as we called the Turkish soldier, was very highly regarded by me and all the men on our side. I never heard him decried, he was always a clean fighter and one of the most

courageous men in the world. When they came there was no beating about the bush. They faced up to the heaviest rifle fire you could put up and nothing would stop them—they were almost fanatical. When we met them at the armistice we came to the conclusion that he was a very good bloke indeed.[1]

After the Turkish attack the front at 'Anzac' settled down as each side recognized the inherent strengths of the other's position.

In the meantime Hamilton was asking for more reinforcements. He was genuinely puzzled by the fact that the campaign was having a negligible effect on Britain's allies. The Allied landings offered countless opportunities, but nothing was happening: '. . . the Balkans fold their arms, the Italians show no interest, the Russians do not move an inch to get across the Black Sea.'[2] On 10 May Hamilton asked for another two divisions, organized as a corps. A week later he raised his requirements and asked for two fully equipped corps. In assessing Hamilton's requests for men it should be remembered that although he had four divisions and a brigade already deployed at Gallipoli, the effective number of bayonets available was greatly reduced because of the high incidence of sickness among his troops. Kitchener replied by sending him one division, the 52nd Lowland Division, a territorial unit which was already substantially below establishment since cadres had been withdrawn for service with divisions in France.

The 52nd arrived at Helles on 5 June, the day after an attack had been launched by the 42nd Division and the French—the Third Battle of Krithia. Progress by the 42nd was invalidated by the French having to retire in the face of a heavy Turkish counter-attack. The 52nd Division went into action on 28 June in a joint attack with the 29th Division which succeeded in achieving minor gains on the left flank a few days after the French had made progress on right flank. However, these advances were relatively insignificant and were followed by ferocious Turkish counter-attacks to regain the lost ground: while the Allies continued to batter their way up the peninsula, the Turks were continually reinforcing their army there and by early June another five Turkish divisions had arrived on the peninsula.

Stalemate in the Dardanelles contributed to a political crisis that erupted in London. An Admiralty proposal for a renewed attempt on the Narrows was the reason for the resignation, on 15 May 1915, of Admiral Fisher, who had long since abandoned his earlier enthusiasm for the Dardanelles venture; a further casualty of the affair was Winston Churchill. The British Government now found that it could not survive without the support of the opposition, and a new coalition was formed.

The conduct of the campaign was entrusted to the Dardanelles Committee. At its first meeting in June it was decided to grant Hamilton the reinforcements he required, and the first three of the divisions of Kitchener's 'New Army', the 10th (Irish), the 11th and the 13th, were ordered to the Dardanelles as soon as shipping was available. The New Army consisted of those men who had joined the colours in the heady days of August 1914. Although their senior officers were all too often old men brought out of retirement, the junior officers, NCOs and ordinary soldiers were keen and raring to go. However, the New Army divisions had not seen combat and would arrive at the Dardanelles in the full heat of summer. Seldom has Britain sent an army overseas which was so youthful and full of hope and yet so hopelessly inexperienced.

The largesse of the Dardanelles Committee was not limited to three divisions. Additionally Hamilton was to receive the infantry from the 53rd (Welsh) Division and the 54th (East Anglian) Division to make up his numbers in view of losses to enemy action and sickness. This windfall of troops was too great for them to be employed in the Helles or 'Anzac' landing zones so Hamilton's staff cast around for alternative sites and times for a single shattering offensive which would break the Turkish forces around his two beach-heads. Hamilton had four options for the deployment of these new troops, which, ironically, mirrored those he faced at the beginning of the campaign. They could be landed at Helles for another offensive there, although Hamilton did not share the optimism displayed by VIII Corps headquarters. They could be landed at Bulair, although the original disadvantages of landing at this location had been exacerbated by the threat posed by German U-boats. A landing on the Asiatic shore was also considered, but since the British and French were ashore in strength on the Gallipoli peninsula another landing in Asia could be no more than a diversion. The fourth option was an adaptation of Birdwood's scheme for a break-out northwards from 'Anzac', and this seemed to offer the best possibilities. The main drawback in adapting Birdwood's scheme was that there was insufficient room (or supplies of fresh water) in the 'Anzac' beach-head for the landing of more troops. The solution was a third landing, either to the north or to the south of the current position. To the south, the area around Gaba Tepe was well defended, but to the north the area around Suvla Bay was lightly held and thus regarded as a better site.

Suvla Bay was well chosen for a landing. To the north of the bay and bordering the Aegean lies a range of hills called the Kirech Tepe Sirt. For six miles the hills climb north-east from Suvla Point, at the northern end of the bay, to Ejelmer Bay, passing the area known as Ghazi Baba (where IX Corps eventually had their headquarters). Midway along the range, and branching off inland for nearly four miles at right angles to it, is the Tekke

Tepe range of hills. At the southern end of this range is the village of Anafarta Sagir, and directly opposite this village, at the northern end of the Sari Bair range, is the village of Biyuk Anafarta. Between these two villages lies a raised area known as the Anafarta Spur. Its northern edge is formed by Scimitar Hill while the southern slopes are formed by Ismail Oglu Tepe. Directly to the west is another range of twin-peaked hills known to the British as Chocolate Hill. Towards to sea lies the Salt Lake, a large dried up area, and the final Suvla Hill called Lala Baba, which tapers away south-west from its central peak towards Nubranesi Point and north to the narrow spit of land which reaches down to the Cut, the shallow ditch where Suvla Bay enters the Salt Lake. Beyond this the ground broadens out again around Hill 10. Within the arc bounded by Kirech Tepe Sirt and Tekke Tepe is the Suvla Plain. It is flat and easy and leads directly to the high ground at the rear. It was the plain which attracted the attention of Hamilton and his staff.

Planning for a landing at Suvla began in June, and de Roebeck's staff were brought in on the operation to discuss the possibility of landing a force at Suvla together with the break-out north from 'Anzac'. The omens for this operation looked good, particularly when de Roebeck offered a number of specially designed motor lighters for landing troops—the precursors of today's landing craft. These had originally been designed for use in Fisher's abortive operation in the Baltic: the only useful by-product of this slightly ludicrous scheme, they were potentially of great value. Each was capable of carrying 500 men, drew only seven feet of water, had armoured sides and was fitted with a bow ramp to permit quick disembarkation on the beach. As such, the craft offered a solution to many of the landing problems experienced on 25 April. On the negative side, however, de Roebeck's staff had studied the shore line at Suvla carefully and found that the bay itself was poorly charted. Fearing the presence of unknown rocks or shoals, they ruled against a landing in the bay but recommended the use of a beach stretching a mile south from Suvla.

The question of who was to command the operation posed some difficulty. Hamilton turned down Kitchener's suggestion that Lieutenant-General Sir Bryan Mahon, GOC 10th Division, be promoted and given command of IX Corps (as the Suvla invasion force would be called). Hamilton considered that, although Mahon was a good divisional commander, he was 'not up to running our Corps out here'.[3] Hamilton then asked for the services of either Lieutenant-General Sir Julian Byng or Lieutenant-General Sir Henry Rawlinson, both of whom were commanding divisions with distinction on the Western Front. Kitchener refused on the grounds that neither of these officers could be spared from their current appointments.

The ludicrous situation then arose whereby, instead of appointing an officer who possessed all the necessary qualities to command an army corps in an amphibious operation, Kitchener remained bound by the question of seniority as defined in the Army List. Since Mahon was the senior divisional commander, it followed that the corps commander must be senior to Mahon. The only two general officers senior to Mahon who were available were Lieutenant-General Sir John Ewart and Lieutenant-General Sir Frederick Stopford. Ewart was commanding Scottish Command and was unfit for service in the Mediterranean and Stopford had been in retirement for five years. The latter was appointed. Stopford had many qualities which had won him professional respect throughout a long career but he had never held a major command in the field, most of his experience was theoretical and he was in poor health. Hamilton had wanted seasoned troops with young commanders; instead, he received new and untried troops led by aged and infirm commanders.

The scheme eventually adopted was a complicated one with three elements—a diversion at Helles, a northwards thrust at 'Anzac' and the landings at Suvla. The diversion at Helles was simply to keep the Turks occupied and guessing as to the real nature of the British intentions. The attack at 'Anzac' was more adventurous. Reconnaissance had established that the area north of the beach-head was lightly held. Lieutenant-Colonel Andrew Skeen produced a plan for a night march through the country north of 'Anzac' followed by the seizure of the heights of the Sari Bair range. If this was successful, the Turks would be outflanked and the Allied advance across the peninsula to the Narrows resumed. To secure these objectives the Anzac Corps would be supported by the 13th Division, which would be landed secretly over three nights.

In the landings at Suvla General Hammersley's 11th Division were to disembark at Nubranesi Point at 2100 on 6 August, capture Lala Baba and Hill 10 and then advance across Suvla Plain to capture Kirech Tepe, Chocolate Hill and the W Hills by daylight. The 10th Division would land at daybreak on 7 August and continue the advance along Kirech Tepe while the 11th Division captured Tekke Tepe. If all went well, by noon on 7 August the British line would stretch from Ejelmer Bay to Chunuk Bair. The Turks on the peninsula would face being cut off from their reinforcements at Bulair, several hours' march away. Having secured the hills to the northern and eastern sides of the plain, Stopford's corps was to swing right and move up the slopes of the Sari Bair range to assist the Anzacs. It followed that the swift seizure of the hills was vital to the success of the plan. This was made clear to Stopford when he received his orders on 22 July. The

instructions were explicit: the seizure of the hills was of the 'first importance'.

Stopford's reaction to the plan was enthusiastic; that of his Chief of Staff,
Brigadier-General H. L. Reed VC, was less so. Reed was a gunner whose
attitudes had been coloured by his service in France. In particular, he
believed that no assault could succeed without massive artillery support.
Furthermore, unlike many British officers in the Dardanelles, Reed had
been attached to the Turkish Army during the Balkan Wars and was familiar
with the courage and discipline of the Turkish soldier, particularly in
defence. These were not negligible criticisms, and it should be remembered
that Reed's objections were the very point that the failure of successive
assaults at Helles had driven home. The irony was that at Suvla there were
but three battalions of Turkish troops. Reed's error lay not in his argument
but in its misapplication. In adhering to it he ignored other principles of war
such as surprise and the value of seizing high ground.

Reed's arguments had an effect on Stopford, who on 26 July asked for his
orders to be revised. The original plan called for the 11th Division's three
brigades to be landed on different sections of the same beach, called New
Beach, which ran south from Nubranesi Point to Aghyl Dere. On Reed's
advice Stopford now requested that one brigade be landed in Suvla Bay, in
order to spare the troops assigned to attack Chocolate Hill from the north a
long night march around the Salt Lake. Reluctantly the naval authorities
agreed, although they feared shoals and rocks. 'A' Beach was thus relocated
to the north and the logical order disrupted so that, from south to north, the
beaches were lettered 'B', 'C' and 'A'.

Reed was now out for a wholesale revision of the plan. Stopford's
confidence wavered and IX Corps' staff managed to scale down the plan
from that of a major undertaking to one of merely securing a beach-head as
a base for further operations. Remarkably, Hamilton and the staff at GHQ
were so absorbed in the planning for the break-out from 'Anzac' that not only
did they fail to object to Stopford's revisions but they actually incorporated
them in revised instructions dated 29 July. These new orders no longer
included the hills at the back of the plain as an objective and downgraded
the task of IX Corps to the simple 'securing of Suvla Bay as a base for all
the forces operating in the northern zone'. There was no reference to the
importance of capturing the hills, and it was obvious that Hamilton and the
staff had failed to convey the very essence of the plan to Stopford; in this
lies the crux of who should bear the blame for the resulting failure. From the
moment Stopford received his orders it became clear that a gulf of
perception existed between his staff and that of GHQ. Stopford did not

believe in the plan, so he did not ensure that his men strove to carry it out. He thus brought about the failure he feared. Yet it was Hamilton's ultimate responsibility to ensure that his plan was carried out when everything about Stopford indicated that he was not up to the task.

By this stage the operation had grown into a mammoth undertaking. Over 100,000 men were to be deployed on three fronts; 20,000 men were to be landed on a hostile shore and another 20,000 were to be smuggled ashore at 'Anzac'. But there was little central control of this operation. Hamilton was allowing his subordinate commanders plenty of discretion to fight their own battles and the result was that the plan degenerated into three separate operations. Hamilton meanwhile was taking a very detached view of affairs —an almost exact repetition of his state of mind at Helles three months earlier.

One of the chief complaints of subordinate commanders was that the operation was so shrouded in secrecy that they knew little of what was expected of them. Hamilton was determined that his plan should not become as widely known as that for the original assault. As a result, brigade commanders were not briefed until 30 July, and some were allowed a speedy excursion past the beaches in a destroyer. Regimental commanders were briefed nearer the date for the operation. The desire for secrecy was commendable but it meant that there was little unity of purpose among the command.

In the event, the Turks did become aware that something was in the wind. The combination of the drying up of the Salt Lake and the patrolling north of 'Anzac' had aroused the Turks' attention. However, their concern focused on the right flank at 'Anzac', the area around Gaba Tepe which was hurriedly reinforced. Nevertheless, the whole Turkish defence was ordered to be on the *qui vive*. The defence of Suvla Bay was entrusted a small unit known as the Anafarta Detachment commanded by a German officer, Major Willmer. It consisted of four infantry battalions (later reduced to three), a pioneer company, a cavalry squadron and nineteen guns. Willmer realized that he could offer only a holding defence until reinforcements arrived. His troops were therefore ordered not to risk being cut off but to retire to the next line of defence, ready to fight again. His forward positions were sited on Kirech Tepe, Lala Baba and Hill 10. Though his troops were well dug in, they lacked barbed wire and machine guns.

The offensive opened on 6 August 1915. At Helles the 29th Division suffered badly in a diversionary attack on part of the Turkish line. A second diversion was carried out by Australian troops at Turkish positions at Lone Pine, at the centre of the 'Anzac' beach-head. Here they captured the Turkish

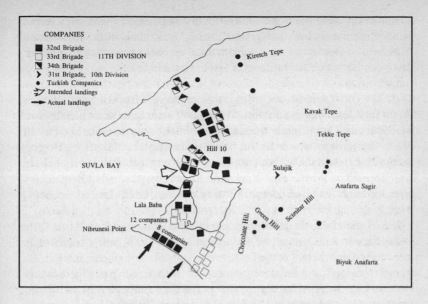

COMPANIES
- 32nd Brigade
- 33rd Brigade   11TH DIVISION
- 34th Brigade
- 31st Brigade, 10th Division
- Turkish Companies
- Intended landings
- Actual landings

Kiretch Tepe

Kavak Tepe

Tekke Tepe

Hill 10

SUVLA BAY

Sulajik

Anafarta Sagir

Lala Baba

Chocolate Hill   Green Hill   Scimitar Hill

12 companies

Nibrunesi Point

8 companies

Biyuk Anafarta

The Dardanelles: Suvla, 7 August 1915

front line but provoked fierce counter-attacks for the next four days. The fighting at Lone Pine was desperate: some measure of its intensity can be gauged from the fact that seven Victoria Crosses were awarded for acts of valour in this action.

During the evening of 6 August the columns from 'Anzac' began their night march. Although some troops became lost among the gullies and ridges, a party of New Zealanders managed to climb within striking distance of Chunuk Bair. However, instead of pressing on they waited for the rest of their brigade to catch up. The Turks used this opportunity to reinforce their defences, and when the New Zealanders resumed the offensive they were beaten back. The failure to take Chunuk Bair had disastrous consequences for the troopers of the Australian Light Horse, who suffered heavily in diversionary attacks on Turkish positions around the Neck on 7 August.[4] In the attack the 'flower and youth of Western Australia' were massacred as they attempted to take the Turkish trenches.

In the early hours of 8 August the Navy laid down a bombardment of Sari Bair and at last the New Zealanders gained the summit of Chunuk Bair. Gurkha troops also made significant progress, but Australian troops who had to seize Hill 971 further north were being held up by Turkish resistance which was stiffening. Eventually the Turks launched a massive counter-attack on 10 August. Some 3,000 fresh troops, led by Mustafa Kemal himself, confronted the exhausted British, Australian, New Zealand and Gurkha forces and drove them back to the slopes below. At 'Anzac' gallantry had been no match for bullets; at Suvla Bay a priceless opportunity was thrown away.

At 2145 on 6 August, according to plan, the first Beetles went ashore at Suvla Bay near Nubranesi Point. Within half an hour the four battalions of the 32nd and 33rd Brigade were ashore without a single casualty. The 7th South Staffordshires and the 9th Sherwood Foresters of the 33rd Brigade secured the right flank without opposition and dug in to their left. Lala Baba was stormed by the 6th East Yorkshire Regiment of the 32nd Brigade just after midnight, but considerable losses were incurred. Indeed, so heavy were these that the battalion was incapable of following up its assault.

Unfortunately, in an uncomfortable echo of the landings at 'Anzac', the 34th Brigade was landed on 'A' Beach some 1,000 yards south of its intended position, right in the middle of shoals. To complicate matters, the troops were landed in the wrong order. The 11th Manchesters were landed close to Lala Baba on the wrong side of the Cut, although they swiftly got themselves sorted out, moved off to the north and by 0300 had secured the northern arm of Suvla Bay at Suvla Point, cleared the area around Ghazi Baba and moved two miles along the Kirech Tepe Ridge, showing what could be achieved by determined leadership.

The other battalions in the 34th Brigade were not so lucky. The 9th Lancashire Fusiliers found themselves facing the wastes of the Salt Lake with no sign of their objective, Hill 10. In vain the officers searched for it, but while they tried to orientate themselves the battalion was plagued by persistent sniper fire. As a result the Fusiliers milled around the Cut going nowhere. The Manchesters had stormed off to the north while the other two battalions had not yet got ashore.

A mile to the south, the 32nd Brigade and half the 33rd Brigade should have moved off towards Hill 10 prior to taking Chocolate Hill and Green Hill. Instead they remained on Lala Baba. The absence of orders stressing the need for speed now made itself felt. Local commanders lacked the flexibility of purpose and mind to take upon themselves the task of capturing Hill 10 when it became clear that the 34th Brigade was unable to do so.

By this stage the 34th Brigade was hours behind schedule. As the tide ebbed, the Beetles were stranded. Brigadier Henry Haggard, in overall command of the 32nd and 33rd Brigades, waited at Lala Baba for the situation to be resolved. Finally, at 0300, he sent a force forward, but despite having at least six untouched battalions at his disposal he only sent four companies north to join the 34th Brigade. Inevitably these became sucked into the chaos around the Cut.

There was now a vacuum at the centre of the British line and the Turks launched a minor counter-attack at 0330 which was beaten back. In the meantime Brigadier Sitwell of the 34th Brigade had finally got ashore, and he determined to restore the situation and capture Hill 10. The 9th Lancashire Fusiliers were ordered to take the hill at dawn, but in the confusion they attacked a sand dune 400 yards to the south of the real objective. As a result they were savaged by enfilade fire from the flank.

The plan was now hopelessly behind schedule. By this stage the 11th Division should have been established in the hills around the Suvla Plain, but, apart from the bold showing of the Manchester Regiment, the troops had hardly moved off the beach. General Hammersley now began to pull the situation together. At 0520 the 32nd Brigade was ordered north to join the 34th Brigade and shortly after 0600 Hill 10 was finally taken.

The next stage in the plan was a swing around the north of the Salt Lake to assault Chocolate Hill from the north. However, most of the battalions had stumbled on to the lower slopes of the Kirech Tepe range instead, a move which reflected the lack of information on the terrain given to battalion commanders. Confusion now turned into chaos. At 0430 the transports carrying the 10th Division arrived to land the troops to consolidate the advance. The obsessive secrecy was now playing havoc with operations as their commander, Brigadier-General Felix Hill, had no idea what he was supposed to be doing nor where he was to do it. Hill went over to the sloop HMS *Jonquil*, which was carrying General Stopford, to receive his orders. Stopford had intended the 31st and 30th Brigades of the 10th Division to have landed at 'A' Beach, but the rapidly shoaling water made this impossible. Instead he directed them to land on 'C' Beach. This created more chaos as 'C' Beach was in the south of the bay whereas the 10th Division's objectives lay to the north.

At this juncture Commodore Keyes indicated that the Navy had found an alternative landing site in the north of the bay which would have been ideal for Hill's troops. Stopford, alas, refused to approve a change of orders, believing that this would only add to the confusion. Thus half of the 10th Division was landed on the wrong side of the bay. At 0730 General Mahon arrived with the rest of his division, was directed to the new beach and was told to push along Kirech Tepe in support of the Manchesters. By 0800 on 7 August the flanks of the beach were secure but the 11th Division, in the centre, was in a muddle with the 10th Division split on either side of it.

By mid-morning on 7 August a stream of contradictory orders and reports was being passed to and from the various divisional and brigade headquarters as Hammersley tried to co-ordinate the attack on Chocolate Hill. Brigadier Sitwell felt that the men of the 32nd and 43rd Brigades were exhausted after the night's activities and needed rest. When Hill's troops reached the Cut late that morning he advised against a further advance on the grounds that he lacked sufficient support. Time and time again orders to take the offensive were cancelled as commanders sought to defer to higher authority. Stopford was in no position to do anything as he was still embarked in *Jonquil* with an injured knee and refused to come ashore. No one was prepared to take any risks and time was slipping away.

Eventually Hill ordered three of his battalions to move round the north of the Salt Lake and take Chocolate Hill, only to cancel the operation shortly afterwards. A larger operation was mounted soon after 1730, this time with the support of all available 11th Division battalions and a naval and artillery bombardment. The three 10th Division battalions were augmented by two battalions from the 33rd Brigade on the right flank which had moved across the Salt Lake, an option which had always been available. With their help the Irish took Chocolate Hill, but after nightfall instead of before daybreak. The advantage gained by the capture of Chocolate Hill was almost instantly nullified by the infantry's spending the night in reorganization instead of pushing on. Indeed, the supporting battalions from the 32nd and 43rd Brigades were recalled to the beach instead of exploiting the opportunity. Meanwhile Willmer's Turks had held Chocolate Hill as long as they dared before falling back to their next position.

To the north, the initial gains made by the Manchesters were not followed up. The three battalions from the 10th Division finally landed at the new, renamed 'A' Beach and moved up to Kirech Tepe shortly after 1430, but on reaching the positions held by the exhausted Manchesters they stopped and dug in. They also made no attempt to link up with the 34th Brigade to the south on the lower slopes but spent they night wearing themselves out digging in amid the rocks when they should have been on a forced march to seize the Kirech Tepe heights at the point where they joined the Tekke Tepe Ridge; it would not have been any easier, but it would have been more useful.

Generally the British troops blundered about in chaos once they were ashore, largely because no one at unit level knew where they were or what they were supposed to do. Yet it must be said that these were untried troops and the constant sniping proved extremely debilitating and demoralizing. Private G. A. Handford of the 8th Duke of Wellington's Regiment wrote:

What an effect these pests had on our progress is best described in the casualties which were mostly the victims of some fiendish snipers . . . Parties would go out in search of these fiends, but all to no good, for generally they would return with the majority of them missing—victims to the snipers.[5]

Although there were not that many snipers in numerical terms, they had a disproportionate effect on the inexperienced, tired British troops on the plain. Another problem was that, in the chaos attending the landings, the water supplies broke down completely, leaving men without water for the whole of the day. The combination of poor leadership, thirst and constant sniping paralysed initiative among the British command.

As night fell on 7 August the objectives of the landing had not been achieved because they had not been attempted. The Turks held all the strategically important points and all the British had achieved was the capture of a few outposts. As after the landings at Helles, the campaign now became a race between the British and the Turks as to who could deploy most troops in the shortest time. Already three Turkish battalions had been ordered to Suvla, but once von Sanders knew the nature of the landing the 7th and 12th Divisions were dispatched from Bulair. After a forced march from Bulair they would reach Suvla late on 8 August or early on the 9th. The success of the campaign rested on how quickly Stopford could seize his objectives. In this respect IX Corps had already lost the battle.

Communications between Stopford and Hamilton were appalling. The former made no attempt to keep the latter in touch with the progress of the operation, and in any case HMS *Jonquil* was barely fitted with communications for the control of an army corps. Finally, on 8 August, Hamilton dispatched two staff officers to Suvla to render a report on progress. Captain C. F. Aspinall and Colonel Maurice Hankey landed to find a holiday atmosphere on the beaches. Worse, after a few minutes' walk across the plain, they found themselves in the front line.

Aspinall pleaded for the offensive to be resumed, but Stopford seemed quite content in that his troops were ashore. In desperation Aspinall signalled to Hamilton:

Just been ashore where I found all quiet. No rifle fire, no artillery fire, and apparently no Turks. IX Corps resting. Feel confident that golden opportunities are being lost and look upon the situation as serious.

Hamilton now decided to go ashore and see for himself. He discussed the situation with Stopford and insisted that an attack be mounted on Tekke Tepe that night. Stopford demurred, saying that Hammersley did not consider an advance at night practical and that anyway he was planning a general attack for the morning of the 9th. Hamilton was having none of this and stormed ashore to see Hammersley himself.

Hammersley had been making progress. He was organizing an assault on the W Hills by the 33rd Brigade for the morning of the 9th when Hamilton appeared. But the curse which seemed to afflict the Gallipoli campaign struck once again. Unknown to anyone, a signaller and an officer from the 6th East Yorkshire Regiment had scaled the heights of Tekke Tepe and found them unoccupied. Hamilton did not learn of this until 1923 hours, by which time the 32nd Brigade were advancing on their own initiative, spread out across the Suvla Plain. The 9th West Yorkshire Regiment were 1,000 yards from Sulajik and the 6th East Yorks were established on Scimitar Hill.

None of this was known, however, at 11th Division HQ, where Hamilton had insisted that the 32nd Brigade were to take Tekke Tepe that night. As a result, orders were given for the brigade to concentrate at Sulajik prior to the attack. This meant that the East and West Yorkshires had to withdraw from their advanced position to re-join the rest of their brigade. After five and a half hours of signalling and manoeuvring the battalions in the dark, the order to advance was not given until 0330 on the 9th.

By this stage the infantry, and the 6th East Yorkshires in particular, were exhausted and in no state to do anything but sleep. To complete the tragedy, the assault on Tekke Tepe coincided with the arrival of the Turkish reinforcements from Bulair. By a supreme irony Hamilton's intervention had ruined Hammersley's plan for a concerted advance which might had succeeded. Instead, what followed was a disaster.

The two divisions from Bulair had now arrived at Suvla. Mustafa Kemal, who been appointed to command the Turkish forces at Suvla in addition to those at 'Anzac' on 8 August, confirmed that one division, the 12th, would counter-attack from the top of Tekke Tepe while the other, the 7th, would head towards Biyuk Anafarta and advance from that direction. The Turks caught the 32nd Brigade spread out on the lower slopes of the hill. Lieutenant John Still was a platoon commander with the 6th East Yorkshires. As his battalion struggled up Tekke Tepe,

> . . . we came under fire from our right flank right from the start. As we moved on and on, up and up, men got lost in the prickly scrub oak . . . and it became increasingly difficult to maintain any kind of formation. But the enemy's fire grew in volume as we mounted, poured into us at ever decreasing range . . . About thirty of us reached the top of the hill, perhaps a few more. And when there were about twenty left, we turned and went down again. We had reached the highest point and the furthest point that British forces from Suvla Bay were destined to reach, but we naturally knew nothing of that.[6]

The retreat caused a rude awakening for the guns of 'A' Battery, 59th Brigade RFA, who were in position on the reverse slopes of Chocolate Hill. Bombardier George Dale remembered that

> Right at dawn the Sergeant Major's cattle-calling bellow drowns the echoes of our last combined snore, 'A Battery-Action!' As Hubert slams the breech on a round the order comes for 'Gunfire!' (As fast as possible with due regard for accuracy) . . . This lasts for two hours…time just stood still. The end comes when each No. 1 reports 'No more ammo, sir'.[7]

And so their guns fell silent until more ammunition could be brought up. The Turkish attack opened up a gap in the British line north of Sulajik which was hastily filled with battalions from the 34th Brigade and the 159th Brigade of the 53rd Welsh Division which had been landed overnight. As reinforcements arrived the Turkish attack subsided. The Turks had gained the Tekke Tepe Heights and were content to look down on the British.

The fate of the landings at Suvla was determined at that point. The fighting continued throughout 9 and 10 August, but after suffering over 8,000 casualties the British occupied roughly the same positions they had held on the morning of the 7th. The delays on the 7th and 8th had been fatal to the outcome of the enterprise.

The débâcle at Suvla cost Stopford his command. Hamilton finally relieved him on 15 August. In his place was appointed General Byng, one of the commanders Hamilton had asked for in the first place. Until Byng could come out to the Dardanelles Major-General H. de Lisle replaced him. Other casualties of the affair included Hammersley, Reed, Sitwell and General Lindley of the 53rd Division.

Hamilton now reinforced IX Corps with the 29th Division and approved an attack for 21 August. The battle was the largest fought during the Gallipoli campaign. The British advanced against the Turks in well dug-in positions and were literally mown down. Over 5,000 casualties were suffered in this attack, which effectively brought the campaign to a close.

Notes to Chapter 4

1. Imperial War Museum, Department of Sound Records, SR4008: Interview with Henry Barnes.
2. Hamilton, *Gallipoli Diary*, p.164.
3. *Ibid*., p.185.
4. An episode immortalized, though not with complete accuracy, in Peter Weir's film *Gallipoli*.

5. Imperial War Museum, Department of Documents, G. A. Hancock: TS account, pp.17–18.

6. Still, John, *A Prisoner in Turkey*, Bodley Head (1924), pp.27–8.

7. Imperial War Museum, Department of Documents, Diary of Bombardier G. E. Dale, 8/9 August 1915.

CHAPTER FIVE

The Reality of Defeat

*Conceive the crowding into the boats of thousands of half crazy men,
the swamping of craft, the nocturnal panic, the agony of the
wounded, the hecatombs of the slain.*—Lord Curzon, predicting the
consequences of an evacuation of the Gallipoli peninsula.

THE failure of the August offensive dashed all hopes for a decisive
breakthrough on the peninsula. On 17 August 1915 Hamilton requested another 95,000 men in new units to reinforce his army. The request
was received by a Government which was increasingly sceptical about the
soundness of the operation. It seemed that everywhere the news was bad: on
the Eastern Front the Russian Army was hard pressed; the Italian summer
offensive against the Austrians had failed; and Bulgaria was just about to
declare against the *Entente*. Moreover, the 'Westerners'—those who believed in the primacy of the front in France over all other theatres—were
increasingly influential.

The Government's response to Hamilton's request came three days later
on 20 August. He was told that he would be allocated 13,000 battle casualty
replacements and 12,000 men in new units, but that he 'must understand that
no reinforcements of importance can be delivered from the main theatre of
operations in France.'[1] Effectively, the Government's answer meant that
the Gallipoli campaign had been downgraded to a holding operation. The
Western Front had centre stage.

At the end of August a French offer of four more divisions, plus a promise
from Kitchener of the British 27th and 28th Divisions, seemed to breathe
new life into the enterprise. Hamilton was jubilant but had not reckoned on
the influence wielded by the 'Westerners': General Joseph Joffre, Commander-in-Chief of the French armies and bitterly opposed to operations
conducted outside France, effectively sabotaged the directive given to him
by his political masters, pleading operational requirements in France, the
lack of information on the intended role for his divisions and the inadequacy
of the officer appointed to command them, General Maurice Sarrail.

Events elsewhere now made their own contribution to the Gallipoli
campaign. The Greeks had asked for assistance from the British and French

in the face of Bulgarian mobilization. Salonika was to be established as a base and Hamilton was ordered to part with three divisions, two British and one French. This was bitterly opposed by Hamilton, who felt that just one more push would be sufficient to drive the Turks off Gallipoli. At the same time he noted with some disgust that British and French casualties in the recent offensives at Loos and Champagne in France had cost over 250,000 killed—more than twice the number of men he had requested. Hamilton was now a depressed and exhausted commander who was losing his grip on the situation in the face of the twin problems of shortage of manpower and the seemingly immovable Turkish infantry.

Conditions on the peninsula were indeed grim. There was an appalling sickness rate of 50 per cent, largely because of dysentery brought about by the lack of hygiene in the trenches, where corpses often formed an integral part of breastworks. There was a chronic shortage of supplies: the artillery were down to two rounds per gun per day for anything other than counter-battery fire or emergencies. There were maintenance problems for nearly all the Army's equipment owing to the lack of large-scale workshop facilities on the peninsula. Moreover, with winter coming, vast amounts of stores would have to be accumulated on the beaches via improvised harbours which would not survive in any kind of rough weather.

On 11 October Kitchener grasped the nettle and asked Hamilton for his estimate of the likely casualties if Gallipoli were evacuated. Hamilton replied that he would expect to lose some 50 per cent of his army in such an operation. This gloomy prediction marked the end of the road for Hamilton. For some time there had been a whispering campaign against him in London mounted by, among others, Lieutenant-General Stopford, who still smarted at his removal from command at Suvla and whose prejudiced and inaccurate account of those operations was accepted verbatim in London. Another opponent of Hamilton was the journalist Keith Murdoch, whose grossly inflated reports about conditions on the peninsula were given far more credence than they deserved. The upshot of all this was a gradual loss of confidence in Hamilton as a commander. On 15 October he was told that he was to return to London with his Chief of Staff and that he was to be relieved by Lieutenant-General Sir Charles Monro. Monro was a 'Westerner' and an officer of some ability who believed that any activity other than on the Western Front was a waste of effort and resources. Monro's appointment effectively meant the end of the campaign: it only remained for the how and the when to be decided.

Hamilton's performance as a commander is open to question. There is no doubt that he possessed the strategic vision to see how the Dardanelles campaign could transform the progress of the war for the *Entente*. However, he possessed little drive and was far too tolerant of his subordinates, as his treatment of Stopford before the Suvla Bay landing showed. He also failed to ensure that his subordinates were fully appraised of his intentions so that, if the plan went awry, they could use their initiative. Both at Helles and at Suvla subordinate commanders did not know what was required of them and paralysis set in. On the other hand, his efforts were continually being suborned by those in Britain who saw the Dardanelles venture as an irrelevance and he was never sent subordinate commanders (Byng, Maude and Fanshawe) of any worth until the campaign had all but ended. Lastly, Hamilton was all too often his own worst enemy, sending optimistic forecasts to London which were seldom matched by results.

Before Monro arrived Lieutenant-General Birdwood took command and his gloomy assessment only served to endorse Hamilton's views. Birdwood informed Kitchener that all units were below strength and that major reinforcements were needed. Furthermore, now that Bulgaria had declared for the Central Powers, the Turks had ready access to supplies of German ammunition. Two-thirds of Turkish shells had failed to explode, thus mitigating the advantage the Turks possessed in overlooking the beaches. However, the prospect of the Turks' being able to direct accurate shellfire on to the peninsula with munitions which would explode every time was not an appealing one. In this situation Birdwood told Kitchener that the only way of remaining on the peninsula would to be drive the Turks back so far that the beaches would be beyond artillery fire. In other words, what was required was another offensive.

Monro arrived at Imbros on 28 October and on 30 October visited Suvla, 'Anzac' and Helles in a day, thus leading to Churchill's jibe that 'He came, he saw, he capitulated'. At each beach-head Monro spoke to the corps and division commanders and quickly established a consensus. The sick and undermanned British and Imperial units on the peninsula would only be capable of a lightning offensive lasting no more than twenty-four hours. Moreover, if the Turks received unlimited amounts of ammunition it would be difficult to predict any outcome. All the divisions were locked into unfavourable positions where it was impossible to build up adequate reserves to sustain an attack or manoeuvre once an offensive had been started. With insufficient artillery and troops incapable of sustaining an significant offensive effort, a successful offensive was out of the question. Accordingly, Monro reported to London on 30 October:

> I am therefore of opinion that another attempt to carry the Turkish lines would
> not offer any hope of success. The Turkish positions are being actively

strengthened daily. Our information leads to the belief that heavy guns and equipment are being sent to the Peninsula from Constantinople. Consequently, by the time fresh divisions, if available, could arrive, the task of breaking the Turkish lines would be considerably more formidable than even it is at the present. On purely military grounds, therefore, in consequence of the grave daily wastage of officers and men that occurs . . . I recommend the evacuation of the peninsula.[2]

Monro's views reflected the professional opinion of the commanders at Gallipoli but those in London were not so sure. Even at this late stage Kitchener had been toying with the idea of a renewed naval attack on the Narrows proposed by Keyes (an idea that was, eventually, firmly squashed by the Admiralty). That Kitchener was undecided was shown by his decision to send Monro to Salonika and appoint Birdwood in command at the Dardanelles (an order which Birdwood managed to conceal from Monro, for whom he had great respect). Surrounded by all this indecision, the War Cabinet ordered another high-level visit and sent Kitchener out to make his own assessment.

Kitchener arrived at Mudros on 9 November and on the 13th his first report was sent to London. Like Monro before him, he accepted the futility of remaining on the peninsula and recommended evacuation. He also reversed his decision regarding command at Gallipoli: Monro was appointed GOC of all British troops in the Eastern Mediterranean outside Egypt and Birdwood was appointed to command the Dardanelles Army (as it was now known), while troops at Salonika were to be commanded by Lieutenant-General Mahon. Ten days later Kitchener returned to Britain. In his absence the General Staff had made a study of the situation and had come to the same conclusion: evacuation was inevitable and essential.

But the Government was unwilling to make a decision, fearing a loss of prestige and the political consequences of such an outright admission of defeat. At a Cabinet meeting on 24 November Lord Curzon, the Lord Privy Seal, argued eloquently for a postponement of any decision about evacuation. Despite a total lack of military knowledge or experience, Curzon frightened the Cabinet with his grim picture of the chaos attending an evacuation:

A moment must come when a final *sauve qui peut* takes place, and when a disorganised crowd will press in despairing tumult onto the shore and into the boats. Shells will be falling and bullets ploughing their way into this mass of retreating humanity . . . Conceive the crowding into the boats of thousands of half crazy men, the swamping of craft, the nocturnal panic, the agony of the wounded, the hecatombs of the slain.[3]

Curzon was successful, for the decision was postponed for a week. But while those in London deliberated, the weather on the peninsula took a turn for the worse. During the evening of 26 November there was an intense rainstorm. Able Seaman Joseph Murray of the RND was in Gully Ravine:

On our side of the Gully the water came so much down the trench that it was cascading over the cliffs into the Gully. The Turks were standing about and so were we. There was no trench to go in, [since] they were all full up with water . . . Everywhere was washed up. Fellows ill with dysentery had fallen down and drowned in their own communications trenches . . . It wasn't till after the storm that we realized what a lot of people were drowned.[4]

Under such conditions personal survival become the sole imperative for friend and foe alike.

The next day the temperature dropped and it began to snow. Snow was followed by freezing rain: the temperature fell below zero and for those in the trenches conditions were unbearable. Private Harold Boughton in the 2/1st London Regiment of the 29th Division on Helles remembered that

We pulled some blankets over our heads, some ground sheets over that, put our arms round each other and sat like that all night with water right over our boots. There was nowhere else to go so we sat there until morning. When we tried to move we could lift these blankets and ground sheets off us like bent sheets of corrugated iron. Our feet, well they were frozen in the water and we could hardly move to pull them out. All around us there were chaps moaning and crying. Some of the sentries standing on the fire steps had frozen stiff and when they were touched fell over, frozen. I had frostbite in my hands and feet. Some of them were so bad that they were told to get down to the beach as soon as they could. That was the only place they could be treated but there was no road and no means of taking them down there. So I saw men crawling on their hands and knees. Grown men crying like babies—even the quartermaster Sergeant of the Royal Marines.[5]

The big freeze ended on 30 December, by which time hundreds of men had died of exposure and thousands had been evacuated with frostbite. It was unthinkable that the British Army could winter on Gallipoli under such conditions. On 7 December, even before the cold spell ended, the Cabinet had come to a decision: the peninsula would be evacuated. Originally it was planned to depart from Suvla, Helles and 'Anzac' simultaneously, and there was much to commend this course of action. However, the Navy lacked sufficient 'lift' to move so many men at once and it was decided to leave from Suvla and 'Anzac' first and maintain Helles until a later date.

Birdwood had begun preparations well in advance of the Cabinet decision. His staff had divided up the evacuation into three stages: Preparatory,

Intermediate and Final. The Preparatory stage involved the removal of non-essential personnel, stores and equipment. By the time the formal decision was received at Army HQ on 8 December the garrisons at Suvla and 'Anzac' had been reduced to a total of 80,000 men, 36,000 at 'Anzac' and 44,000 at Suvla. Birdwood proposed leaving the implementation of the Intermediate stage to his two corps commanders. At Suvla Lieutenant-General Byng proposed to effect a gradual withdrawal of his corps to new positions set up around the areas from which the troops would embark. This raised the prospect of a fighting withdrawal, with all the consequences foreseen by Lord Curzon. However, Lieutenant-General Sir Alexander Godley, who had taken over the Anzac Corps from Birdwood, proposed a different and more subtle plan. Godley argued that if the troops departed without 'ostentation', it should be possible to deceive the Turks up to the last minute. The strength of the garrison would be gradually reduced until only a few select troops would be left holding the front line; these would slip away during the last night. Godley's plan was ingenious and commended itself so much to Birdwood that he ordered Byng to abandon his plan for a phased withdrawal and adopt the Anzac proposal.

The Royal Navy had sufficient 'lift' to evacuate 10,000 men a night from both 'Anzac' and Suvla. Accordingly, the Intermediate stage was intended to reduce each garrison to a total of 20,000 men, who would be removed during the nights of 18/19 and 19/20 December. It was vital that the Turks should not get wind of what was being planned, so daily routines were altered to allow for the gradual run-down in numbers. Instead of zealously maintaining control of no-man's land, soldiers were now ordered not to fire at night unless their positions were attacked: however, if and when this occurred, these attacks were to be fiercely driven back. In this way the Turks would become accustomed to silence at night.

At the same time the façade of normal routine had to be maintained. Tents, though empty, were left in position. At night mules and limbers made the usual racket delivering non-existent rations. Fires were lit in evacuated bivouacs to preserve the appearance of normality. Sergeant William Kirk of the Army Service Corps was employed in such tasks:

> I was told to go down to where headquarters had been, find their dugouts and pick up all the paper, boxwood, old sacking—anything that would burn. I was to light fires where they'd usually done their cooking to send up smoke to make the Turks think they were still there. But they weren't—the headquarters had been evacuated.[6]

Kirk was also responsible for destroying supplies which could not be moved. Food was purposely spoiled, though the British soldier baulked at destroying jars of rum. As a result there was a certain amount of hilarity in Kirk's work party, which earned him a reprimand to the effect that all the rum should be destroyed next time.

Fortunately the operation was blessed with good weather and the long nights of winter darkness. On the last day of the operation most of the garrison were given 'parts' to play and were employed in schemes to confuse the Turks still further. Private William Cowley, in the Army Service Corps, 11th Division, was given some mule carts loaded with empty water tins and told to '... take up as near to the Turkish front line as you can, Piccadilly Circus, and run them around; make as much noise as you like to let him think we were bringing stuff up.'[7] The Turks caused a last-minute alarm at Suvla when a battery of recently arrived Austrian 6-inch howitzers began laying very accurate fire on the spot which had been chosen as the main forming-up point for troops on their way down to the beach. Some fifty rounds were fired, each of which exploded with perfect detonation. However, the numbers remaining were so thin that there was only one casualty and the damage to the pier was quickly repaired. This bombardment resulted in some counter-battery fire from the few guns remaining, which served to heighten the illusion that everything was as normal on the beaches.

The naval aspect of the evacuation was organized by Admiral Wemyss. Captain C. F. Corbett RN in HMS *Anemone* was appointed to take charge at Suvla, while Captain the Hon. A. D. Boyle RN was in charge at 'Anzac' in HMS *Honeysuckle*. Captain Edward Unwin VC, that doughty veteran of 'V' Beach, was to be Naval Transport Officer at Suvla and Captain C. M. Staveley would exercise the same role at 'Anzac'. Ten of the Beetles were assigned to each beach, together with large numbers of other craft. After being taken off the beaches the troops would be transferred to the battleships *Magnificent* and *Mars*, supported by fifteen shallow-draught steamers, for the voyage to Imbros. In addition, a squadron of four such steamers, each capable of holding 1,000 men, was to be retained at Imbros in case of emergencies. To preserve the appearance of normality strict orders were given that all craft engaged in evacuation must be clear of the beach by daybreak and that only the usual number of warships were to remain visible from the shore.

The arrangements worked perfectly. During the night of 18 December 9,000 men were lifted from 'Anzac', leaving 10,040 for the final night. Although nine guns were abandoned they were rendered useless; in any case, their barrels had been worn smooth from ceaseless firing. The next night the troops were divided into three groups. A party of 4,000 men left as soon as darkness had fallen. The 6,000 remaining then spread themselves to cover the whole of the front, maintaining the usual amount of bombing and sniping. Considerable use was made of 'automatic rifles', to give the illusion of strongly held trenches. A can of water dripped into another, underneath which was attached the trigger of a gun. As the water dripped the weight increased and the trigger was pulled. To vary the rate of firing, more water was put in some cans than in others. At 2100 the 4,000 men of 'B' Party sneaked away and the front was held by the 2,000 'Last Ditchers' of 'C' Party.

The evacuation was proceeding so well that it was possible to advance the moment for the last men to leave. At 0240 Lone Pine, the scene of such desperate fighting, was vacated, the last batch of men leaving trenches only five yards from the Turkish front line. At 0255 Quinn's Post and Pope's were evacuated, leaving Russell's Top as the only occupied front-line position. This was abandoned at 0314, and at 0330 the entire garrison was clear of the hills and a mine was fired on Russell's Top. At 0400 the last lighter cleared the beach and at 0410 Captain Staveley and a few other officers stepped into a picket boat and headed out to sea. 'Anzac' was Turkish again.

At Suvla a similar plan was followed. The front line was held until 0130, with small parties stationed in two reserve lines which had been prepared to cover the two halves of Suvla Bay. These lines would be held until all the front-line troops had passed through and been accounted for, when they too would fall back to the beaches. Because of the flooded Salt Lake area, the Suvla garrison was effectively split into two. In the southern half, the troops, the 13th Division and the 2nd Mounted Division, had all gone by 0400. In the north the evacuation of the 11th Division, the 88th Brigade (29th Division) and the 39th Brigade (13th Division) was complete by 0500. It was vitally important that, on the southern sector, the closest co-operation should be maintained with the left flank of the Anzac Corps. The left-flank battalion of the Anzac Corps retired under the command of IX Corps in order to ensure that there was no break in the line. There was nothing left but mounds of burning stores, which finally alerted the Turks to what had happened.

The evacuation had been a triumph of organization. No fewer than 83,048 officers and men, 186 guns and 4,695 animals had been evacuated from 'Anzac' and Suvla under the direct observation of the Turks. Only one casualty was sustained, and that was a soldier who had taken too much rum that had escaped destruction and 'fallen over'. All of Curzon's dire prophecies could be discounted.

Notes to Chapter 5

1. Hamilton, *Gallipoli Diary*, pp.132–3.

2. Aspinall-Oglander, *History of the Great War: Military Operations, Gallipoli*, Vol. II (1932), p.403.

3. *Ibid.*, p 430

4. Imperial War Museum, Department of Sound Records, SR8201: Interview with Joseph Murray.

5. Imperial War Museum, Department of Sound Records, SR8667: Interview with Harold Boughton.

6. Imperial War Museum, Department of Sound Records, SR9778: Interview with William Kirk.

7. Imperial War Museum, Department of Sound Records, SR8866: Interview with William Cowley.

CHAPTER SIX

Stealing Away from Gallipoli

Come into the lighter, Maude,
For the fuze has long been lit.
Come into the lighter, Maude,
And never mind your kit.
—Gallipoli doggerel

THE evacuation from Helles posed altogether different problems. The British were in a difficult if not impossible position at Cape Helles. If they stayed it could only be a matter of time before the Turks mounted a major offensive. The weather was worsening, and if the British tried to leave there was every chance that the deception which had worked so well at 'Anzac' and Suvla would not work again. To quote a German military axiom of the period, *'Zweimal ist nicht einmal noch!'*[1]

Able Seaman Thomas MacMillan of Drake Battalion RND summed up the position quite perceptibly:

> It was common talk that our divisional commander had reported to his superiors that the men of his division were anxious to remain on the peninsula until operations were brought to a satisfactory conclusion. If our divisional commander was reported correctly , either he did not know the mind of his men, or it was a case of wishful thinking on his part. Our position appeared hopeless to any man with a spark of intelligence.[2]

General Monro, however, was in no doubt as to the course of action to be taken. Directly the last soldiers were evacuated from 'Anzac' and Suvla, he advised London that Helles should be evacuated without delay. This time he found an ally in Admiral Wemyss, while General Birdwood, too, favoured evacuation. On 23 December Lieutenant-General Sir William Robertson was appointed Chief of the Imperial General Staff. Robertson was an ardent 'Westerner' and had no faith in the Gallipoli campaign. On the day after his appointment he ordered Monro to begin preparations for the evacuation of Helles, subject to nothing being done which would actually prejudice the Army's ability to stay there if decided. When this signal was deciphered at Lemnos it was received with some pleasure. It was as if the decision to evacuate had some cathartic effect on those involved. Now that the political and strategic wrangling was dispensed with, the issue became a straightforward exercise in staff work: preparations could start in earnest.

Eventually, on 27 December, the Cabinet agreed. Robertson informed Monro that Helles was to be evacuated as soon as possible but at his discretion. There followed a reshuffle in the British command. De Roebeck relieved Wemyss as Commander-in-Chief, while Birdwood relieved Monro, who went to France in command of the First Army—an appointment after his own heart. It seemed that everyone was dissociating himself from Gallipoli and the graveyard of men and reputations it had begun. The evacuation, the last and most painful act of this tragedy, was left to the three commanders who had been there from the beginning—Birdwood, de Roebeck and Keyes.

Lieutenant-General Sir Francis Davies, GOC VIII Corps, decided that the evacuation should follow the plan established at Suvla and 'Anzac'. Dardanelles Army Order No 2, issued on 1 January 1916, outlined an Intermediate stage lasting over a number of nights and a Final stage scheduled to take place on the nights of 6/7 and 7/8 January. Troops were to be embarked off Gully, 'X', 'W' and 'V' Beaches, with a naval patrol established on both flanks to rescue any stragglers. However, once the Intermediate stage had got under way, the covert withdrawal of troops and equipment, Birdwood became concerned about the wisdom of drawing out the final stage over two nights. Fearful that the unpredictable weather would play havoc with his plans, he investigated the possibility of conducting the Final stage on one night. At first Davies demurred: he believed that the number of men the Navy could lift in one night would not be sufficient for him to hold the peninsula in the event of a delay. However, improvements to the piers and the breakwaters meant that the Navy could lift 17,000 men in a night—a number which Davies considered adequate. On 6 January a new Army Order was issued to this effect and stipulated a number of other changes: 'X' Beach was not to be used and only 400 men were to come off from Gully Beach; all the rest would come away from 'W' and 'V' Beaches. The Final stage would begin on the night of 8/9 January.

Evacuation began in January 1916 and the French colonial troops were the first to leave. However, their departure left such a gap in the British line that Birdwood had no option but to order the remnants of the 29th Division, which was down to half strength after the August battles and which had just been taken off from Suvla, to hold the line at Helles. Whatever the numerical strength of the 29th Division, its reputation for steadiness and courage was undimmed, and after only one or two days' rest on Lemnos the men found themselves landing again on the beaches they had taken at such cost eight months before. At the same time it was decided that, to avoid the dangers of an evacuation with a divided command, the remaining French infantry on the right flank should be evacuated, their place being taken by the Royal Naval Division. The weakest British division at Helles, the 42nd, was relieved by the 13th Division, also just taken off from Suvla. Private Harry Boughton of the 2/1st London Regiment was not pleased to be back on the peninsula after having been evacuated from Suvla:

> I came off in the boat with Major Nathan. "Well, scrape the mud off your boots, Boughton, that's the last of the Dardanelles!" We were back at Cape Helles within a week![3]

Major John Gillam of the Army Service Corps with 29th Division was also not particularly pleased to be going back. He received the news while anticipating a gentle passage back to Egypt in the transport *Southland*:

> We learn that the 86th have passed to Helles and soon we are to follow. Good Lord! This is the unkindest cut of all. So we are not done with it yet. Well, I don't suppose the Turks will let us get off scot-free this time. I draw food for the men on board and at 7.30 p.m. go down to dinner. The last time I dined in this saloon was in those days in April, just before the original landing. The officers of the KOSB's were dining here then, and their bagpipes played them into dinner, many for the last time in their lives.[4]

Thus there were four British divisions deployed at Helles. On the left flank, facing the Aegean, was the 13th Division, then, running left to right across the peninsula, there were the 29th, 52nd and Royal Naval Divisions.

The effects of the evacuation of Suvla and 'Anzac' were clearly felt at Helles. Firstly Turkish artillery fire increased, and then, as their infantry were moved south, there was an increase in patrolling. Second Lieutenant J. S. Millar, serving with the 1/5th KOSB, noticed this increase, just after Christmas 1915:

> The rifle and machine-gun fire from the Turkish positions appeared to increase and reconnaissance and fighting patrols became more active, probing into our positions with determination and vigour . . . The casualties were again steadily mounting . . . Obviously the Turks were now bringing troops on to the Helles front and we were beginning to feel the effect.[5]

As with the previous evacuation, secrecy was paramount. As part of the illusion Davies issued an order to all ranks to the effect that VIII Corps would soon be relieved by IX Corps, thus allowing preparations for the evacuation to be conducted under the cover of a routine rotation of units. However, many troops guessed the true nature of what was afoot and believed that IX Corps did not exist; in fact, IX Corps was the force evacuated from Suvla, so the ruse was a genuine one. Lieutenant A. M. McGrigor of the Royal Gloucestershire Hussars was based at Imbros at Army HQ. In his diary for 30 September he wrote:

> Although it is not supposed to be known, one can't help putting two and two together, and the latest decision is that Helles is to be abandoned. It does not do to criticise and it is not polite, but it does strike one as weird that the decision could not be come to before, and that the three places [could have been] given up together . . . By Jove, though, this new operation will be ticklish in the extreme. one can surely not hope to get away a second time without fighting.[6]

Some of the factors which were causing concern can be seen in a letter written by Lieutenant-Colonel Norman Burge, in command of Nelson Battalion, RND, on 4 January 1916:

> Since the Anzac and Suvla shows are no more, and the Turks have full liberty to concentrate on us here, things have not been too pleasant. In fact, they have been, and are, most damnably uncomfortable. We get shelled far more than we've ever had before and with heavier guns. We wallow in the mud and wish we were flatter.[7]

Lieutenant Lavell Leeson, a Royal Army Medical Officer in 17th Stationary Hospital, was concerned that the wounded and the medical staff would be left behind. His fears were compounded by the issue of notes to the medical staff, in French and Turkish, which read: 'I am not a fighting soldier; my only work is in connection with the wounded and sick in hospital and in the field under the protection of the Geneva Convention.' The staff of 17 Stationary Hospital were gradually whittled down, so that by the beginning of January there were only eight officers and twenty-four other ranks remaining.

The evacuation now proceeded with a momentum all of its own. Lieutenant Leeson wrote: 'We were stunned by the finality of all the arrangements; it seemed to fit into such a tidy pattern with absolutely no room for a mistake.'[8] What were known as 'periods of silence' were now introduced. Able Seaman Thomas MacMillan explained how these worked:

> Throughout the campaign it had been a first principle with us on taking over trenches to secure fire mastery: for every shot fired by the enemy, we returned

two where possible. Now during the hours from dusk to dawn he was allowed to fire to his heart's content without challenge. This made him inordinately curious, and patrol after patrol was sent towards our line. Orders were given that the Turks were to be allowed right on to our wire and that, even then, fire was to be opened only on the instruction of a responsible officer.[9]

To help make these 'periods of silence' as effective as possible, the troops were ordered to wrap their feet in sandbags, a process which Able Seaman Joseph Murray of Hood Battalion, RND, described as 'bloody awkward'.

The 42nd Division were the first formation to leave in early January 1916. The once busy peninsula suddenly became a strange place, as Joseph Murray recalled:

It was really frightening. We leave Fusilier Bluff . . . and then come down Geoghegan's Bluff, you see. That's all right, but there was nobody behind us . . . there were no troops to be seen anywhere and we just used to walk down to the [ammunition] dump through empty trenches. Nobody there, and I thought to myself, 'Well, I don't know where the hell everybody's gone!'[10]

Lieutenant Leeson watched the stream of men and animals heading down to the beach:

There were sounds and signs of withdrawal all about us, in spite of the seemingly strong security that we were following. It was a sobering thought, watching the men slipping down the cliff's edge to the beach and becoming aware that their disappearance meant that we were less protected every minute.[11]

The measures taken by the 17th Stationary Hospital to disguise the fact that its staff were gradually stealing away are typical of those used throughout the peninsula throughout this period:

The Red Cross flags continued to flutter bravely and outwardly our tented white city looked as busy as ever: there were stretcher-bearers supposedly bringing in patients from the front, there were parades and work parties and we even took the precaution of keeping lights ablaze at night to lull the Turks into believing that our lives went on as usual.[12]

On the beaches there was a hive of activity as troops, guns, stores and equipment were prepared for evacuation and while what had to be left behind was prepared for destruction. At the same time, in keeping with the deception plan, activity on the beach had to seem normal. Thus empty ammunition boxes were unloaded from lighters to simulate the daily re-supply of ammunition. Heavily camouflaged tree trunks were dragged around the beach to simulate artillery. A constant ship-to-shore traffic was maintained, whereas in reality the traffic was all going the other way. Parties of officers and men were detailed to supervise the work on the beaches. One such officer was Lieutenant Patrick Campbell of the Ayrshire Yeomanry:

> I have had the rather less pleasant but none the less honourable duty thrust upon us of being left behind and attached to the embarkation staff, fortunately under a brick of a general, beside whom it would be an honour to be killed should the worst come to the worst. It is a most wonderfully calm and cool staff this, considering the difficulty and extent of the operation and the most unwelcome attention of Asiatic Annie, Puking Percy, Quick Dick and sundry other long-barrelled visitors.[13]

The 'brick of a general' was Brigadier-General J. W. O'Dowda, who had been appointed to take charge of 'W' Beach on 1 January. He recalled that he

> . . . found a great deal of confusion and lack of organisation reigning on the beach. This I proceeded to remedy, parcelling off areas of the shore to my various assistants and advising them how to create some order out of chaos.[14]

The embarkation staff faced a perplexing task, as Lieutenant Campbell recalled, with some frustration:

> We are engaged, as you may judge, in infernally difficult work and on two nights the weather has played the deuce with everything. I have never had more difficulty in keeping my head in my life. Dealing at night with refractory piers, refractory boats, refractory Indians, refractory Mules, and meanwhile shells at the rate sometimes of three a minute, from two different directions, and from as many as seven guns, is just about the limit.[15]

There were other problems for the harassed evacuation staff to deal with, including the looting of the copious amounts of stores lying around. O'Dowda

> . . . noticed a good deal of looting going on. I therefore had to arrange for the police and the patrols to look after the dumps to stop this practice. Not that I minded the stores being taken, for I realised that thousands of tons would have to be destroyed, but it was very bad for the discipline of the area. But on one occasion a very exalted General Officer and his staff paid us a visit to see the progress we had made and on their departure the General asked for some bales to be opened when he knew what their contents were, and in front of a considerable crowd of onlookers he and his staff proceeded to loot them properly.[16]

What could not be brought off, or looted, would have to be destroyed. Near 'W' Beach a large cavern in the cliff was packed with surplus guncotton, shells, small-arms ammunition, grenades and other ordnance, all waiting be blown up. Around 'W' Beach there were over twenty-five dumps of stores which, on the night, would be drenched with petrol and set alight. Further inland a variety of preparations were in hand. Lieutenant-Colonel Burge of the RND recalled:

We hope that, even if they do discover that we are retreating from our front lines pretty soon after we have commenced to go . . . they won't come after us too quickly. In fact we are discouraging little schemes of that kind by leaving large numbers of contact mines behind us and various other little booby traps which should throw a considerable amount of cold water [otherwise melanite] on any thrusting and inquisitive spirits.[17]

Should the Turks advance before the evacuation was complete, their progress was to be made as difficult as possible. Barbed-wire entanglements were prepared, to be placed across all routes and tracks after the last troops had passed through. All dug-outs and trenches were to be filled with barbed wire. Trip and tread mines were to be laid liberally all over the peninsula.

These preparations made movement around the peninsula very difficult. Joseph Murray remembers the frustration of finding familiar routes suddenly blocked:

We'd been up and down these trenches hundreds of times and—bless my heart and soul—we come off today carrying our rations and, 'Oh, trench blocked, what the hell's done that?' And you have to go, walk back and find another way and find that one blocked. We got lost because all the trenches we knew were blocked.[18]

The final element of the preparations was the improvement of the defences around the beaches in case of a final breakthrough by the Turks. O'Dowda described those at 'W' Beach:

The far side of the crest of the semi-circular beach was fully entrenched and strengthened by a double apron barbed wire fence. Six hundred men, naturally called the Die Hards, held these trenches to the last.[19]

All was proceeding smoothly. By this stage some 18,350 officers and men had been taken off and the Turks were none the wiser. Or were they? Colonel Burge heard the story of a note thrown in the trenches occupied by 52nd Division which said, 'Goodbye, you swine! We know you are going!' Perhaps it was wishful thinking on the Turks' part. However, it was with some apprehension that on 7 January the Turks began a heavy bombardment on the Fusilier Bluff sector of the front. The atmosphere in the British trenches was extremely tense as the defenders waited for the assault which could ruin all their plans.

In the event, although the bombardment went on for most of the day, it was not followed up by an infantry attack. Numerous troops could be seen in the Turkish trenches, but their officers were unwilling or unable to persuade the infantry to go over the top. Only around Fifth Avenue and Fusilier Bluff was an infantry attack pressed home, and this was repulsed by the North Staffordshire Regiment, whose commanding officer, Lieutenant-Colonel F. Walker, was killed.

January 8 was the last day for the British Army on the Gallipoli peninsula, and it began with an orgy of destruction of such equipment that could not be evacuated. Even the traction engine was booby-trapped. The troops worked with a will, one observer noting that they seemed to revel in the destruction. A less happy task was that fifteen horses and a number of mules had to be shot. Not everyone was willing to co-operate in the slaughter of their animals, and a number of soldiers turned their horses loose rather than shoot them. Major John Gillam led the last Army Service Corps detachment, consisting of five men, off 'W' Beach:

> It is now the beginning of Z day and we three stand on W Beach waiting orders to go on No 1 Pier. As we stand in the heavy sand, my thoughts immediately go back to the night of April 25th where in the same place as I am now standing we were labouring carrying boxes of supplies up the beach. I feel as if I have gone around in a complete circle.[20]

The final stage of the evacuation had been meticulously planned to take place in three waves, with the RND and 52nd Division leaving from 'V' Beach and the 13th Division from 'W' Beach. The first wave would leave their positions after dark and embark soon after 2000. The second wave would follow three hours later and the third wave would embark between 0200 and 0300. Lieutenant-Colonel Burge was detached from his battalion to help with the organization of these precise arrangements. His first task was to organize the evacuation of the 2,000 men of the RND who were deployed either side of the Krithia Road where it crossed over Krithia Nullah:

> The difficulty was that they must arrive on the beach in bodies of 100 exactly, and as no unit was exactly that number it meant adding a few of this battalion on to a few of that and chucking in a few Royal Engineers as a make-weight. Still not so difficult so far. *But* I'd only got one narrow road to form those troops up on—no one could move or show himself till 5.45 p.m. and the whole body must start at 6.15. So it meant falling in in the dark and detaching bodies to join other bodies and in short doing most unmilitary things which, if I'd done [them] in a promotion exam, would have ploughed me straightaway . . . At 6.10 they began to move off and at 6.20 the bivouacs were clear.[21]

After dispatching the first 400 men, Burge was to remain at the RND rendezvous point and stay there until the last man of the RND had passed through at 0230. At 2100 the second wave, drawn mainly from the support troops, passed through, a little early because, as Burge noted, there was very little loitering.

Able Seaman Joe Murray left his trench shortly after dark and began making his way down to the beach:

> All the gear we had which jangled—water bottles, entrenching tools, even your bayonet scabbard—was taken away because it made a noise. We still had sandbags on our feet and we were told, 'Empty the breech and you've got to make your way to Kirthia Road.[22]

Murray's feelings on leaving were mixed and shared by many who made their way down to the beaches that evening:

> I thought to myself, I don't like sneaking away like this after all this trouble. I was really distressed in my own mind. I thought to myself, we're stealing away. We stole away from Blandford, stole away from Egypt and now we're stealing away from Gallipoli.[23]

Murray made his way down to 'V' Beach, where he embarked in a lighter via the hulk of the *River Clyde*:

> We were so packed we couldn't move our hands up at all. We couldn't! I remember the chap in front of me was sick as a dog. Half of them were asleep and leaning. We were packed up like sardines in this blinking lighter . . .[24]

Lieutenant-Colonel Burge was still at the RND Rendezvous Point. After the second wave had passed through came the most anxious time. The firing line was barely manned at all, and if the Turks attacked there would be no stopping them. At 2345 the last of the RND were withdrawn. Able Seaman Thomas Macmillan was covering the extreme left flank of the division's front:

> Running as fast as my legs would carry me, I eventually got up with my party as they were leaving the communications trench for the open. There we halted and removed the blanket strips from our feet. When free from our fetters the gallop was resumed . . . We found that the road had been broken up purposely by our engineers, and at frequent intervals we were precipitated at times headlong into holes of considerable depth. On clearing the road, from which it was impossible to stray by reason of directing belts of wire, we were halted at the first blockhouse. The officer in charge accounted for our party to cool and calculating engineer non-commissioned officers and on we passed to the next blockhouse.[25]

At the rendezvous point Burge watched every man of his division file through:

> During this last period I had naturally been very busy, as I found the best way was to count every individual man who passed my bridge. Sketchley was in a dugout—Control Station—close near and knew, of course, exactly the numbers of each party due. So after the last feller-me-lad passed according to my reckoning, I went and checked over the numbers with him. The staff arrangements were perfect—and more than perfect—because they were foolproof. There were small control stations dotted about everywhere that knew who and how many to expect (these were between my place and the firing line) and they phoned into Sketchley's place as each lot passed. So that if any small party had gone adrift it would be known that it must be between two definite points. Well, we checked our numbers—said 'Damyer, ole man, its all right' or some such nonsense to each other—the four signallers packed up their instruments and we made for the beach feeling pretty happy.[26]

All of the RND together with the 52nd Division got away safely from 'V' Beach without a single casualty.

On 'W' Beach General O'Dowda controlled the evacuation of the 13th Division:

> The troops were met at the entrance of the defence works which were on the top of the cliffs. From that point they were guided to forming-up places, where they were sorted out and detailed for their respective troop carriers. Then they were marched to the beach by guides and either sent to the hulks by the floating pier or embarked in lighters alongside the jetties.

Everything proceeded according to plan, but there was one factor which lay outside the control of the command—the weather. The improvised bridge which linked the pier to the hulks, alongside which came the ships embarking the troops and on which the evacuation from 'W' Beach depended, took a battering from wind and waves. Despite attempts at repair, the bridge was eventually carried away after two lighters crashed into it. Henceforth the evacuation from 'W' Beach would have to be by means of lighters. Despite the destruction of the bridge, the schedule of the evacuation was maintained.

Chief Petty Officer P. Powell was in command of motorized lighter *X152*, which was working from No 2 pier on 'W' Beach:

> By 11 p.m. the wind had freshened, blowing from the south, and a slight sea got up and was causing much inconvenience on the beach. A floating bridge got carried away on W Beach, necessitating us to make a trip to the destroyer with troops. The Turks seem very quiet. I only noticed about six shells fired

up to the present, but I found that one of these shells dropped on to the last section that was coming on board my lighter; one was killed three injured.[27]

This would seem to contradict the oft-made assertion that Helles was evacuated without loss, although one killed and three wounded is but a slight price to pay for the evacuation of four divisions.

Powell and *X152* worked through the night ferrying troops from the beach out to the transports:

[By] 11.15 p.m. we were busy being loaded up as full as possible; still, we made progress and by 11.45 I moved out after some difficulty for the wind and sea were blowing right on. I was ordered to . . . HMS *Mars* but it was rather a long trip, uncomfortable for us and certainly for the soldiers who had marched down five miles through trenches. We had great difficulty in getting alongside . . . It was hard work for the troops to climb the ladders with 100lb packs and rifles, for the sea was very nasty.[28]

Second Lieutenant Herbert Lamb from 2/1st London Regiment was taken out to the cruiser HMS *Talbot*:

About three a.m. we were taken out to HMS *Talbot*—a very difficult and dangerous job getting on board. Wind and sea rising; the sailors swung wooden ladders over, on to which we had to cling for dear life as the lighter was swept at intervals away from the ship's side. We had full kit on and a roll of blanket in our hands which made it more dangerous: one man fell into sea between ship and lighter but was rescued. Five hundred of us got on board up those ladders.[29]

Despite the difficulties with the floating bridge at 'W' Beach, everything had gone according to plan. The second wave from the 13th Division from Gully Beach had arrived along the beach road in time and had been successfully embarked. Behind them, engineers closed the road with barbed wire entanglements and laid mines. The final group of men from the 13th Division, including the divisional commander, Lieutenant-General Maude, were due to embark directly from Gully Beach by 0200 on 9 January. However, the seas coming in from the Aegean were so rough that before the lighter carrying Maude and his staff could clear the shore it was driven aground. Although the lighter was refloated, it could not approach the shore a second time to pick up him and 160 other men left on the beach. There was no alternative but for Maude and the others to head for 'W' Beach on foot, carrying their kit—a journey of over two miles in the dark that was not made any easier in that the peninsula was thoroughly 'closed' by the activities of the engineers.

At 'W' Beach Brigadier-General O'Dowda was just about to embark when

> ... a GSO, very disturbed, rushed up and told me that General Maude had not yet arrived ... I asked what had happened and was informed that, after they had left Gully Beach, General Maude had discovered that his bedding roll had been left behind. He said that he was hanged if he was going to leave his bedding roll for the Turks, got two volunteers with a stretcher and went back for it ... The time was now 3.50 a.m. and there was no sign of the missing general. I therefore sent an officer and a couple of men who knew every inch of the beach, and gave them ten minutes to retrieve him. Fortunately they found him almost at once.[30]

Lieutenant Leeson was waiting on 'W' Beach with the remnants of 17 Stationary Hospital, where they had established a dressing station for any wounded during the evacuation, when he heard the general approach:

> In the darkness we heard the general, his fellow officer and a wheeled stretcher carrying his suitcase. Having been in a state of near panic over the idea of leaving a general behind, the embarkation officer had composed a little verse:

> > *Come into the lighter, Maude,*
> > *For the fuse has long been lit.*
> > *Hop into the lighter, Maude,*
> > *And never mind your kit.*[31]

On the beach General O'Dowda was clearing the final stragglers into the last three lighters. Time was pressing, for at 0400 the fuzes set in the beach stores and ammunition packed into caverns in the cliffs would explode. Lieutenant Patrick Campbell was one of the last British soldiers to step off the Gallipoli shore:

> We pushed off in some excitement for the last men to leave the firing line had done so four hours before and the Turks might be expected at any time. The glare showed us up very clearly to Asia, and why they didn't shell us is a mystery still; then the magazine fuse has been lit and was due to blow up any minute. As we let loose the wind caught us and for some moments we drifted back to the shore and straight to where the magazine was, within fifty yards of the beach. For some seconds we thought all was up, but the skipper succeeded in getting the nose of the lighter into the wind again just in time and we began to make our way safely out to sea.[32]

The last lighter on 'W' Beach was the hospital lighter for the medical staff. Lieutenant Leeson made a desperate rush for that last boat:

We scrambled to reach the hospital lighter tossing in the cruel waves, helping each other with supplies and kit bags. Were we in time? 'Leeson!' shouted Thomas. 'Get down!' I saw Thomas crumpled on the deck and the air was filled with mud, sand, clods of earth, pieces of shrapnel and the most incredible noise I had ever heard.[33]

The stores and ammunition had exploded on time and as arranged. The explosion was shattering. General O'Dowda recalled:

We had not gone 200 yards from the jetty when the expected terrific explosion nearly blew us out of the water. Thousands of tons of debris, rock, shell cases, bits of limber wheels and other oddments hurtled over our heads. I could never understand how we escaped injury . . . the beach was lighted up like a carnival, and would have delighted Mr Brock of fireworks fame. It was a truly magnificent sight.[34]

The evacuation was over. It had been successful in that Helles had been evacuated with minimal losses—but it had been a close thing. The moment the stores on the beach were set off, the Turks began a violent bombardment of the beaches from positions on the peninsula and the Asiatic shore. The evacuation was, and has been since, hailed as a brilliant example of successful planning and a model of how to disengage from a hopeless military position. But satisfaction with the outcome of the operation could not overcome the magnitude of the campaign's failure. Gallipoli was a great victory for the Turks.

The British and Imperial troops would soon be in action again. The three divisions which had landed on 25 April—the 29th, the Anzacs and the Royal Naval Division—would all be ordered to France, where they would arrive in time for the July 1916 offensive on the Somme. Later on they would be joined by the 11th and 42nd Divisions. The 13th Division went further east to Mesopotamia while the remainder stayed in Palestine and fought their up to Damascus under Allenby.

While the troops rested and were re-equipped they were prey to mixed emotions. Lieutenant C. S. Black of the 1/6th Highland Light Infantry wrote:

Cape Helles had no happy memories for us; no-one wanted to see the place again. But what of them we were to leave behind us there? The good comrades, who had come so gaily with us to the wars, who had fought so gallantly by our side, and who would now lie forever among the barren rocks where they had died . . . No man was sorry to leave Gallipoli but few were really glad.[35]

At a rest camp in Egypt on 20 January 1916 Major John Gillam concluded his Gallipoli diary:

> Of those who sailed from England so light-heartedly in March, few are left, but those that remain are attached to each other by invisible fetters. Those strange months—dull, exciting, tragic and humorous, spent under the eye of an enemy under an alien shore—form a common bond between us. All of us now know the full meaning of life and all of us have walked not once, but many times, with death on the grim Peninsula. We have been beaten—not so much by the enemy as by climate and geographical conditions; but beaten we are.[36]

Notes to Chapter 6

1. Twice does not mean once again!
2. Imperial War Museum, Department of Documents, Papers of AB T. MacMillan: 'The War to End War, 1914–1918', pp.109–10.
3. Imperial War Museum, Department of Sound Records, SR8667: Interview with Harry Boughton.
4. Gillam, John, *Gallipoli Diary*, Unwin & Co, (London, 1919), p.298.
5. Imperial War Museum, Department of Documents, TS memoir of Lieutenant-Colonel J. S. Millar.
6. Imperial War Museum, Department of Documents, Papers of Captain A. M. McGrigor: diary entry, 30 December 1915.
7. Imperial War Museum, Department of Documents, Papers of Lieutenant-Colonel N. O. Burge: letter, 4–10 January 1916.
8. Imperial War Museum, Department of Documents, Papers of Lieutenant-Colonel L. H. Leeson, p.115.
9. Papers of AB T. MacMillan, p.115.
10. Imperial War Museum, Department of Sound Records, 6201/42, Reel 27: Interview with Joseph Murray, 1985.
11. Papers of Lieutenant-Colonel L. H. Leeson, p.126.
12. *Ibid.*, pp.126–7.
13. Campbell, T. A., *Letters from Gallipoli*, p.89.
14. Brigadier-General J. W. O'Dowda's TS notes on the evacuation of Gallipoli, quoted in Campbell. *op. cit.*
15. Campbell, *op. cit.*
16. *Ibid.*
17. Papers of Lieutenant-Colonel N. O. Burge: letter, 4–10 January 1916
18. Interview with Joseph Murray, 1985, Reel 27.
19. O'Dowda's notes, *op. cit.*
20. Gillam, *op. cit.*, p.320–1.
21. Papers of Lieutenant-Colonel N. O. Burge: letter, 4–10 January 1916.
22. Interview with Joseph Murray, 1985, Reel 27.
23. *Ibid.*
24. *Ibid.*
25. Papers of AB T. MacMillan.

26. Papers of Lieutenant-Colonel N. O. Burge: letter, 4–10 January 1916.

27. Imperial War Museum, Department of Documents, Papers of Coxswain P. Powell.

28. *Ibid*.

29. Imperial War Museum, Department of Documents, Diary of Second Lieutenant H. A. J. Lamb, 9 January 1916.

30. O'Dowda's notes, *op. cit.*, pp.14–15.

31. Papers of Lieutenant-Colonel L. H. Leeson, pp.150–1.

32. Campbell, *op. cit.*, pp.96–7.

33. Papers of Lieutenant-Colonel L. H. Leeson, pp.151–2.

34. O'Dowda's notes, *op. cit.*, p.16.

35. Thompson, Lieutenant-Colonel R. R., *The Fifty Second (Lowland) Division 1914–1918* (Glasgow, 1923), p.106.

36. Gillam, *op. cit.*, p.325.

CHAPTER SEVEN

South to the Natkong

If some of us die, we will die fighting together.
—General Walter Walker

THE American landings at Inchon on the west coast of Korea in September 1950 represent a dramatic illustration of how a successful amphibious operation can transform the nature of a campaign. Before the landings the United Nations (UN) forces in Korea were demoralized and pinned into a narrow perimeter around the town of Pusan in the south of the country; after Inchon the UN forces romped northwards as far as the Chinese border. A subsequent development, namely the entry of Chinese 'volunteers' into the war, negated any advantages gained by the landings, but that does not invalidate this particular triumph of American arms.

Amphibious warfare was, and is, an art at which the US armed forces excel. The gathering, organization and deployment of large numbers of men and equipment is an American speciality and these skills were developed and honed during the Pacific War in a series of operations which saw US forces advance across the Pacific on two fronts using their mobility and strength to storm those Japanese strongpoints that required to be taken while by-passing and isolating those whose capture was unnecessary. In September 1945 the Americans possessed all the means and expertise necessary to conduct a major amphibious campaign.

It was therefore both sad and surprising that in the five years between the end of the Second World War and the outbreak of the Korean War the Americans practically turned their backs on amphibious warfare. In 1945 the US Navy had 610 AW ships in commission; by 1950 there were only 91 left. In 1948 a total of 510 landing ships and craft of all types were sold or scrapped and only one new craft was commissioned. Also in 1948 the Fleet Marine Force (FMF) was reduced from 35,000 to 23,000 men; by 1950 there were plans to reduce it to six infantry battalions and supporting arms with eleven aviation squadrons. Amphibious warfare (AW) was a backwater in which no career-minded officer would want to stay for very long. Op-343, that section of the Navy Department dealing with AW, was headed by a captain while other department heads were flag officers. In short, AW lacked clout in the higher reaches of the US Navy command and was declining in terms of resources. That this run-down took place against a difficult international situation with the United States and the Soviet Union coming to terms with a new world order is all the more amazing.

The cause of this run-down was, simply, the atomic bomb. It is impossible to underestimate the effect that the bomb had on American strategic thinking in the post-war period. US planners such as General Curtis le May believed that opponents could simply be bombed into submission. Though evidence from the Second World War showed that mass bombing was not as successful as the planners hoped, Americans believed that the nuclear weapon would give them the edge where conventional bombing had failed. From a political perspective, the atomic bomb appeared cheap compared to maintaining a large force of men and ships. This was an important card to play, and one which the officers of the newly formed US Air Force exploited to the limit in Congressional hearings.

By the late 1940s the belief that the A-bomb was some kind of panacea for all America's worldwide problems was widely held. In 1949 General of the Army Omar Bradley testified to the House Armed Services Committee: 'I predict that large-scale amphibious operations will never occur again.' For a general who had witnessed his army transported and landed on the Normandy beaches only five years earlier, this was an astonishing admission. Worse was to come. The Secretary of Defence, Louis Johnson, declared to Admiral R. L. Connolly, Chief of Naval Operations:

> Admiral, the Navy is on its way out. There's no reason for having a Navy or a Marine Corps. General Bradley tells me that amphibious operations are a thing of the past. We'll never have any more amphibious operations. That does away with the Marines. And the Air Force can do anything the Navy can do nowadays, so that does away with the Navy.

It was unfortunate to say the least that this run-down in American 'conventional' arms should have occurred at the same time as a major change of foreign policy by the Truman administration. Since the end of the Second World War the United States had stood by and watched the seemingly inexorable advance of communism, firstly in Eastern Europe, where country after country became part of the Soviet Empire, and then in 1949, in China when the communist forces under Mao Tse-Tung finally defeated the US-backed Nationalist government led by Chiang Kai-Shek. There were those in the US administration who believed that American foreign policy was soft on communism, that the communists had been allowed to advance unchecked and that there were liberal elements in the State

Department who were not averse to this situation. After some barely concealed coat-trailing in the journal *Foreign Affairs* (a journal which often serves as the mouthpiece for the expression of opinions by Federal employees), the policy finally surfaced as document NSC-68, better known as 'Containment'. Henceforth the US would not merely stand by while the Soviets 'rolled up' one state after another but would intervene as far as the situation warranted. 'Containment', the reduction in forces and the decision by the communist government of North Korea to invade the south in an attempt to unify the country by force all came together during the night of 25 June 1950 when the North Korean People's Army (NKPA) smashed through the ill-equipped and poorly trained South Korean (ROK) forces and, in the words of General MacArthur, 'struck like a cobra'.

On the face of it, Korea was the last place anyone would think of in terms of superpower conflict. Yet all the ingredients were there for those who chose to look. Korea had been a Japanese protectorate since 1910. During the Second World War the Koreans had, despite an avalanche of postwar propaganda to the contrary, co-operated fairly enthusiastically with the Japanese. In particular, Korean guards earned an evil reputation in prisoner-of-war camps. Korea did not figure in any American plans for the conduct of the war in the Far East, but the sudden end to hostilities following the dropping of the two atomic bombs and the entry of the USSR into the war against Japan caused a substantial revision of this view. The Red Army was sweeping through Manchuria and fears were expressed in the State Department and the War Department about the strategic consequences of a Soviet occupation of the entire Korean peninsula. In a complete reversal of policy, the US Army's XXIV Corps, barely rested after the gruelling fighting on the island of Okinawa, was dispatched to Korea as a garrison. As a result Korea was divided into the Soviet and American zones, with the 38th Parallel as the boundary between them. The development of government in each zone proceeded on separate lines, with a nominally 'democratic' regime under Syngmann Rhee set up in the south with US backing while in the north the Soviets installed a hard-line communist administration under Kim il Sung.

In an attempt to bring the two sides together, a meeting of the Council of Foreign Ministers in Moscow in December 1945 urged the creation of a single government for all Korea, but nothing came of this proposal. In 1947 the United Nations proposed free and fair elections throughout the country, but this proposal, too, collapsed when the USSR refused to allow the UN Election Commission into the north. By 1948 the country was effectively split, with development proceeding along diverging lines in north and south. Both sides claimed sovereignty over the whole of Korea and in 1948 a UN resolution favoured the south. But all of this was just talk: Korea was as effectively partitioned between the superpowers as Germany was in Europe. Finally, in 1948 both the United States and the Soviet Union withdrew their armed forces from Korea.

There is no evidence at all about the motives behind the North Korean invasion or what degree of support Kim il Sung received from the USSR. Such evidence is not likely to be forthcoming from Pyongyang, capital city of the last, most impenitent communist government.

The NKPA advanced south in four columns, driving all before them. The South Korean Army was American-equipped and trained but in reality was little more than an armed gang. It was no match for the NKPA's armoured columns spearheaded by T-34 tanks. The ROK Army fell back amid columns of refugees while Syngmann Rhee's government appealed to the United States for help. Rhee did not find his ally wanting in this time of crisis. After it became clear to the planners in Washington that this was no Korean panic over a larger-than-usual border raid, President Truman promised US air and naval support on 27 June. Somewhat later General Douglas MacArthur was to note:

> I could not help being amazed at the manner in which this great decision was being made. With no submission to Congress, whose duty it is to declare war, and without even consulting the field commander involved, the members of the executive branch . . . agreed to enter the Korean War.

All the risks inherent in this decision—including the possibility of Chinese and Russian involvement—applied just as much then as later.

Truman's next move was to tie the United Nations to the South Korean cause. By a stroke of luck the Soviet delegate to the Security Council was absent, having walked out over a disagreement about Nationalist China, so the resolution calling for all member states to render assistance to South Korea went through with only Yugoslavia abstaining. Thus, for its first outing, the new US 'get tough on communism' policy was to be wrapped in the blue and white colours of the UN.

The Americans would be providing the largest element of the UN forces in Korea and so it was logical that the overall commander should be American. In this case that was General of the Army Douglas MacArthur. There can be no neutral feelings for the historian writing about General MacArthur: his life was a parade of superlatives. He was ambitious, vainglorious and convinced that only his own eastern-orientated view of US strategy was correct. He surrounded himself with a court of sycophantic hangers-on and he had a considerable talent for self-promotion. On the other hand, there were very few US military commanders who had his strategic grasp and tactical skill. His island-hopping campaigns in New Guinea and the south Philippines were classic examples of the use of amphibious warfare and mobility. Above all, MacArthur was an exponent of 'total war'. He believed that, once a political decision had been made and given to him to execute, there should be absolutely no restraints on how he achieved the objective.

From his headquarters in Tokyo MacArthur had been slow to grasp the reality of what was happening in Korea, but once he had grasped it there was no stopping him. He flew to Korea on 29 June to survey the scene and saw the burning buildings of the capital, Seoul, which had fallen the previous day. On his way back to Tokyo, having told fifteen dismayed American officers from his staff that they were to stay and 'put some backbone into the Koreans', MacArthur urged that all American forces which could be spared for Korea—whatever their condition—should be committed. He saw no value in waiting for the training or equipping of units: the NKPA's advance had to be stopped. It is clear that even at this stage MacArthur was thinking not merely of evicting the NKPA from South Korea but of inflicting absolute defeat upon them. Because of the time difference it was 0300 when MacArthur's recommendations rattled off the teleprinter in Washington. The Army Chief of Staff, General Lawton 'Lightning Joe' Collins, wanted to wait until office hours to brief the President but MacArthur insisted that Truman be woken immediately.

Truman concurred with MacArthur's recommendations and he gave approval for units of the US army of occupation in Japan to be airlifted to Korea. At the same time he declared a naval blockade of Korea and announced the commitment of the US Air Force in the Far East. Within hours the first men of the 24th Infantry Division (Major-General William Dean) were being roused from their billets and emplaning for Korea. However, in truth, the leading elements of the US Army heading for Korea were little better than the ROK Army they were going to aid. They had grown soft on occupation duty in Japan and their scales of equipment were insufficient for training let alone a major war against a determined enemy.

Dean's division deployed to Korea in a hurry, without time for proper briefing, and units were simply thrown into the line south of Seoul, battalion commanders being told simply to deploy their men in blocking positions across the NKPA's advance. It was inevitable that the Americans found themselves outclassed by the NKPA. Time and time again US positions would be attacked by NKPA armour while infantry worked round their flanks and infiltrated them. American troops were trained to fight as part of a large army with mutually supporting elements and with a large superiority in *matériel* over their opponents. In Korea, US infantry found themselves alone, with their flanks unsupported and usually with some distance between them and the nearest friendly formation. It was not surprising that many men simply abandoned their positions and fled. Thus was a new term, the 'bug-out', added to US military terminology as hundreds of American units, finding themselves outflanked and infiltrated, simply retreated, leaving all behind them.

Further reinforcements from Japan included the 25th Infantry and 1st Cavalry Divisions. The 25th came ashore between 10 and 15 July, followed by the 1st Cavalry on the 18th. By 22 July both were deployed so that the remnants of the 24th might retire through their ranks. Yet these formations fared no better than the 24th in combat. Close fighting with the NKPA was a shattering experience for most US soldiers, even those who had fought against the Japanese. Repeatedly, a column of refugees trudging towards an American position would be swept aside to reveal NKPA infantry, while the suicidal 'human wave' attacks were extremely unnerving. The communists acknowledged no adherence to the rules of war and Americans were shocked beyond measure when the first photographs of executed GIs, their hands bound with wire, were discovered and subsequently published. Perversely, the news of communist atrocities served to stiffen many units as the knowledge became widespread that they were more likely to receive a bullet in the back of the head if captured than be transferred to a PoW camp conducted under the rules of the Geneva Convention.

On 10 July MacArthur was formally appointed UN Commander-in-Chief, though not without some misgivings on the part of a number of UN member-states who sought to have the war directed by a 'co-ordinating committee'. Since the Americans were providing the largest number of troops, the UN command structure closely mirrored the existing US command in all aspects. Reporting to MacArthur were his service commanders, Lieutenant-General Walton Walker (land forces commander in Korea and commander of the Eighth Army); Lieutenant-General G. E. Stratemayer (Air Force); and his three naval commanders, Admiral Radford, Commander-in-Chief of the Pacific Fleet (who was somewhat removed from proceedings as his headquarters was in Pearl Harbor), Vice-Admiral C. T. Joy, Commander Naval Forces Far East, and Vice-Admiral A. D. Struble, Commander 7th Fleet. Beneath these were the appropriate unit and national commanders, for eventually eleven other countries responded to the appeal to send forces to Korea—Australia, Belgium, Canada, France, Greece, the Netherlands, New Zealand, the Philippines, New Zealand,

Thailand, Turkey and Great Britain. The various national contingents added a colourful, though not always efficient, element to the campaign: one French ship arrived with five months' supply of wine but no cipher machine!

Though the US/ROK forces were still compelled to retreat, the influx of men and *matériel* into Korea did slow the advance of the NKPA. The latter had also suffered heavier losses than was realized at the time—more than 58,000 killed or missing in the period 25 June to early August. Nevertheless the retreat continued. The 25th Division held ground in the centre of Korea until forced to withdraw on 30 July. The 1st Cavalry was outflanked around Yong Dong and likewise forced to retreat. A large Korean flanking operation in division strength steamed in from the west and threatened the port of Pusan on Korea's south-east coast. If Pusan fell, then the Americans would be encircled; moreover, they would have lost the only port capable of handling large amounts of cargo—a grim prospect. Walker was forced to move part of the 25th Division to halt the NKPA thrust outside Masan, only 30 miles from Pusan.

By now both sides had run out of room for manoeuvre. From the high ground behind the Natkong river, around the port of Pusan, the Americans occupied a position of great natural strength. Here, with their backs to the sea, they would have to stand and fight. As General Walker said,

> There will be no more retreating, withdrawal, readjustment of lines or whatever else you call it. There are no lines behind which we can retreat. This is not going to be a Dunkirk or Bataan. A retreat from Pusan would result in one of greatest butcheries in history. We must fight to the end. We must fight as a team. If some of us die, we will die fighting together.

For the next six weeks Walker's army submerged itself in what became known as the Battle of the Pusan Perimeter. Half the length of his 130-mile perimeter lay behind the Natkong river, which varied from a quarter to half a mile in width. Armour and artillery were being positioned in strength, and as the front stabilized the task of the forward air controllers became much easier. However, Walker's problems lay in the poor morale and motivation of his troops and in the fact that there were not enough of them to cover the whole perimeter adequately, given that the river was shallow enough in many places to be forded. He was forced to keep his best units, like the 27th Infantry under the command of Colonel John 'Iron Mike' Michaelis, back as a mobile 'fire brigade', to be inserted into the line at moments of crisis (of which there were to be many over the next six weeks). Yet all the time reinforcements poured into Pusan, including the British 27th Brigade and the US Marine Brigade. Walker also had 45,000 men in the ROK Army (though these were of doubtful military value). His forces outnumbered those of the NKPA, but so great was the latter's psychological dominance that most Americans would not have believed it.

The NKPA, too, had its problems. Its commanders knew that Pusan had to be captured before the US/UN forces arrived in vast numbers. As a result they launched an offensive on 5 August, the Battle of the Natkong Bulge, which drove deep across the Natkong, but after three weeks of heavy fighting they were forced back by the weight of American firepower, especially from the air. Whatever other shortcomings Walker was faced with, a lack of air support was not one of them.

The ferocity and recklessness of the NKPA tactics gave the impression of an Asian horde with limitless supplies of firepower and armour, but in reality the NKPA was squandering its resources in armour, artillery and trained troops. Consequently there was a pause in operations in late August while it regrouped. But it struck again on 31 August, and this time Walker's thinly stretched troops could not hold it. On 5 September he was forced to order a general withdrawal. But even as Walker's headquarters was preparing to move, reports began to come in that the NKPA offensive had run out of steam. Walker's army, perhaps the least professional and poorly motivated ever fielded by the United States, had held the Pusan Perimeter.

The Eighth Army troops regarded themselves as forgotten and ignored. They wanted to know what was being done to help them. Major Floyd Martin of 1/21st Infantry complained: 'We knew we weren't doing very well, but we kept saying to ourselves, "Well, we are here and we've been here a month, and where the hell is the rest of the United States Army?"' Even as the NKPA launched its last offensive on 31 August, news reached the beleaguered defenders of Pusan of a major offensive to be mounted from Japan, and their spirits rose accordingly.

CHAPTER EIGHT

Crushing Them

*No, General, we don't know how to do that. Once we start ashore
we'll keep going.*—Rear-Admiral James H. Doyle, briefing
MacArthur on the landings at Inchon

ONE of MacArthur's greatest attributes as a commander was, as one of
his subordinates later recalled, the ability to 'get going and hit quick'.
MacArthur wanted a grand gesture, a single thrust which would restore
strategic freedom. While reinforcements poured into Pusan, he made a
fundamental decision. He would not attempt to lead a counter-offensive
from Pusan. He considered, probably correctly, that Walker's troops were
not prepared for an offensive and that they had let the NKPA gain moral
ascendancy. In any case, from the start of the campaign MacArthur had
envisaged an entirely different scenario for reversing the course of the war
in Korea. He wished to land at Inchon on the east coast of Korea, strike
inland and cut the NKPA in half. Because the United states had total,
unopposed command of the sea, the NKPA moved their supplies by road
down the length of the Korean peninsula. The concentration of the NKPA
lay deep in the south, around the Pusan Perimeter. Its supply lines were
extended and totally exposed. Faced with a landing at Inchon, the NKPA
would therefore have to choose between being surrounded or retreating.

By a stroke of luck MacArthur found himself with a naval staff possess-
ing an unrivalled knowledge of amphibious warfare. MacArthur was
unique among US Army commanders in his belief in amphibious warfare,
and in the summer of 1950 he had requested the services of an amphibious
training group from the Pacific Fleet for routine purposes. This tiny training
force, insignificant in itself, consisted of an LST, an AGC, an AKA, an APA
and a fleet tug. He also borrowed various USMC training cadres, but the
jewel in the crown was the staff and commander of Amphibious Group One,
Rear-Admiral James H. Doyle. Like MacArthur, Doyle possessed a genuine enthusiasm for, and professional grasp of, amphibious warfare and
during the Second World War had been operations officer to Vice-Admiral
Kelly Turner, the admiral who more than any other had masterminded the
amphibious aspects of America's Pacific war. From the moment the NKPA

crossed the border, Doyle became the amphibious commander for the Seventh Fleet. His staff formed only a nucleus, but their skills gave MacArthur the ability to plan a major amphibious assault while the situation on the ground in Korea seemed akin to a total collapse.

MacArthur chose Inchon for a number of strategic reasons. The city is the port for the Korean capital of Seoul: to be able to capture Seoul soon after a landing at Inchon would be a significant victory. Moreover, Seoul was the focal point of the Korean railway system (which was excellent and extensive) and the country's telephone and telegraph services. The largest and best airport in Korea, at Kimpo, lies between Inchon and Seoul. However, from an amphibious point of view Inchon was the last—the very last—place that a planner would choose.

In 1950 the US Navy laid down seven criteria which had to be satisfactorily met in any amphibious landing:
1. The ability of naval forces to support the assault and follow-up operations;
2. Shelter from unfavourable sea and weather;
3. The compatibility of beaches and their approaches to size, draft manoeuvrability and beaching characteristics of assault ships and landing craft;
4. Offshore hydrography;
5. The extent of 'mineable' waters;
6. Conditions which might affect the enemy's ability to defeat mine-clearance efforts; and
7. Facilities for unloading and how these may be improved.
Inchon did not measure up to any of the criteria. In the words of Lieutenant-General Edward M. Almond, commander of X Corps, Inchon was 'the worst possible place where we could bring in an amphibious assault.' Yet, despite Almond's dire assessment, Inchon was the only plausible site for a landing: Kunsan was too close to Pusan, Chinnampo was too far north and Posung Myon lacked scope for the exploitation of the landings. However, the problems were formidable.

To begin with, the tidal range at Inchon is one of the largest in the world—32 feet between high and low water. When the tide is out the port can only be approached through tortuous channels set in acres of dull, flat mudbanks. The currents in these channels are rarely less than 3 knots and in the main channel, called Flying Fish Channel, the current reaches 7 to 8 knots—close to the speed of an LCVP. If one such craft were sunk in the channel, or disabled there, the wreck would completely block it from below and pen in any ship above. Despite the currents, the waters off Inchon are capable of being mined with little difficulty and are overlooked by commanding heights which would make ideal gun positions, rendering minesweeping operations impossible to carry out.

As for beaches, there were none at all at Inchon. There were several miles of wharves, breakwaters and sea moles which would have to do. Beach exits were through the go-downs, railroad yards and congested, narrow streets of an oriental city. If the city were stoutly defended, the landing could get bogged down in days of street fighting. The approaches to the 'beaches' (for want of a better term) demanded a tidal height of 23 feet for an LCVP and 29 feet for an LST. At Inchon such conditions occur only once a month for a three- to four-day period. In the immediate calendar only on 15 and 27 September and 11 October would the tide be high enough to get the landing craft ashore. Thereafter the imminence of the typhoon season would hamper operations considerably. To cap it all, the tides dictated that the landing could take place only during the late afternoon, leaving just two hours of daylight for the troops to get ashore and consolidate the beach-head. Small wonder that Inchon was considered the worst place for a landing.

MacArthur originally wanted to land the 1st Cavalry Division at Inchon, but the needs of Walker's army came first. The 1st Cavalry Division could not be held back while the situation in Korea crumbled. MacArthur would have to look elsewhere for his troops (and not only troops, but ships to carry and support them), and this confronted him with as many problems as the selection of a landing site. The only troops in the American armed forces with any familiarity with amphibious operations were the US Marines. However, by the autumn of 1950 the Marine Corps was looking at abolition and the last thing anyone in the Pentagon or the White House wanted to see was a successful campaign conducted by the Marines. By another of those coincidences which blessed the Inchon operation, the Commandant of the Marine Corps, General Clifton B. Cates, was observing events in Korea with some care and believed that the Marines would have to be used: the only problem was persuading those in authority of this. Cates was unable to secure a formal interview with his superiors, but by chance he 'ran into' Admiral Forrest Sherman, Chief of Naval Operations, on 29 June. The upshot of their meeting was that MacArthur was persuaded (not without much difficulty) to request the GCS to send a Marine Corps Regimental Combat Team (RCT) together with supporting aviation. MacArthur's request arrived on 3 July and was approved by the JCS and the White House, although to the end General Hoyt Vandenburg, Chief of the Air Staff, tried to strip the force of its air wing.

Cates was not satisfied merely with mobilizing an RCT. On his own initiative he had placed the 1st Marine Division on war alert. Lieutenant-

General L. C. Shepherd USMC, prospective commander of Fleet Marine Force Pacific, was another Marine officer who was not going to wait to be asked. Cutting short his vacation, he returned to Honolulu on 2 July and poured all his energies into preparing the RCT for deployment. On 9 July he went to Tokyo with G-3, to brief MacArthur and arrange for the Marines' employment. After the usual pleasantries the conversation went something like this: MacArthur—'I wish I had the entire 1st Marine Division under my command as I have a job for them to do.' Shepherd—'Why don't you ask for the 1st Marine Division, General?' The deed was as good as done.

MacArthur's request to the JCS for a full division was sent on 10 July, with a reminder sent on 15 July. Meanwhile the private Marine Corps network was running smoothly: Shepherd flew to the United states to brief Cates and the result was that from 12 July the headquarters of the Marine Corps began preparing for a full mobilization, since to assemble a war-strength division from a Corps with a total strength of 70,000 men would require the recall of reservists. On 19 July MacArthur sent his third request for the 1st Marine Division, and this was considered by the JCS. They had little choice in the matter: as they deliberated, the NKPA was driving the Americans out of Taejon and administering a drubbing to the 24th Division. Time was of the essence, so that afternoon President Truman signed the necessary papers and mobilization began.

MacArthur was told on 20 July that he could have the division, but it would not be ready until November. This was not good enough for MacArthur, and on the same day he replied:

> Most urgently request reconsideration of decision with reference to 1st Marine Division. It is an absolutely vital requisite to accomplish a decisive stroke and if not made available will necessitate a much more costly and longer effort both in blood and expense. It is essential the Marine division arrive by 10 September 1950 . . . There can be no demand for its potential use elsewhere that can equal the urgency of the immediate battle mission contemplated for it.

The Chiefs of Staff had now received four messages from MacArthur, each more insistent than the last. However, they were not prepared simply to watch the biggest mobilization since the Second World War without being told why MacArthur wanted the troops in the first place. MacArthur's response was a masterpiece of evasion:

> Operation planned mid-September is amphibious landing of two division corps in rear of enemy lines for purpose of enveloping and destroying enemy in conjunction with attack from south by Eighth Army. I am firmly convinced

QUEBEC
Above left: Major-General Sir James Wolfe, the brilliant but mercurial land commander at Quebec.
Above right: Admiral Sir Charles Saunders, the naval commander at Quebec, whose achievement has been overshadowed by that of Wolfe.
Below: Boats carrying the Grenadier Company of the 40th Foot land at the Anse de Foulon, 13 September 1759.

Left: The French commander, the Maquis de Montcalm, whose numerically superior forces were out-manoeuvred by the British.
Below: The death of General Wolfe. He was killed at the moment of victory.

THE DARDANELLES
Left: Winston Churchill,
First Lord of the
Admiralty and an
enthusiastic advocate of
the Dardanelles cam-
paign—and its principal
victim. (IWM Q.42037)
Below: A view of the
harbour at Mudros on
the island of Lemnos.
The British and French
possessed excellent
advance-base facilities
near to the beaches.
(IWM Q.13657)

Above: The French battleship *Bouvet* sinking on 18 March 1915. She was one of three such vessels sunk in the abortive attempt to force the Dardanelles. (IWM SP.682A)

Below: A 9.4-inch gun in a Turkish fort above 'V' Beach at Cape Helles dismounted by a direct hit from a 15-inch shell fired by HMS *Queen Elizabeth* on 25 May 1915. (IWM Q.13223)

Right: Marshal Liman von Sanders. He believed that he could strengthen the Dardanelles defences in eight days; in the event, the British gave him three weeks. (IWM Q.95324)

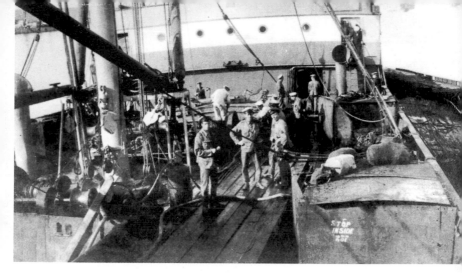

Left, upper: Inside the ruined fort at Sedd-el-Bahr above 'V' Beach, showing dismounted Turkish guns. The bombardment failed to clear the fort of Turkish infantry and their machine guns. (IWM Q.13235)

Left, lower: British commanders at Gallipoli. From left to right are Commodore Roger Keyes, chief of staff to Vice-Admiral de Roebeck; Vice-Admiral John de Roebeck; General Sir Ian Hamilton; and General Braithewaite, chief of staff to Hamilton. (IWM Q.13560)

Above: Preparations on board the *River Clyde* prior to the landings. Two of the machine gun positions fitted to the upper deck can be seen on the port side. (IWM Q.50484)

Below: The scene at 'V' Beach on 25 April 1915, from the bridge of the *River Clyde*. In the foreground, dead of the Munster Fusiliers and the Hampshire Regiment are lying on the lighter, while huddled in the lee of the sandbank are survivors of the Dublin Fusiliers. (IWM Q.50473)

Left, top: A photograph of the *River Clyde* taken after the landings. The ports cut in the ship's side through which the Munsters and the Hampshires disembarked can clearly be seen. (IWM Q.50468)

Left, centre: A photograph of 'W' Beach, where the Lancashire Fusiliers came ashore, taken after the landings. (IWM Q.61099)

Left, bottom: Men of the 1st Battalion the Essex Regiment come ashore at 'W' Beach, 25 April 1915. The battalion had originally been scheduled to land at 'V' Beach but were switched to 'W', unfortunately compounding the chaos there. (IWM Q.37880)

Above: Troops in a drifter pass HMS *Implacable* off 'X' Beach. The close support to the troops given by this battleship contributed much to the success of the landings at 'X' Beach. (IWM Q.13220)

Below: Looking north from the Helles beach-head. Achi Baba is in the background: this hill was the objective for the troops who landed at Helles. (IWM Q.13546)

Left, upper: A view of 'Anzac' Beach, looking north. Note how steeply the cliffs reach down to the shore, and that there is very little room on the beach itself. (IWM Q.13603)

Left, lower: North Beach at 'Anzac' in August 1915. On the horizon are the hills of the Kirech Tepe Sirt range, the northern boundary of the Suvla Plain. (IWM Q.13618)

Above: The scene at 'Anzac' Beach at 0730 on 25 April 1915. Men of the 4th Battalion are coming ashore from the transport *Lake Michigan*. (IWM Q.58078)

Right: Mustafa Kemal, the Turkish commander whose energy and decisiveness on 25 April did much to halt the Australian and New Zealand troops at 'Anzac'. (IWM Q.10174)

Above: The terrain looking north from 'Anzac'. In the foreground are the hills of the Sari Bair range, while in the background is the Suvla Plain, bounded to the north by the Kirech Tepe Sirt range. (IWM Q.13429)
Below: Turkish dead on the parapet of an Australian trench at 'Anzac' following the Turkish offensive of 19 May 1915. (IWM HU.53359)
Right, upper: Manufacturing bombs using discarded tins of bully beef and jam before the Third Battle of Krithia, June 1915. The troops at Gallipoli lacked much of what was considered to be essential equipment for trench warfare. (IWM Q.13281)
Right, lower: Trench warfare at Helles, June 1915. A Royal Irish Fusilier holds his hat on a stick to encourage a Turkish sniper to give away his position. (IWM Q.13447)

Left, upper: Filtering water at Cape Helles. The supply of fresh water was a constant problem on all three beaches. (IWM Q.13448)

Left, lower: Hot and tired, men of the Lancashire Fusiliers return to the beach through Gully Ravine, June 1915. (IWM Q.13315)

Above: Troops ashore at Suvla Bay, 7 August 1915. The lack of urgency and direction is apparent. (IWM Q.13456)

Below: Gunners of the 4th Glasgow Battery attached to the 52nd (Lowland) Division at Suvla in August 1915 with a 5-inch howitzer. There was a shortage of artillery and ammunition at Gallipoli, and this was an important factor in the inability of the British and French to break out of their beach-head. (IWM Q.13644)

Above: Troops at Suvla Bay in an improvised shelter made from biscuit boxes and straw. The advent of severe winter conditions made the British positions at Gallipoli almost untenable; these men are suffering from frostbite. (IWM Q.13644)
Below: Field Marshal Lord Kitchener at 'Anzac', in company with General Birdswood, returning to the beach from Russell's Top on 13 November 1915. (IWM Q.13595)

that early and strong effort behind his front will sever his main lines of communication and enable us to deliver a decisive and crushing blow . . . the alternative is a frontal attack which can only result in a protracted and expensive campaign.

The word 'Inchon' was not mentioned once: no wonder the Army Chief of Staff, General Lawton J. Collins, felt constrained to remark, '. . . frankly, we were somewhat in the dark.' Nevertheless, on 25 July MacArthur got his Marine Division, together with its attached aviation wing—a victory for the Marines over the Air Force, who had engaged in a shabby campaign to deny the division its organic aviation. However, MacArthur was not going to be given *carte blanche*. In August he received a visit from Admiral Sherman and General Collins, who were to find out exactly what he had in mind.

The meeting, held on 23 August in the sixth-floor conference room in the Dai Ichi Building (MacArthur's Tokyo HQ), was a momentous occasion. In addition to MacArthur, Sherman and Collins, the following were present: Rear-Admiral Doyle, amphibious force commander; Admiral Arthur W. Radford, CinC Pacific Fleet; Vice-Admiral C. Turner Joy, Commander US Naval Forces Far East; Major-General Edward M. Almond, MacArthur's Chief of Staff; and Generals Ruiffner, Wright and Hickey, all on MacArthur's staff. Curiously enough, no representatives of the 1st Marine Division were present—either by oversight or design. Otherwise the only notable absentee was Vice-Admiral A. D. Struble, Commander 7th Fleet, who was at sea engaged in operations.

The meeting began with a detailed briefing on the problems confronting the planners. Doyle had insisted on this since in previous meetings MacArthur had not shown any interest in the minutiae of the operation. Doyle concluded his eighty-minute presentation: 'General, I have not been asked nor have I volunteered my opinion about this landing. If I were asked, however, the best I can say is that Inchon is not impossible.' After hours of discussion, during which the normally monosyllabic Sherman was manoeuvred into saying that he would not hesitate to take a ship up the Flying Fish Channel to Inchon ('Spoken like a Farragut,' replied MacArthur), MacArthur drew the meeting to a close. Then, in a forty-five minute peroration delivered without notes or other aids, he held his distinguished audience spellbound while he argued the case for Inchon. While recognizing the validity of the objections and reservations, he pointed out that a deep cut across the NKPA's communications would deprive communist forces around Pusan of munitions and fighting power. Inchon would be the anvil on which the Eighth Army would crush the NKPA from the south. MacArthur concluded his mesmeric performance by lowering his voice and declaring: 'We shall land at Inchon and I shall crush them.' 'I wish I had that man's optimism,' commented Admiral Sherman the next day.

Sherman and Collins returned to Washington to report to Bradley and Vandenburg. In reality they had no choice but to approve MacArthur's plan, despite their objections: to reject it would be a public rebuttal of their senior commander in the Far East (who would be certain not to take the affront lightly), which would have the most unimaginable political consequences. On 28 August MacArthur received the approval he wanted:

> We concur in preparations for executing a turning movement by amphibious forces on the west coast of Korea, either at Inchon in the event the enemy defences there prove ineffective, or at favorable beach south of Inchon if one can be located.

Operation 'Chromite' (the name chosen for the landings) was now a fact.

However, it was not simply a matter of alerting the 1st Marine Division and mounting the assault. The division should have had three constituent regiments ready for service: in fact only one, the 5th Marines, was up to strength and they had been allocated to Walker's Eighth Army. Walker was loath to release them, but in the end had no choice and they finally joined their division at sea on 13 September, two days before the operation. The other two regiments, the 1st and 7th Marines, existed as paper formations. To bring them up to strength the entire Marine force on the Atlantic Coast, the 2nd Marine Division, was stripped down to a skeleton. Moreover, from hundreds of Marine Corps establishments all over the world, men were given their orders for Camp Pendleton in California, where the 1st Marine Division was assembling. One battalion of the 7th Marine Regiment was even scrounged from the Fifth Fleet in the Mediterranean and joined the division via the Suez Canal. In four frantic days in August 1950 over 9,000 officers and men reported for duty to bring the division up to its war strength of 22,343 officers and men. Fortunately, equipment was not a problem. After the Second World War the Marines had carefully salvaged their (and other units') trucks, guns, amphibians and weapons and shipped them to Barstow in California, where they were overhauled, painted olive green (to disguise previous ownership) and mothballed. This miser's paradise of military equipment now came into its own.

Commanding the 1st Marine Division was Major-General Oliver P. Smith. Smith was an intellectual who had attended the US Army's Infantry School at Fort Benning (an unusual assignment reserved for the most studious officers in the Corps) and the French Army's *École Supérieure de Guerre* in Paris. In the Second World War he had seen combat at New

Britain, Peleliu and Okinawa. He was a cautious man and a practising Christian; his byword was 'You do it slow, but you do it right'. His subordinates were more flamboyant and included Colonel Ray Murray of the 5th Marines, an outstanding tactician, and Colonel Lewis B. 'Chesty' Puller of the 1st Marines, a cigar-smoking extrovert who led from the front but whose tactical carelessness exasperated his superiors. The commanding officer of 7th Marines, Colonel Homer Litzenburg, was slower but no less competent. All these officers and their staffs possessed the experience of the Second World War to guide them through the planning and execution of the operation.

If the Marines were in a sorry state, then the 7th Infantry Division (Major-General David G. Barr), who would land after the initial assault, were in total chaos. The 7th were an occupation division in Japan but had had their ranks stripped—naturally, the best and most experienced had been selected—to provide reinforcements for the Pusan Perimeter, so that on 26 July, the day the unit was formally warned that it would be required for Inchon, the division was short of 416 officers and senior NCOs and 8,701 other ranks. General Barr, an officer renowned for his common sense and practicality, commented that his unit was not fit for training let alone an operation.

The shortfalls were made up with over 8,000 South Korean volunteers. Each Korean was 'attached' to an American who would be his 'buddy' and show him the ropes as they went along. The situation can only be described as farcical: the Koreans could barely speak English and even the simplest tasks, such as the use of a Western-style latrine, had to be explained to them. However, on a more positive note, the reinforcements that Barr's division received from the United States were of the finest quality. Against strident howls of protest from Pusan, Barr succeeded in acquiring not only the entire flow of infantry replacements (390 officers and 5,400 enlisted men) but also cadres of experienced officers and NCOs from the US Army's artillery and infantry schools at Fort Sill and Fort Benning. However, Barr did have to lose one regiment to replace the 5th Marines at Pusan.

Appointed to command both divisions as Commanding Officer of X Corps was Major-General Edward M. Almond. The decision to divide military command in Korea between X Corps and the Eighth Army was responsible for so many of the problems encountered later in the war. MacArthur's reasoning is difficult to follow. He believed, probably correctly, that the Eighth Army commander was incapable of leading the imaginative and daring assault planned for Inchon. However, Almond was MacArthur's protégé and Chief of Staff, and nepotism, of which MacArthur was so often accused, cannot be ruled out. As a third option, it could have been that MacArthur knew, as he told O. P. Smith, that the landing at Inchon would be won by the Marines and that the question of corps command was a matter of protocol.

Almond was a driver of men who got results, despite having been a rather undistinguished corps commander in Italy from 1943 to 1945. However, he was supremely arrogant, describing amphibious warfare as 'just a mechanical option' and calling General O. P. Smith 'son'—which was hardly a good start. Even worse, the corps headquarters had absolutely no experience of amphibious warfare and for this reason only entered the battle once the landings had been completed. Almond and his staff would embark on a transport without a proper communications suite and would simply wait for the Marines to do the job. Thus the planning for Inchon was all rather lopsided. Instead of responding to operational directives issued from above, the planners, Doyle and Smith, produced their schemes and sent them up the chain of command, anticipating the requirements of their superiors. Thus Smith issued his first order on 27 August, whereas X Corps' Operational Order No 1 (which should have been Smith's directive) was not issued until 30 August.

General Smith arrived in Tokyo on 22 August and boarded the USS *Mount McKinley*, Doyle's command ship, to begin detailed planning of the operation. He was formally told what he had already heard rumoured—that his division was to land at Inchon on 15 September and that serious problems remained unresolved. Their first task was to define the operational parameters for the landings:

1. Seize the port of Inchon and establish a beach-head;
2. Advance rapidly and seize Kimpo airfield;
3. Cross the Han river;
4. Seize and occupy Seoul; and
5. Occupy blocking positions north, north-east and east of Seoul.

These five objectives were assigned to the Marines. With the landings complete, the 7th Infantry would land and advance on the Marines' right, the southern flank, and form the anvil on which the NKPA would be smashed. Aircraft from the 1st Marine Air Wing (General Harris) and the fast carriers of Rear-Admiral Ewen's Task Force 77 would provide tactical air support. Vice-Admiral Arthur D. Struble, who had assumed command of all forces engaged as Commander Joint Task Force 77 (the title was a concession to the concept of 'jointness'—Army, Navy and Air Force working together—which was the fashionable military thinking in Washington), was concerned that the Air Force lacked the skill and ability to support the amphibious force properly. Experience is a great influence on decision-making: Struble was a veteran of Omaha Beach in Normandy, where, despite all the promises made by the Eighth Air Force, air support was ineffective and minimal. Accordingly, Struble ordered that there should be no Air Force operations in the Seoul–Inchon area during the assault, although participation in the deception around Kunsan would be allowed. This decision was not accepted with good grace and was the subject of some lobbying (ultimately unsuccessful, since MacArthur was no lover of the Air Force) by Lieutenant-General George E. Stratemayer, the Far East Air Forces commander.

The first problem confronting the planners was the seizure of the island of Wolmi-Do, the tactical key to Inchon which commands both the harbour and the city. Everything was complicated by the tides, so in the end the planners opted for an assault on Wolmi-Do to take advantage of the morning high tide just after sunrise, with the main assault going ahead in the evening. One problem leads to another, and the capture of Wolmi-Do was no exception.

The island would have to be taken by a force of at least battalion strength. Usually such a force would be embarked in a single-screw transport (APA) with their stores in an attack cargo vessel (AKA) and their vehicles in an LST. These ships were too cumbersome to navigate Flying Fish Channel at night and, moreover, lacked navigational radar. The problem appeared insurmountable but for Captain Norman Sears USN, Doyle's Chief of Staff. Sears argued that, since the battalion would not be laden with too much of its equipment for the assault, the troops could be carried in APDs (destroyer-escorts rebuilt for amphibious duties) and such vehicles as they required in an LSD (Landing Ship Dock). These ships were manoeuvrable, had sufficient power to stem the currents of Flying Fish Channel and had adequate navigational aids.

Sears' idea was accepted and the staff worked out a minimum load for the Marine battalion, to be selected from the 5th Marine Regiment (the 5th Battalion was eventually allocated). In addition to the Marines, the force would include engineers, artillery (to support the main landings from positions on Wolmi-Do) and reconnaissance troops. This force would be carried in three APDs and one LSD, with destroyers and rocket-armed landing craft in support. Sears convinced Doyle that this idea would work and then volunteered himself for the job of commanding the landing force.

The landing site at Wolmi-Do was labelled 'Green' Beach. For the main assault at twilight the remaining two battalions of the 5th Marines would attack on 'Red' Beach, extending north from the causeway joining Wolmi-

Do to the mainland. They would then proceed to take a necklace of hills extending through Inchon and would link up at daylight on 16th with the 1st Marines. The latter regiment were to land on 'Blue' Beach south of the town and would then hook left and north to join the 5th Marines. Both regiments would then attack eastwards towards Yongdungpo. The landing force reserve would be provided by the 1st Regiment Korean Marine Corps (KMC) since Smith's third USMC regiment, the 7th Marines, was still in transit and would not reach Japan until after the operation.

Throughout the night following the landings, as much of the division's supplies as possible would be landed. Forty-seven LSTs would beach themselves on the evening high tide and stay there until they could retract on the high tide the next morning. This would call for supreme qualities of navigation and seamanship on behalf of the LST crews since they would have to beach in darkness, avoiding the horde of smaller landing craft which would be scurrying about while a major land battle raged a matter of yards away inland. Because of the beach gradient, each LST was restricted to 500 tons of cargo apiece. Two of the LSTs were configured as ambulance ships to handle the expected casualties.

Finding the forty-seven LSTs proved something of a problem. The United States possessed a huge fleet of these capable craft at the end of the Second World War but they had been disposed of with abandon in the postwar years. The US Navy could only supply ten craft, many of these in less than 100 per cent operational condition. The balance came from the Japanese Government, who had chartered a large number of these craft as inter-island ferries (most Japanese transports having been sunk or bombed and the losses not yet made good). By another stroke of luck with which the Inchon operation was blessed, General MacArthur's staff had earlier insisted, against some opposition, that these craft be given routine maintenance by the US Navy in the event of their being required again.

Within four days of General Smith's boarding the *Mount McKinley*, the draft plan for the landings was complete. It was an astonishing performance by any standards and testament to the vast reservoir of knowledge of amphibious operations present in the Navy and the Marine Corps. However, one of the drawbacks of working to such a tight schedule was that the opinions of important subordinate commanders could not be obtained. In this case the schedule was complicated by the fact that, of the two assault regiments, one was fighting in Korea and the other was crossing the Pacific. When the regimental staffs were given the plans there was some feeling that the divisional staff had usurped their prerogatives in doing so much detailed planning, though when the cold, hard realities of the timetable were made known it was accepted that, had they not done so, the schedule might not have been met.

Crucial to the success of the landings was the level of gunfire and air support on hand. The Marines believed in the effectiveness of 'softening' the landing area before and during an assault and liked to be generous in their disposal of these assets. However, the Army planners preferred to rely on total surprise, trusting to their own artillery once ashore. The dispute over air cover has been referred to: the Navy and Marines would provide air cover. The air planners then began to organize a series of strikes up and down the length of the west coast of the Korean peninsula so as to keep the Koreans guessing where an assault might come. The Americans assumed that Korean intelligence would list an amphibious landing as a more than likely possibility given MacArthur's known inclinations. Therefore the preliminary bombing had to be fairly lavish and indiscriminate. However, as the day of the operation drew near, the air strikes would concentrate on the Inchon–Seoul area.

The gunnery bombardment posed more serious problems. The gunnery officers on Doyle's staff had worked out, from photo-reconnaissance and other intelligence, that there were 106 hard targets such as weapons positions or fortifications. Of these, 80 per cent were sited so that they could command one or more of the three beaches. The gunnery specialists on Doyle's staff had considered that several days' worth of bombardment would be necessary to ensure complete destruction. However, this requirement had to be balanced against the need to achieve surprise on the day: too heavy and concentrated a bombardment might well indicate the landing site to the Koreans. The debate about the gunnery plan—how much to fire and when to fire it—went back and forth until 8 September, almost the eve of the landings. Then Doyle agreed a compromise. On D–2 (13 September) destroyers could begin to work over Wolmi-Do from the closest possible range, while cruisers bombarded Inchon from further out to sea. If the Koreans showed some signs of fighting, then at least twenty-four hours remained before the assault for a thorough bombardment to take place.

At this juncture, with the plan complete and all the pieces falling neatly into place, the whole operation nearly came to a grinding halt because of General Walker's refusal to release the 5th Marine Regiment from the Pusan Perimeter. Walker argued that he needed the Marines too much, that they were one of his most seasoned and combat-effective units and that their departure would have an adverse affect on the morale of the other defenders at Pusan. Walker was supported by General Almond, and the discussion rapidly degenerated into an Army-versus-Navy/Marine Corps argument with the debate being conducted on strictly partisan lines. Almond offered Smith the services of the 32nd Infantry Regiment from the 7th Division, a unit without any amphibious training and 40 per cent of whose strength was made up of Korean 'volunteers'. Smith was indignant and threatened to cancel the 'Blue' Beach landings and attack over 'Red' Beach using the 1st Marine Regiment alone. Finally Struble suggested a compromise: let Walker have the 32nd Regiment as the Army Reserve in return for releasing the 5th Marines. It was a compromise which all could agree to.

Even at this stage, 3 September, with less than two weeks to the landings, Washington could not stop interfering. On 7 September the JCS asked MacArthur to reconsider the plan. General Omar Bradley, chairman of JCS, should have known the mettle of his subordinate and realized that MacArthur would never have given in: 'There is no question in my mind,' replied MacArthur, 'as to the feasibility of the operation, and I regard its chance of success as excellent.'

CHAPTER NINE

The Decisive Stroke

*We'll find out what's on the beach when we get there . . . We're
going to work at our trade for a little while. We live by the sword and
if necessary we'll be ready to die by the sword. Good luck, I'll see
you ashore.*—Colonel Lewis 'Chesty' B. Puller, 1st Marine
Regiment, at a pre-assault briefing

AN amphibious assault usually demands painstaking rehearsal, but
there was no time for such luxury with the mounting of Operation
'Chromite'. The assault troops mounted out from Kobe (1st Marine
Division, less the 5th Marine Regiment), Yokohama (7th Division) and
Masan (5th Marines, when disengaged from the Eighth Army). The main
convoy of troops transports left Yokohama on 5 September—a convoy of
260 ships, many of Second World War vintage and some crewed by
Japanese officers whose last taste of combat had been under the red and
white ensign of the Imperial Navy (one of the masters of the LSTs on charter
from the Japanese Government had been the commanding officer of a
Japanese capital ship).

The main convoy was joined by the ships bringing the Marines from Kobe
and Masan. At sea they had the misfortune to run into Typhoon 'Kezia': in
the tank decks of the LSTs tanks and soft-skinned vehicles broke loose and
frantic efforts were required to secure them. The 70,000 American and
Korean troops just had to endure the discomfort in their swaying, heaving
ships and quite a few must have wished themselves ashore. En route the
command ship *Mount McKinley* diverted into Sasebo to collect MacArthur
and his staff, much against Doyle's judgement for he felt that there was
insufficient room for the general and his entourage. The ship sailed in the
small hours of 13 September, the anniversary of Wolfe's victory at Quebec.

Intelligence gathered from NKPA prisoners and other sources had shown
that Inchon was defended by some 2,000 men, mainly conscripts of the
226th Marine Regiment, and two batteries of 76mm guns manned by the
918th Coast Artillery together with engineer and other specialist units.
Further intelligence was gained by the insertion of a seven-man party under
the command of Lieutenant Eugene F. Clark USN on the island of Yonghung-

Do, just fourteen miles out of Inchon. The NKPA had not garrisoned this island and when the omission was discovered the Americans acted quickly.

Yonghung-Do acted as an excellent base, from where intelligence about Inchon could be gathered—from prisoners, usually Korean civilians who had had enough of the terror of the NKPA, and by reconnaissance (on one occasion Clark found himself floundering about on mudbanks outside Inchon, confirming that they were impassable). Clark also supplied the rather sorry news that the US Navy's tide tables for the west coast of Korea were hopelessly inaccurate but that those produced by the Japanese Navy were much better. He was also able to send a string of agents into Inchon to measure the height of the sea wall and gather intelligence on troop numbers and concentrations, and he even managed to place an agent on the island of Wolmi-Do, a restricted area. His activities did not, alas, go unnoticed. The 300-man NKPA garrison of Taebu-Do attempted to eliminate Clark's party on 8 September but were driven off, and a bombardment by the destroyer *Hanson* on 9 September meant there was no further trouble from that quarter. Clark's last act was to ascertain that the light on the island of Palmi-Do would work, and he offered to light it on the night of 14/15 September. His departure from Yonghung-Do was timely, for as he and his party left in an ancient sampan the NKPA landed in strength. They found nothing but executed the fifty inhabitants.

Preliminary operations began against Wolmi-Do on 10 September when Marine Corps aircraft dropped 95 tanks of napalm on the island in an attempt to destroy buildings and defoliate the landscape before the assault. Subsequent air reconnaissance showed that the raid had been successful.

On 13 September the main bombardment began. The advance group, consisting of the cruisers USS *Rochester* (flying the flag of Admiral Struble, CJTF.7), USS *Toledo* (flying the flag of Rear Admiral John M. Higgins, CTG.90.6), HMS *Kenya* and HMS *Jamaica*, preceded by the destroyers *Mansfield*, *De Haven*, *Swenson*, *Collett*, *Gurke* and *Henderson*, entered Flying Fish Channel at 1030. Bombarding conditions were almost perfect: visibility was excellent and only a fresh easterly wind ruffled the waves. Fortunately the ships approached Wolmi-Do at low water, as one of Doyle's worst fears was realized: a number of floating mines were seen. However, it proved easy to destroy them by gunfire: had the approach been conducted at high water the mines would have been covered. Even worse, when the destroyers took up their position off Wolmi-Do, a large number of mines were sighted piled on the causeway ready for laying; they had not been deployed because the dispatcher at Chinnampo had neglected to send their harness cables.

The cruisers arrived at their bombarding position arranged in a south-easterly line from Palmi-Do at 1245 and opened fire a quarter of an hour later. Only one aircraft had been assigned to each pair of ships for spotting purposes and this proved unsatisfactory. Eventually the British cruisers agreed to relinquish 'their' aircraft to the two American cruisers and concentrate on indirect fire. Meanwhile the destroyers had proceeded right up to Inchon and anchored abreast off Wolmi-Do, which they began to bombard from a point-blank range of 800 yards. The reason for bombarding at close range was to force the NKPA defences to reveal themselves. The aim was successful: very heavy fire was returned—'a necklace of gun flashes sparkled round the waist of the island,' wrote an Associated Press correspondent. *Collett* took most of the fire, suffering five hits which wrecked the wardroom, the plotting room and main battery computer as well as cutting fuel lines. Nevertheless her 5-inch armament went into local control and she kept firing.

The destroyer bombardment lasted just under an hour (1253 to 1347). In that period 998 rounds of 5-inch were fired at Wolmi-Do and selected targets on Inchon. Then, with the defences thoroughly aroused, the warships retired, going astern through the channels and the mudflats and swamping small local craft with their wakes while their after batteries continued to engage enemy positions. Sadly, during the retirement *Swenson* suffered the only casualty of the bombardment when a junior lieutenant in the 40mm director was killed by splinters. His name was David H. Swenson, son of Captain Lyman K. Swenson, the destroyer's namesake. The destroyers retired under cover of fire provided by the cruisers and at the moment of their disengagement Marine Corps aircraft came into deliver another strike on Wolmi-Do. After the air strike the cruisers continued to fire for another half an hour before retiring at 1645.

At a conference that evening between Admirals Struble and Higgins, with Captain Halle C. Allen of the destroyers in attendance, two subjects were uppermost. First, Inchon was defended and would require a major effort by the bombarding forces on the 14th. Second, the sighting of mines had given everyone a nasty jolt: if Inchon harbour was indeed mined, the whole operation could grind to a halt. Nothing could be done except to order the minesweepers to leave their convoy and hasten forward at their best speed.

The next morning the bombardment recommenced with the same dispositions as the day before. Aided by air strikes from TF.77, the fast carrier group, the destroyers lobbed 1,732 5-inch shells on to Wolmi-Do, only slightly fewer than the number fired at Omaha Beach in Normandy in June

1944. By 1215 the defences of Wolmi-Do had been silenced. The cruisers then switched fire to precise targets inside Inchon; on this occasion the air spotting arrangements, by Marine Corps Corsairs, worked and considerable fire was laid down for an hour before the ships withdrew under air cover. The final report on the condition of Wolmi-Do was from a Marine Corps pilot of VMF-323, who commented that the island looked as if were no more than a 'worthless piece of real estate'.

During the night of 14/15 September the advance group and main assault convoy approached Inchon. The advance group, under the command of Captain Norman W. Sears USN, consisted of the three APDs, *Diachenko*, *H. A. Bass* and *Wantuck*, which carried the men of the 3rd Battalion of the 5th Marine Regiment (under the command of Lieutenant-Colonel Robert D. Taplett USMC) in grossly overcrowded conditions—200 per cent capacity, according to one commanding officer. The fourth ship of the group, the LSD *Fort Marion*, carried the regiment's vehicles and supporting armour.

Just after midnight the advance group joined up with the bombardment ships at the entrance to Flying Fish Channel. Leading were the destroyers *Mansfield*, *De Haven* and *Swenson*, followed by the amphibious group. Then came three support landing craft, *LSM(R)401*, *403* and *404*, armed with bombardment rockets, followed by the second division of destroyers, *Southerland* (in place of the damaged *Collett*), *Gurke* and *Henderson* and then the headquarters ship *Mount McKinley* (where MacArthur, Doyle and Smith were already up), to watch the passage of Flying Fish Channel. The cruisers *Toledo*, *Rochester*, *Jamaica* and *Kenya* brought up the rear. The darkness was almost impenetrable as the ships threaded their way up the channel, but it was suddenly relieved by the shining of a regular beam of light from the island of Palmi-Do. Lieutenant Clark had succeeded in activating the old French lighthouse and was sitting on the roof, wrapped in a blanket, as the invasion fleet sailed past him. So surprised were many, including MacArthur, to see the light burning that they believed it had inadvertently been left on by the North Koreans.

By first light Marine Corps aircraft from the USS *Sicily* and the USS *Baedong Strait* began the first air strikes on the island, followed at 0540 by the destroyers and at 0545 by the cruisers with a final gunfire assault. At 0520 Admiral Doyle had the traditional signal, 'Land the Landing Force', hoisted and Taplett's Marines began filing down into the landing craft and heading for the rendezvous area, roughly one mile from 'Green' Beach. At 0615 the three rocket ships began swamping the beach, each delivering a thousand 5-inch projectiles: *LSM(R)404* and *401* attacked the rear of the island from a position just off 'Red' Beach in case the NKPA had positioned

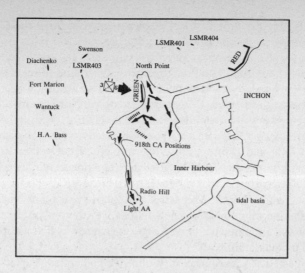

Inchon: The Assault on Wolmi-Do

artillery or mortars on the reverse slopes while *LSM(R)403* struggled against the 3-knot current to deliver her rockets right on to 'Green' Beach.

L-Hour, the time the troops were expected to land, was 0630. At 0628 the destroyers' guns fell silent as thirty-eight Marine Corps aircraft from VMF-214 and VMF-323 gave the island a final working over. As the aircraft departed the destroyers opened up again, this time firing VT-fuzed shell and taking targets in the city of Inchon. At 0633, three minutes behind time because the air strikes had run somewhat late, the LCVPs carrying 'G' and 'H' Companies touched down. The Marines ran ashore under cover of the Corsairs, which kept strafing the ground only yards ahead of the advancing troops. 'G' Company was to swing right and storm Radio Hill while 'H' Company (Captain Patrick E. Wildman) advanced to their front across the island while clearing North Point using a couple of squads. 'H' Company quickly seized their objectives and were soon dug in at the end of the causeway leading to the mainland while engineers laid anti-tank mines to prevent the NPKA sending reinforcements from the city. Once the seaward end of the causeway was secure, Wildman turned his company and worked down the east shore of the island, meeting light opposition. Meanwhile one platoon of 'G' Company had attacked the summit of Radio Hill while the other two platoons were working gown the west coast of the island to seal off the causeway leading to So Wolmi-Do, a 500-square-yard knoll at the south end of the island containing little other than a lighthouse and warehouses. By the time Colonel Taplett landed at 0650 the Stars and Stripes were flying from the top of Radio Hill.

The two secondary waves had now also come ashore—six M26 Pershing tanks from the 1st Tank Battalion, together with a flame-thrower tank, two tankdozers and a recovery vehicle in the second wave, followed by 'Item' Company in the third. 'Item' Company went to clear North Point in the wake of 'How' company and in doing so located an NKPA force on the reverse slope overlooking 'Red' Beach. The Americans were not disposed to engage in long and fruitless close-quarters combat. Captain Robert A. McMullen summoned up the M26 tanks and a tankdozer. While the Marines and the M26s gave cover, the tankdozer filled in the NKPA positions on top of their occupants. Then the M26s fired into each cave at point-blank range: if the inhabitants chose not to come out, they were entombed. At the same time an NKPA armoured car moved on to the causeway and was promptly destroyed by tank gunfire.

As soon as NKPA resistance on Wolmi-Do had ended, Taplett ordered 'George' Company to take So Wolmi-Do. Though resistance on Wolmi-Do had been desultory, the defenders of So Wolmi-Do put up a stiffer fight. As the Marines advanced across the causeway the NKPA laid down a withering fire using double-barrel 76mm anti-aircraft guns. From the summit of Radio Hill Taplett could see his men caught out in the open and he called in air support. Eight Corsairs of VMF-214 worked the island over with 20mm cannon fire followed by napalm. Then the Marines advanced again and took the island. Seventeen NKPA dead were found, together with nineteen prisoners; the remainder of the garrison had jumped into the sea and swum for Inchon when the Corsairs roared over.

With the island taken, the Americans were amazed at how well defended it was. Wolmi-Do was criss-crossed with trenches, dug-outs and emplacements. Mines and booby traps were liberally scattered all over the terrain. A number of 76mm guns were found intact which could have had a devastating effect if used on the thin-sided landing craft. Fortunately the calibre of the defenders, 400 men from the 226th Regiment and the 918th Regiment Coastal Artillery, was not of the same calibre as their defences.

Watching the landings were MacArthur and his staff from the *Mount McKinley*. This was MacArthur's moment of glory: the operation was his plan, his creation. He had fought the plan through the various stages of American bureaucracy and was to be on hand to see it come to fruition. He sat in the Captain's chair on the bridge of the *Mount McKinley* with all the familiar accoutrements—the gold braided cap, the corncob pipe, sunglasses and leather jacket. This was to be his last triumph before defeat, disillusionment and disappointment began to eat away at his ego and reputation. Once Wolmi-Do was secure, MacArthur rose from his seat and said, 'That's it, let's get a cup of coffee.' However, he did not go below without paying tribute to the Marines and sailors who had made his triumph possible. He asked Doyle to make a signal to the entire force: 'The Navy and Marines have never shone more brightly than this morning.'

However, when Admiral Struble announced his intention of taking a closer look at Inchon from his barge, MacArthur could not decline the invitation to come along. So he and the entire staff of the 1st Marine Division and X Corps, together with the attendant press contingent, piled into Struble's barge and headed for the beach. MacArthur stood prominently in the bow and made no attempt to adopt a more cautious stance, even when the barge lay less than 1,000 yards off 'Red' Beach. Finally General Shepherd warned him that it was unwise to thus expose himself and the barge turned around and headed back to the safety of *Mount McKinley*.

At noon the tide began to recede, revealing the acres of black mud between the invasion fleet and the shore. The Marines on Wolmi-Do, cut off from the fleet, consolidated their positions and requested approval, which was denied, to carry the advance over the causeway into the city of Inchon. Instead they had to be content with laying down mortar and machine-gun fire at anything which moved ashore while aircraft from TG.77 continued to roam inland within a 25-mile radius of the town, shooting and strafing targets at will. The two escort carriers of TG.90.51, the *Baedong Strait* and the *Sicily*, in particular were operating a very demanding flying programme. Although there was no shortage of aircraft, there was a shortage of pilots and two, sometimes, three missions a day were required of each man. One tactical air co-ordinator spent sixteen hours in the air on 15 September.

What was the reaction of the NKPA? The authorities at Inchon had warned their superiors in Seoul of developments at Inchon but were not taken seriously: the Americans were conducting so many bombardments along the west coast of Korea that it seemed no more than one among many such actions. If anything, the NKPA felt that Kunsan would be the likely site for a landing, believing that Inchon offered two many obstacles. Moreover, the NKPA were too busy with the 're-education' of South Korea and the removal of all those who backed Syngmann Rhee. All this changed with the capture of Wolmi-Do: the 700th Regiment was ordered to Seoul from Suwon and the 18th Division, which had been en route for the Natkong, was ordered back to Seoul. None of this would be of immediate use to the defenders of Inchon, which was now held only by the remnants of the 918th Coast Artillery Regiment.

At 1430 the bombardment increased in intensity while on the attack transports *Henrico* and *Cavalier* the assault battalions of the 5th Marine Regiment were boarding their LCVPs. The two battalions, the 1st and the 2nd, were to land abreast on the left and right sections of the 'beach' which showed on the photographs as a quay with a stone sea wall. The last photographs showed a cluster of pillboxes and bunkers while a spur jetting out from the sea wall provided an ominous reminder of Tarawa. By 1704 the LCVPs carrying the leading companies ('A' from the 1st Battalion and 'E' from the 2nd) were a mile off shore on the line of departure. The Marines could see the objectives clearly: the 1st Battalion (Lieutenant-Colonel George S. Newton USMC) were to seize Cemetery Hill and then the northern slopes of Observatory Hill, a large redoubt commanding the harbour. The 2nd Battalion (Lieutenant-Colonel Harold S. Roise USMC) were to take British Consulate Hill overlooking the harbourmaster's office and the southern slopes of Observatory Hill. While waiting for the final command to go, the cruisers *Rochester* and *Toledo* increased the tempo of their bombardment, hurling 260-pound, 8-inch shells into the city of Inchon to prevent NKPA reinforcements from arriving. Meanwhile the destroyer *Mansfield* began to lay down a murderous hail of 5-inch air-burst shell over 'Red' Beach while *De Haven* fired on Observatory Hill and *Swenson* fired on Cemetery Hill and various port installations. The noise was intense and was soon augmented by the roar of *LSM(R)403*'s 5-inch rockets.

At 1724 the first wave of eight LCVPs was ordered in and the bombardment fell silent. Instead Taplett's Marines on Wolmi-Do, who enjoyed an excellent view over 'Red' Beach, put down a curtain of mortar, machine-gun, tank and captured NKPA 76mm fire. So good was their position that they could continue their barrage without any risk of hitting the assault troops. To the fire from Wolmi-Do was added the last strike from the Corsairs of VMF-214 and 323 and Skyraiders from the Navy. The air co-operation was excellent: a forward air controller with the 1st Battalion spotted a target while on board the LCVP during the run-in and was able to have it under attack before the LCVP touched down. The Skyraiders flew so close that the Marines were pelted with spent 20mm cases as the aircraft flew by.

The bombardment was so intense that the beach was wreathed in smoke as effectively as if a smoke screen had been laid down. Precisely at 1733 the first LCVPs carrying 'A' Company of the 1st Battalion hit the sea wall. As the craft touched the wall, the coxswains kept them in position using the engines while the Marines threw out hastily made ladders or nets fitted with grappling irons and climbed over the wall. The left flank of the company was quickly bogged down by NKPA fire, a situation not helped by the fact that half the 1st Platoon were still drifting around the bay, their LCVP having broken down. The 3rd Platoon landed amidst the men of the 1st. First Lieutenant Baldomero Lopez took out the bunker that was holding up the advance with a lone grenade attack and was just about to deal with a second bunker in similar fashion when he was mortally wounded. The grenade he was carrying was primed but Lopez clutched it to himself to save his comrades: for this selfless act of gallantry he was awarded the Medal of Honor.

On the right, Second Lieutenant Francis W. Muetzel led the 2nd Platoon through a breach in the wall and took his men towards their objective, the Asahi brewery. This objective figured prominently in the minds of the Marines since they had been promised a good 'binge' should they take it—which they did. (They were to be denied their 'binge': during the night the brewery caught fire and its stock of good Asahi beer was destroyed.) But Muetzel could not rest on his laurels, nor enjoy the fruits of his labours. The company commander, Captain John R. Stevens USMC, ordered his men back to the beach. With the left flank still pinned down, Cemetery Hill had to be taken or the beach could not be secure. As Muetzel moved back he realized that the reverse slopes of Cemetery Hill were easier to climb than the slopes facing the beach. Without waiting for approval, he re-formed his platoon and went straight up the hill, clearing out a large number of NKPA prisoners including a support company from the 226th Regiment. From the newly won ground on top of the hill, Muetzel could bring down fire on the bunker which was holding things up on the left flank. Just as he was about to lay down fire, he saw the bunker eliminated by a flame-thrower. The Marines below advanced and Cemetery Hill was taken, but the cost to 'A' Company was eight dead and 28 wounded.

On the right of 'A' Company, 'E' Company of the 2nd Battalion had landed at 1731, three minutes earlier. Their landing was almost unopposed and by 1845 were holding British Consulate Hill, the lower slopes of Observatory Hill and the landward end of the causeway to Wolmi-Do. The right flank of 'Red' Beach was secure.

There now followed the most audacious aspect of the landing on 'Red' Beach. Within sixty minutes of H-Hour, eight LSTs, carrying 3,000 tons of supplies and heavy equipment, made their way towards the beach. The LSTs would drive themselves against the sea wall and then remain on the mudflats for the night while they were unloaded. They ran a serious risk of being hit during the run-in, and while lying immobile on the beach. *LST859* led the way, followed by the others at five-minute intervals. As the LSTs

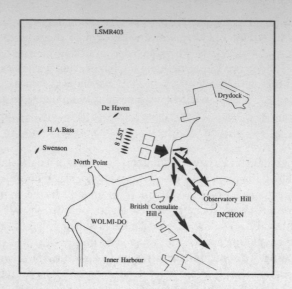

Inchon: The Assault on 'Red' Beach, 15 September 1950

approached, they could see the firefight in progress and *LST914* and *857* were hit, by whose fire is not known. The sailors returned fire but, instead of choosing targets, put down an indiscriminate barrage of 3-inch, 40mm and 20mm on 'Red' Beach which resulted in one Marine dead and 23 wounded. So sweeping was the barrage that Lieutenant Muetzel and his men on top of Cemetery Hill moved down on to the reverse slopes, preferring to take their chances with a NKPA machine-gun post engaging them from Observatory Hill than with the hail of shellfire coming from the sea. Fortunately, as soon as the LSTs were beached, they were boarded by irate Marines who swiftly restored order to the situation, and soon the supplies started coming ashore.

The next and final task for the 5th Marines was the capture of Observatory Hill, for until this hill was secured 'Red' Beach was under continual fire from the NKPA on its summit.. The northern half was assigned to 'C' Company of the 1st Battalion while the southern half was assigned to 'D' Company of the Second Battalion. 'C' Company landed in disorder behind 'A' Company. The beach was under continual fire from NKPA and gunfire from the LSTs as they approached the beach. The small LCVPs had to move out the way quickly or be crushed by the large LSTs as they grounded. Moreover, the landing craft carrying the company commander, First

Lieutenant Paul F. Pederson, was late on the beach, having diverted en route to rescue an LCVP carrying men of 'A' Company which had broken down and was drifting. It was a recipe for chaos.

Fortunately, training and the Marine Corps' spirit carried the occasion. Two junior officers, Second Lieutenants Byron L. Magness and Max A. Merritt, managed to get the 2nd Platoon and the Mortar Platoon organized and headed for Observatory Hill. Despite being held up by a lone NKPA machine-gunner as they dashed through the darkened streets, the two platoons rushed up the hill and at 1845 found themselves on the saddle which joins the north and south horns of the hill. However, when Magness tried to fire the flare to indicate that the objective had been taken, there was no result: his only flare cartridge was a dud.

Down on the beach, with darkness falling amid the chaos, Colonel Newton had no way of knowing that his Marines had secured their objective. Believing that the attack had been halted, he ordered his reserve company to take the hill. As the Marines pushed up the hill they encountered intermittent resistance from the NKPA but got to the top by 2000, where they were very surprised to be greeted by the Marines of 'C' Company. Meanwhile 'D' Company of the 2nd Battalion had run into trouble. First Lieutenant H. J. Smith believed, erroneously, that the men of 'E' Company had already taken the hill. He therefore ordered his men to move up to their positions in columns in order to get there more quickly. As the Marines went up the hill they encountered an NKPA force which engaged the Marines with machine-gun fire and grenades. The column quickly went to ground and a general free-for-all ensued. However, the men of 'D' Company were seasoned soldiers after their weeks on the Pusan Perimeter, and once their initial surprise was over, they quickly regrouped and drove the NKPA off the hill.

By the time Observatory Hill had been secured it was dark and the regimental commander, Lieutenant-Colonel Murray, felt that to push forward into Inchon in darkness would be foolhardy. So the Marines dug in while 'F' Company, the reserve company, were sent to secure the east end of the tidal basin, thus consolidating the Marines' perimeter. The only other event of the night was the capture of a very frightened North Korean soldier by an equally surprised Marine officer who had been about to relieve himself when the Korean crawled out of a foxhole directly beneath him!

Further south, the 1st Marine Regiment was landing on 'Blue' Beach. The 5th Marines may have been the élite of the Marine Corps, but if any one man was the living embodiment of the Corps' spirit it was the regiment's commanding officer, Colonel Lewis B. 'Chesty' Puller. Puller was one of the great fighting soldiers of the American history: he had won two Navy Crosses before the 1939–45 war and would win another two during it while commanding the 1st Marine Regiment (he would win a fifth Navy Cross in Korea). He was an iron disciplinarian who was resolute in battle, and the scourge of the desk-bound staff officer. When the war broke out, Puller was employed in an administrative post but besieged General Cates for a combat command with, reportedly, $19 worth of telegrams.

He was successful, for Cates appointed him to re-form the 1st Marine Regiment (which had been disbanded after the end of the Second World War) from the mixture of East Coast Fleet Marine Force units, Navy Yard guards, reservists and the inevitable infusion of men from military detention who were gladly accepted: Puller noted that some of the best fighting men came out the brig. No matter—most of the men had served in the Second World War and were tried and tested.

The 1st Marine Regiment's mission was to land south of Inchon and secure a beach-head covering the approach the city proper, from which the regiment could advance inland to Yongdungpo and then Seoul. It would land two battalions abreast, the 2nd (Lieutenant-Colonel Sutter) on 'Blue' Beach 1 on the left and the 3rd (Lieutenant-Colonel Ridge) on 'Blue' Beach 2 on the right. The 1st Battalion (Lieutenant-Colonel Hawkins) would land over 'Blue' Beach 2 when the 3rd Battalion was clear.

If 'Red' Beach had been an unsuitable landing spot, then 'Blue' Beach was doubly so. To begin with, the whole area of 'Blue' Beach lay within a bight a mile wide, bounded on the northern side by the island of Won-Do and at the southern end by Tok Am Point. If these two positions were held by the NKPA, then fire could be poured on to the LVTs during their run-in with devastating effect. A further gift to the NKPA was that the approach to the beach involved a 45-minute run over two and half miles of open mudflats, during which time the LVTs would be exposed to fire from the shore. At the other end the beaches were poor. 'Blue' Beach 1 consisted of a small strip of foreshore overlooked by a steep hill sited only a few yards inland. The only exit from the beach was a dirt track which wound around the left side of the hill. The right side of the beach was bounded by a foetid drainage ditch (testifying to the Korean habit of fertilizing crops with human excrement). 'Blue' Beach 2, which joined the right flank of 'Blue' Beach 1 was little better. It was in fact not a beach at all but rather a sea wall which on the right flank went back on itself to form a cove characterized by more mudflats. Yet 'Blue' Beach did have some advantages. There was more open ground inshore and therefore more room to manoeuvre. The area was not as built up as 'Red' Beach and it was hoped that it would not be as well defended, although intelligence was so scanty that it would be up to the Marines of the 1st Regiment to find this out for themselves.

The pre-assault bombardment was provided by the cruisers HMS *Kenya* and HMS *Jamaica*, the destroyers USS *Gurke* and *Henderson* and *LSM(R)401* and *404*. The two cruisers concentrated on laying down fire behind 'Blue' Beach and on Tok Am Point. The necessity of their actions was validated by *Jamaica* hitting what must have been a NKPA munitions dump: the resulting explosion was heard for miles. The American destroyers concentrated on Won-Do and on pouring direct fire on to the beaches. From 1445 the Marines began boarding their LVTs while Skyraider aircraft from TF.77 worked over the beaches with rocket and cannon fire.

The defences were active. Guru and the first wave of Lets were fired on, though to no effect. Some of the Japanese-manned LSTs which were launching LVTs requested permission to abandon their charges and retire when the shells began to fall around them, though this request was indignantly denied. However, counter-fire from the destroyers was extremely effective. An NKPA gun had but to fire one round before it was smothered in accurately directed 5-inch shells. At 1705 the LVTs, 172 of them, began their final run-in to the beach, covered on either side by the two LSM(R)s wearing outsize Stars and Stripes so as not to be wrongly identified.

It was at this stage that the plan went awry—through no fault of those carrying it out. 'Blue' Beach lay downwind from 'Red' Beach and so the smoke from fires burning on 'Red' Beach, in the town of Inchon and on Wolmi-Do drifted down and across the beach, forming a virtually impenetrable curtain. This itself was a recipe for confusion, but the shortages of basic equipment which represented the shabby way in which the Marines had been treated since the end of the Second World War now made themselves felt. There were not enough guide boats. Guide boats were required to shepherd the landing craft (which had little or no navigation equipment) to the beach, making sure that they did not stray from their allotted boat lane. A landing on the scale of that at 'Blue' Beach called for at least 32 guide boats, one for every five or six landing craft. At 'Blue' Beach there were precisely four such craft. In good visibility four guide boats might just have managed, but in the dense smoke which shrouded the beach on 15 September even 32 would not have been enough.

The first three waves of the 2nd and 3rd Battalions were carefully shepherded on to their beaches by the guide boats. Thereafter chaos set in. The USS *Wantuck*, the control vessel for 'Blue' Beach and responsible for landing craft organization, could not see the beach through the murk. Waves

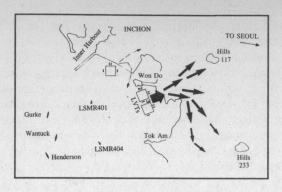

Inchon: The Assault on 'Blue' Beach

of LVTs and amtraks wandered around without guide boats and without precise navigational data, their position made even more difficult by a strong cross-current which ran left to right across the beach and which was equal to the speed of advance of the LVTs.

Fortunately professionalism and improvisation carried the day. The first three waves, which landed on time and in the right place, were able to surmount the chaos. On 'Blue 1', 'D' and 'F' Companies, the assault companies of the 2nd Battalion and the battalion commander landed without opposition. 'D' Company's advance around the left of the hill behind the beach was blocked; the terrific pre-assault bombardment had started a landslide which had obstructed the road. However, 'F' Company quickly got ashore and made the top of the hill which overlooked the beach. Colonel Sutter had 600 men of his battalion ashore, and while he was wondering where the rest of the battalion were he reorganized the forces immediately available to him.

As twilight came Sutter realized that he could not wait indefinitely for the rest of his battalion to come through the smoke. There could be no more hesitation. He had been allocated two objectives, coded 'A', a road junction, and 'B', a hill numbered 117 which commanded the road from Inchon to Yongdungpo. 'D' Company set off to take objective 'A', which they did just as night fell, while 'F' Company secured Hill 117 just after 2200. Fifteen NKPA prisoners were taken and 50 enemy dead were estimated. The 2nd Battalion's casualties were one killed and nineteen wounded.

On 'Blue 2' the position was much the same. The Army LVTs had failed to go on the beach but lay offshore, exchanging the occasional burst of fire with NPKA forces. 'George' Company, the left flank assault company, headed up the drainage ditch while the amtraks carrying 'Item' Company, the right flank assault company, lay alongside the sea wall while the Marines climbed up scaling ladders or nets. As the Marines went forward Colonel Ridge immediately checked the cove on his right flank to see if it was suitable for amtraks to use. It was, and thus was 'Blue' Beach 3 born. Marine signallers on the sea wall directed the remaining LVTs and amtraks to turn right and land via the cove.

The 3rd Battalion's objectives were 'C' and 'D', Hills 94 and 223 respectively, which dominated the right flank. In addition 'G' Company had to secure an avenue of approach leading from the south-east to the centre of 'Blue' Beach. Like Sutter, Ridge could not wait for the rest of his battalion to arrive, so he set about capturing his objectives with what he had. 'G' Company secured the approach to 'Blue' Beach while 'Item' had been swung to the right to take the western side of Hill 233 before night fell. Fortunately 'H' Company had just managed to come ashore over 'Blue' Beach 3 and were sent to fill the gap between 'G' and 'I' Companies. The 1st Platoon drove an NKPA company off Hill 94 after a brief firefight while the 2nd Platoon failed to reach the eastern side of Hill 233. In view of the darkness and unfamiliar terrain, the platoon commander was allowed to dig in where he was.

Meanwhile, in the confusion raging in the smoke offshore, the 1st Battalion were trying to land. Their landing craft had been misdirected by a searchlight aimed from Wantuck at what they thought was 'Blue 2'. In fact, the bearing was wrong and the beam was shone to the north-east of the correct bearing. The result was that, although the LVTs and amtraks carrying 'A' Company and part of 'B' Company were redirected to 'Blue' Beach, most of the battalion ended up by landing in the tidal basin in Inchon docks, from where they walked to 'Blue' Beach the next morning—accompanied by a large file of prisoners. Only 'C' Company landed on time on 'Blue' Beach; they were patiently waiting for their commanding officer when he finally caught up with them.

While the beaches and their immediate objectives were being secured, the follow-up operations began. Artillery and armour had to be landed. Engineers wanted to clear and extend the beaches. Supply dumps had to be established and filled. The teeth of the army were ashore: now its logistic tail, without which the teeth would soon be blunted, had to follow.

The original plan had called for the 11th Marines' 105mm guns to be landed on Wolmi-Do following the morning assault. In the event the plan was considered complicated enough without artillery. Observers would land with the initial assault on Wolmi-Do and begin identifying targets for the guns which would arrive that evening. The 105mm guns were to be landed from LSTs in DUKWs. Despite the strong currents which all but overpowered the DUKWs, the guns were ashore by 2150 and ready to respond to requests. By then, however, the gloom and lack of clear targets meant that there was little for the gunners to do. Likewise the armour was held on its ships (minus one company which had landed to support 'Red' Beach) until 17 September.

Clearing and expanding the beaches was the responsibility of the 1st Shore Party Battalion commanded by Lieutenant-Colonel Harry P. 'Jim' Crow USMC. Korea was Crow's third war and he was as much a legend in the Corps as Colonel Puller. His first task was to guide the eight LSTs up on to 'Red' Beach. Once beached, the first vehicles out of the LSTs were bulldozers which began to demolish parts of the sea wall and use the rubble to make an improvised road for the vehicles on the LSTs to roll ashore. The timetable was inflexible. The eight LSTs had to be unloaded during the night, no matter what was happening elsewhere. The eight LSTs had to be empty so that they could retract on the next morning's tide, to make way for more ships carrying more supplies. Within four hours, despite having to work under bright arc lights which drew enemy fire, the engineers and Marines were in control of the situation and supplies were flooding ashore.

By midnight on 15 September 13,000 men and their equipment were ashore. Total US casualties amounted to 21 killed, one missing and 174 wounded. No accurate figures are available for the NKPA. Historians have made much of the confusion which attended the landings, particularly on 'Blue' Beach, but no amount of revisionism or 'new analysis' can deny that the landings were made on time, that the objectives were captured and that the NKPA was so taken by surprise and struck so hard that they were incapable of organized resistance. That this happened was due to the professionalism and expertise of the sailors and Marines who made it look so simple and who were thus able to rise above any immediate difficulties. 'The reason it looked so simple,' General O. P. Smith observed, 'was that professionals did it.'

CHAPTER TEN

To Seoul and Beyond

It is fatal to enter any war without the will to win it.—General
Douglas MacArthur, 1952

SEPTEMBER 16, D+1, began with the Marines from 'Red' and 'Blue'
Beaches advancing forward to the Force Beachhead Line (sometimes
known as Line O-3), a line at right angles to the two landing beaches
pointing like an arrow at Seoul. The boundary between the 5th Marines and
the 1st Marines was the Inchon≈Seoul road. While the 1st Marines headed
for Yongdungpo, a grim industrial suburb of Seoul, the 5th Marines looped
left and took the airfield at Kimpo. Mopping up NKPA resistance in Inchon
and securing the city was left to the ROK Marines—a task which was
accomplished with grim efficiency. At the same time Corsair aircraft from
the USS *Sicily* began probing inland to find from where and in what strength
the expected NKPA counter-attack would come.

Near to a small hamlet called Kamsong-Ni the aircraft sighted a column
of T-34s, which they attacked with cannon-fire and napalm. Six tanks were
destroyed in the first strike and another two were destroyed an hour later,
with heavy casualties inflicted on the infantry accompanying the tanks. On
18 September the 5th Marines secured Kimpo airfield and its 6,000-foot
long runway, although not before one intrepid Marine aviator had already
landed on the field before it had been cleared safe . Once the airfield was
secured Marine squadrons VMF-212, VMF-312 and VMF(N)-542 deployed ashore to provide close ground support for the troops.

Meanwhile, in the south, the Eighth Army was finding it difficult to go
on to the offensive. The NKPA were withdrawing, but it was the fear of
encirclement that was making them do so rather than any activities of the
Eighth Army. Yet there was a gross disparity in numbers between the forces
engaged on the Pusan Perimeter—140,000 UN troops, of which 60,000
were American, against 70,000 NKPA, of which half were unwilling
conscripts from South Korea. The drubbing which the NKPA had inflicted
on the Eighth Army in June, July and August was still having an effect.

Regardless of what was happening around Pusan, the Marines pressed
on. The momentum of the advance had to be maintained to keep the enemy

in a constant defensive posture and not allow him to consolidate, regroup and launch a counter-attack. The Marines were driving on Seoul in a two-pronged assault: the 5th Marines would cross the Han river and attack the city from the north-west while the 1st would take the suburb of Yongdungpo and enter the city from the south-east. The 5th Marines' left flank was guarded by the Korean Marines while the right flank of the 1st Marines was guarded by the 32nd Infantry Regiment from the 7th Infantry Division, which had followed the Marines ashore at Inchon from D+3 onwards.

The 5th Marines began their crossing of the Han river during the night of 19/20 September. There was no bridging equipment available, so the men from the 3/5th and 2/1st Marines would have to cross in amtraks. Before the main attack a reconnaissance company and assault frogmen were sent over to indicate likely landing sites on the north bank. They gained the far shore, but when the first wave of amtraks set out the North Koreans laid down a fearsome curtain of fire with machine guns and mortars. Reluctantly Colonel Murray called off the attempt. Five hours later the Marines made a second attempt and this time were successful. The 2/5th Marines reached the north bank, followed by the 2nd Battalion Korean Marine Corps. The Marines then swung right and began clearing the bank and preparing crossing sites from the 1st Marines fighting their way through Yongdungpo.

Puller's 1st Marines were having a harder time of it. Until the 32nd Infantry came up to cover his flank, Puller always had to provide forces from his regiment for this purpose, which weakened his advance. In the night of 19 September the 1/1st Marines relieved the 1/5th—the latter was required for the crossing of the Han river—on three hills between Kimpo and Yongdungpo which the 1/5th had captured. However, the handover took place at night and the 1/1st did not occupy their new positions until daylight on the 20th, by which time they found that Hill 80 and Hill 85 had been reoccupied by the NKPA. Both hills were retaken by the Marines on the 20th, but only after fierce fighting in which Second Lieutenant John A. Commiskey won the Medal of Honor for single-handedly clearing two NKPA machine-gun positions.

The 1st Marines' drive on Yongdungpo was slowed by street fighting in the outskirts of the suburb. However, a group of 200 men from 'A' Company, the 1/1st, under Captain Robert A. Barrow, somehow went through a gap in the NKPA perimeter and found themselves in the centre of Yongdungpo. They then ran into NKPA infantry, returned fire and dug in. For some reason Colonel Hawkins neither supported them nor sought to exploit the opportunity Barrow's advance had offered him. Meanwhile Barrow's men were withstanding attacks by NKPA infantry supported by armour but were offering grim resistance. At dawn on 21 September there were over 300 NKPA dead piled high around the Marines' positions. By then the 1/1st and 3/1st were advancing and drove the NKPA out of Yongdungpo, securing the whole of the south bank of the Han.

On 22 September the final assault on Seoul began. It was characterized by the wanton destruction which was soon to become typical of the liberation movements in South-East Asian conflicts. The British war correspondent of the *Daily Telegraph*, Reginald Thompson, vividly described the scene:

> It is an appalling inferno of din and destruction with the tearing noise of dive bombers blasting right ahead, and the livid flashes of the tank guns, the harsh fierce crackle of blazing wooden buildings, telegraph and high tension poles collapsing in utter chaos of wires. Great palls of smoke hang over us as massive buildings collapse in showers of sparks, puffing masses of smoke and rubble upon is in terrific heat . . . Few people can have suffered so terrible a liberation.

By the time the last NKPA soldier had fled from Seoul there was little left but the ruins. The 5th Marines would attack Seoul from the north-west. As it happened, the Koreans' strongest defensive positions lay directly across the 5th Marines' line of advance. These defences were manned by men of the 25th Brigade and 78th Independent Regiment. They were experienced troops, many of whom had fought the Japanese as partisans. They would not simply break and run in the face of the Marines' advance: they would have to be driven out. In fierce fighting the Marines pressed on, and on 23 September took a position known to them as Hill 56. Without realizing it, they had just captured the single most important position in the NKPA's defensive perimeter. The following day the 1st Marines crossed the Han river to positions already prepared by the 5th Marines, while the 7th Marine Regiment, a composite unit formed from USMC detachments all over the world and which had only recently landed at Inchon, swept north around the rear of the 5th Marines to guard their flank and cut off the NKPA's escape.

At this stage, with the capture of Seoul becoming an all-Marine affair, General Almond, who was nominally in command of the whole operation as General Commanding X Corps, suddenly intervened. Almond did not come ashore until 21 September, an absurdly long time after the landing considering that during the Second World War no American Corps commander got ashore later than D+1. The appointment of Almond as commander of X Corps is perhaps the least understandable of MacArthur's decisions, especially as a 'ready-made' corps commander and headquarters were present in the shape of General Shepherd of the Fleet Marine Force.

Almond, though without doubt a competent soldier, was not a Marine and had no experience of amphibious operations. Consequently he was content to remain in his transport until the Marines were established ashore. Moreover, he had retained his previous appointment as MacArthur's chief of staff and it was not until the latter left the theatre to return to Japan that Almond felt that he could devote himself wholeheartedly to his new command.

The situation was an invidious one and it is hardly surprising that a mutual antipathy developed between the staff of X Corps and that of the 1st Marine Division. The latter looked upon the soldiers as a bunch of 'johnny come latelys' and poured scorn on Almond's luxurious command complex with its air conditioning units, showers, silver service and fresh food flown in daily from Japan. In return the soldiers viewed the Marines as little more than plodders who were incapable of an imaginative movement and who were being needlessly slow in the taking of Seoul.

When Almond reviewed the tactical situation he was dissatisfied with the speed of the Marines' advance, particularly as he had made the somewhat rash promise to MacArthur that he would be in Seoul by 25 September, three months after the North Korean invasion. Almond decided that what was required was an enveloping movement around Seoul from the south-east. He proposed that the 1st Marines be used for this purpose instead of having them slog through the streets of Yongdungpo, but when the idea was put to General Smith the latter rejected it. Smith did not want the 1st and 5th Marines coming face to face in Seoul from opposite directions. Moreover, the reports from Murray's 5th Marines and Puller's 1st Marines confirmed his impression that the NKPA were going to defend Seoul to the last building, regardless of any flanking movement by the Americans. Smith thought that the soundest plan was to carry on with what he was already doing—to advance through Seoul street by street and to manoeuvre his division as one solid, co-ordinated formation.

Almond, understandably, was furious, and had Smith been an Army general there is no doubt that he would have been relieved there and then. Smith, however, was a Marine, and the Marines were still enjoying the laurels of their success at Inchon. Almond was not defeated and instead of the 1st Marines selected the 32nd Infantry Division backed by ROK troops (for psychological and political reasons) to make the manoeuvre. He shrewdly reckoned that the use of a US Army formation might spur the Marines on, while having the Army present at the fall of Seoul would give it some positive publicity. Even on the field of battle there is always room for inter-service rivalry

General Smith was angry when he heard of Almond's decision, particularly as it was communicated to the regimental commanders without Smith having been informed first (a fact which Almond subsequently denied). Smith was not just annoyed; he was worried too. He felt that taking the 32nd Infantry away from protecting the Marines' southern flank while replacing them with the 31st Infantry would leave the flank dangerously undefended. The NKPA still had some fight in it, and a swift counter-attack could sever the Inchon–Seoul road and capture Kimpo airfield. Smith felt that the chance of taking Seoul by 25 September was not worth the risk involved by weakening the southern flank.

Smith's objections were overruled and on 25 September the Americans advanced into Seoul from three directions, the 5th Marines from the north-west, the 1st Marines from the south west and the 32nd Infantry from the south-east. The last had to endure General Almond's presence in the command post nearly all day. Almond was not above castigating battalion commanders directly for their tardiness, and under this avalanche of constructive criticism the 32nd Infantry seized the South Mountain, the highest point in Seoul.

At this point Almond felt that he could announce that Seoul had been liberated. This was nothing more than a propaganda *tour de force*: a further two days of savage street fighting followed before MacArthur invited Syngmann Rhee to resume the government of his country at a moving ceremony in the ruined capitol in Seoul on 28 September. Even then, as MacArthur spoke, those present could hear the rattle of small-arms fire as the last pockets of NKPA resistance were flushed out.

What of the Eighth Army? Walker had failed to make any progress and it was only after MacArthur threatened a second landing at Kunsan using two of Walker's divisions that the latter was stung into action. The break-out began sluggishly and the Americans were not across the Natkong in strength until 19 September. Bad weather then hampered the Air Force's ability to provide close air support, but once the weather cleared the advance quickened in pace. It was not until 27 September that elements of the 1st Cavalry met up with the 31st Infantry just beyond the town of Osan. The link up between X Corps and the Eighth Army was 'official'.

The Eighth Army, however, did not break out from Pusan. Walker's men were able to pursue an enemy compelled to withdraw because of the landings at Inchon. The NKPA divisions around the perimeter simply melted away—their own version of 'bug-out' fever. Walker's tardiness meant that one of the objectives of the Inchon landings was not accomplished. MacArthur had wanted to trap the NKPA between X Corps and the

Eighth Army. But Walker moved too slowly and the NKPA slipped away, either into the hills to form guerrilla bands or north to regroup. The so-called 'trap lines' Walker threw across the peninsula in successive vain attempts to ensnare the NKPA were too few and came too late. It is impossible to estimate how many of the NKPA troops escaped, but the official US Army history guessed that between 25,000 and 30,000 got away. The true figure was probably much higher. Those who got away were more than likely experienced combat troops rather than conscripted South Korean levies and their numbers were more than sufficient to form the nucleus of a new army.

The taking of Seoul and the rout of the NKPA brought the Korean War on to a new course. The aim of the UN resolution of 27 June 1950—the re-establishment of the Syngmann Rhee government—had been achieved. Before the Inchon landings the planners in Washington had given some thought to the matter, which emerged as document NSC81/1. This provided for the conduct of operations north of the 38th Parallel, the border between the two Koreas, to ensure the destruction of the NKPA. The factor dominating all discussion on the matter was how the Chinese would react if military operations were conducted close to or on the Chinese border with North Korea along the Yalu river. The Chinese were an unknown quantity, and apart from some vague pronouncements made through the Indian Government had so far given little away of their attitude. After a consider-able amount of discussion operations up to the Chinese border were approved, but it was specifically stated that in order not to provoke the Chinese all such operations should be conducted only by ROK troops.

The smashing victory at Inchon created a vacuum as far as intelligent planning for the campaign went. It was a classic example of how a military opportunity becomes the driving force behind a policy with total disregard for the political consequences. MacArthur had won a notable victory and his forces were romping north toward the 38th Parallel. He himself had no doubts that his aim was the complete destruction of the NKPA and the reunification of Korea. In this he was backed, up to a point, by the Joint Chiefs of Staff. In the glow of victory following the Inchon landings, the diplomats and the politicians were simply dragged along behind. On 29 September, in an 'eyes only' signal, MacArthur was given the authority to conduct operations north of the 38th Parallel but was told to be discreet about crossing the border into North Korea for fear of arousing difficulties in the United Nations.

ROK forces crossed the 38th Parallel on 28 September and by 8 October the main force of the Eighth Army was streaming across. The NKPA tried to hold ground but on 16 October they broke and fled. Meanwhile MacArthur had decided on a fundamental realignment of his forces. X Corps were to be moved by sea around the peninsula and were to land at Wonsan on the east coast. This would provide for a two-pronged thrust up the peninsula, the Eighth Army in the west and X Corps, supported by ROK units, in the east. The decision was the cause of more bitterness among Walker's staff: not only were the ROK units dealing successfully with the NKPA on the east coast, but it was thought that the move was nothing more than blatant patronage for MacArthur's protégé, Almond, and an opportunity for him to take more of the limelight. The Eighth Army felt that they had been in Korea since the beginning and that they now wanted their share of the glory.

In the event the landings at Wonsan on 25 October were a farce. When the Marines got ashore they found that ROK troops had taken the town on 10 October. Even the Marines' technical and administrative units had arrived by air two days earlier. The final insult, which has since entered Marine Corps legend, was that the entertainer Bob Hope had given a show there on the night before the landings.

On 25 October the first ROK forces reached the Yalu river. By now MacArthur was hell-bent on annihilating the NKPA. Directives were issued to Walker and Almond which gave them the authority to manoeuvre their forces right up to the Chinese border. This was a flagrant violation of the orders MacArthur had received from Washington. Yet Collins, the Army Chief of Staff, made no move to curb his unruly subordinate. MacArthur was certain that the Chinese would not intervene and he convinced everyone with whom he dealt of this—even President Truman, who had summoned him to Wake Island for a conference on 15 October. MacArthur's contempt for intelligence, for the cardinal virtue of prudence in an unknown situation, has seldom been matched in twentieth century warfare.

MacArthur was wrong: the Chinese were moving. Alarmed by the advance of the UN forces in Korea and by the visibly strengthening relationship between the US administration and the Chiang Kai-Shek government in Taiwan, the Chinese had decided to act. Marshal Peng Tei Huan was placed in command of XIII Army Group—consisting of 130,000 men, who were called 'volunteers' in order to prevent full-scale hostilities with the UN—which was ordered to move into North Korea and deploy in support of the NKPA. One of the most remarkable aspects of the Korean War is that the Chinese managed to move the 130,000 men together with their equipment into North Korea without being detected by the UN forces, who, after all, held complete air superiority. In this the American command was supremely careless: by now they were so confident of victory that they saw only what they wanted to see.

The Chinese first went into action between 1 and 3 November against the US 1st Cavalry Division and against the ROK II Corps. They attacked with great skill and determination using small arms, mortars and Katyusha rockets. The 3rd Battalion of the 8th Cavalry Regiment was effectively destroyed and the other battalions in the regiment severely mauled. Yet no sooner had the Chinese struck than they melted away and withdrew from 6 November onwards.

MacArthur and his staff were inclined to think that the attack on the 1st Cavalry was the last effort by a smashed and routed NKPA. The truth was exactly the opposite. After several days' hard fighting, during which they had seized the initiative, the Chinese chose to break off the engagement. Modern sources in China claim that the disengagement was on account of logistic problems and co-ordinating the various Chinese forces in the field. This is plausible, but the reasons run deeper than mere problems of supply. The Chinese did not want a conflict with the United Nations forces. It must be remembered that they had only just finished nearly twenty years of fighting in civil wars and against the Japanese. The economy was in ruins. What was needed more than anything else was a period of stability and reconstruction. On the other hand, the Chinese were not prepared to tolerate the establishment of an anti-communist regime on their borders. Thus the attack launched at the beginning of November was a warning. China was saying, in effect, 'We are here. We can strike you and we can defeat you. Halt the advance now and that will be the end of it.' Unfortunately this warning was not heeded in the UN command. The offensive, the drive for the Yalu river, would continue. In turn, the Chinese made preparations to meet it.

The Chinese struck on 25 November. Eighteen divisions smashed through the three divisions of the ROK II Corps, tearing an eighty-mile gap between the Eighth Army on the west coast and X Corps in the east. The Eighth Army faced the prospect of being cut off from the south, so Walker ordered an immediate retreat. The retreat turned into another rout, a repeat of the events of five months earlier when the Eighth Army had fled before the NKPA. In the east the 1st Marine Division had reached the Chosin reservoir when they were attacked during the night of 27 November. The journey of the 1st Marine Division from the reservoir to the Korean port of Hamhung, where they were evacuated on 24 December—General O. P. Smith described it as 'advancing in another direction'—is an epic in military history. Alone among the American forces, the Marines retired in good order and kept most of their equipment with them. Even their dead were brought back rather than abandoned on the field where they fell, a

Above: Troops and a field gun being evacuated from Suvla in daylight, December 1915. (IWM Q.13637)
Below: Stores burning on the shore at Suvla Bay after the last troops had been taken off. The photograph was taken from HMS *Cornwallis*, the last ship to leave the bay. (IWM Q.13679)

Above: Stores being prepared for destruction on 'W' Beach, Cape Helles, in January 1916. (IWM Q.13692)

INCHON
Left: Major-General O. P. Smith, Commanding General 1st Marine Division, with Admiral James H. Doyle, Commander Amphibious Group 1, and Colonel Krulak, Marine Corps Operations Officer, on the headquarters ship USS *Mount McKinley* before the Inchon operation. (US Navy)
Right: General of the Army Douglas MacArthur. He was single-minded in the implementation of his plan for a landing at Inchon. (US Army)

Left: The destroyer *Lyman K. Swenson* retiring from the bombardment of Wolmi-Do on 14 September 1950, seen from the cruiser HMS *Kenya*. (IWM HU.57482)

Below: A Marine using a flame-thrower blasts an NKPA emplacement on Radio Hill, Wolmi-Do. (US Navy)

Right: An NKPA 76.2mm gun on Wolmi-Do destroyed by shellfire from HMS *Kenya*. (IWM HU.57484) **Below:** A Marine road block on the causeway leading from Wolmi-Do to the town of Inchon. In the distance some of the objectives off 'Red' Beach can be seen: Cemetery Hill is on the left of the causeway and Observatory Hill is on the right. (US Navy)

Above: A photograph of 'Red' Beach from Wolmi-Do, taken before the landings. (US Navy)
Below: The first waves of the 5th Marines head past the destroyer *De Haven* on the run-in to 'Red' Beach. (US Navy)

Above: Lieutenant Baldomero Lopez of the 5th Marines clambers up and out of his LCA on to 'Red' Beach. Shortly after this photograph was taken Lopez was killed, the circumstances of his death resulting in the posthumous award of the Medal of Honor. (US Navy)
Below: Amphibious tractors carry men of the 1st Marines towards 'Blue' Beach. (US Navy)

Left: Colonel Lewis B. ('Chesty') Puller, Commanding Officer of the 1st Marine Regiment, seen before the landing on 'Blue' Beach. (USMC)

Below: 'Blue' Beach seen from the sea. Fires are burning and explosions from rocket salvos are apparent. (US Navy)

Right, upper: LSTs resting on the mud at 'Red' Beach and discharging supplies. Wolmi-Do is in the background on the left. (US Navy)

Right, lower: Major-General Edward M. Almond (wearing baseball cap), the commanding general of X Corps. Although nominally responsible for the conduct of the landing, Almond did not go ashore until some days after it had taken place.

Above: A photograph of the Korean capital, Seoul, taken from across the Han river. (US Army)
Below: The crossing of the Han river. Amtraks can be seen making their way across the water under fire. (USMC)
Right, upper: An officer from HMS *Kenya* inspects a knocked-out NKPA T-34/85 tank on the road to Seoul. (IWM HU.57435)
Right, lower: Men of the 1st Marines engaged in street fighting in Yongdungpo. (USMC)

Above: Men of the 5th Marines raise the Stars and Stripes outside the capitol building in Seoul. The flag was later replaced by Korean colours out of political expediency. (USMC)

THE FALKLANDS WAR
Right, upper: Rear-Admiral John ('Sandy') Woodward in his quarters on board HMS *Antrim* during the voyage south. (IWM FKD.212)
Right, lower: Brigadier Julian Thompson and some of the staff of 3 Commando Brigade. Major Ewen Southby-Tailyour, the officer whose detailed knowledge of the Falkland Islands proved indispensable, is seen on the left of the photograph. (MoD)

Left, upper: HMS *Hermes*, Admiral Woodward's flagship, leaves Portsmouth, 5 April 1982. (MoD)

Left, lower: Workmen completing the installation of *Canberra*'s forward flight deck. (IWM FKD.374)

Above: The Amphibious Group at Ascension. Visible in the photograph are five Royal Fleet Auxiliary LSLs, an RFA tanker, RFA *Stromness* acting as a troopship, an assault ship, an unidentified Type 21 frigate and, on the left, the RMAS tug *Typhoon*—the first vessel to leave for the Falklands and the last to return. (MoD)

Below: The advance group of warships heads south. From left to right are *Glamorgan*, *Brilliant* and an unidentified Type 21 frigate, with *Yarmouth* in the background. Of the ships in the photograph, only *Yarmouth* would return unscathed. (MoD)

Above: Wideawake Airfield on Ascension Island. An RAF Hercules is on the tarmac together with a huge amount of stores. Ascension played a vital role as a supplies base, situated as it is roughly half way between Great Britain and the Falklands. (MoD)

Below: A landing craft loaded with Marine Commandos passes *Canberra* at Ascension. The period of time spent at Ascension was the only opportunity the troops had to practise final landing-craft drills. (IWM FKD.386)

practice which some observers found macabre but one which testifies to the close comradeship binding the Marines together.

By the end of 1950 the UN forces were virtually back where they had started. Another two and a half years of bloody fighting followed before an armistice was agreed on 27 July 1953 at Panmunjon. The new border between the two Koreas was not so very different from the one which had been swept aside on 25 June 1950. One casualty of the war was, of course, MacArthur, who was dismissed by President Truman on 11 April 1951.

While MacArthur was winning, his military and political superiors in Washington were content to let him run his command in his own way. However, the defeat inflicted by the Chinese on the Americans and UN forces in the winter of 1950 caused those in Washington to reflect on their country's commitment to the Korean War. It was now felt that Korea was not the place to begin World War III, and in December 1950 MacArthur was told that he could expect no more reinforcements and that he would have to manage the situation in Korea with such forces as were available. This, of course, was anathema to MacArthur. His pronouncements against the Truman administration for its lacklustre policy were almost as vitriolic as those directed at Peking and the North Koreans. Slowly and steadily a gap widened between the wishes of the UN commander in Korea and those of his superiors in Washington. MacArthur wanted total war against China using massed air power and amphibious landings on a scale which dwarfed Inchon; he even proposed creating a no man's land between Korea and China by dumping piles of radioactive waste.

The final straw came on 5 April when MacArthur's infamous letter to Representative Joseph Martin was read out on the floor of the House of Representatives:

> It seems strangely difficult for some [wrote MacArthur] to realize that here in Asia is where the communist conspirators have elected to make their play for global conquest, and we have joined the issue thus raised on the battlefield; that here we fight Europe's war with arms while the diplomats there still fight it with words; that if we lose this war to communism in Asia, the fall of Europe is inevitable; win it, and Europe most probably would avoid war and yet preserve freedom. As you have pointed out, we must win: there is no substitute for victory . . .

It was enough. After discussions with the Chiefs of Staff, Truman dismissed MacArthur on 11 April and replaced him with Lieutenant-General Matthew B. Ridgeway. There were many who regretted the manner of his departure, yet MacArthur had lost touch with the realities and with the thinking of the administration he was pledged to serve.

The retreat from the Chosin reservoir, the dismissal of MacArthur and the ambivalent end to the Korean War have all served to cloud Inchon's claim to be the most audacious and successful amphibious operation of all time, Yet since 1950 the Inchon landings have been forgotten—or, when remembered at all, recalled amidst a haze of inaccuracy. Inter-service rivalry brought about the first attempt to rewrite what happened. The Department of the Army withheld its Distinguished Unit Citation from the 1st Marine Division and it was not until December 1951 that the Navy Department issued the Presidential Unit Citation to the Marines, even though they had been under Army command. The United States Air Force was equally quick off the mark when General O. P. Wayland claimed that air attacks on the NKPA had had more effect than the Inchon landings and that the 1st Marine Division and the 7th Infantry Division would have been better employed at Pusan. President Truman, no admirer of the Marines, omitted to mention the Corps in his victory message to the troops. Yet without the Marines and their back-up from the US Navy Inchon could never have happened: the US Army did not possess that level of expertise in amphibious warfare.

Another form of revisionism came from MacArthur's off-hand (and unintentional) remark that the odds against 'Chromite''s succeeding were 5,000 to 1. This impromptu remark has been taken by some as a serious estimate by MacArthur. Inchon, therefore, was a gamble, an inexplicable success, and one which should not be taken as an example when planning future operations. Finally, in what can only be described as a process of guilt by association, the success of 'Chromite' has been 'discredited' by the subsequent débâcle on the Yalu and the dismissal of MacArthur. 'Chromite' did not win the war: therefore the operation is of no consequence.

Yet Operation 'Chromite' succeeded in all its immediate objectives. It caused the withdrawal of the NKPA forces around the Pusan Perimeter. It brought about the destruction of the NKPA in the fighting around Seoul and the subsequent advance to the 38th Parallel. It preserved the Republic of South Korea and, for the first and only time since 1945, it restored a city captured by the communists to freedom. Moreover, it restored, albeit temporarily, the prestige of American arms, which had been badly dented in the series of 'bug-outs' following the NKPA invasion.

Perhaps most importantly of all, the landings at Inchon reminded the Pentagon planners of what they had tried so hard to forget since 1945—that the United States is a maritime power. Only through the exercise of maritime power could the course of this little war in a faraway country have been reversed in a matter of weeks. The success of the Inchon landings broke the hypnotic spell which atomic weapons had placed on the Pentagon since 1945. The Korean War had forced the United States to consider the use of nuclear weapons and the Americans had backed down. The retreat from the Yalu and the prospect of using nuclear weapons had made those in Washington realize that America needed conventional forces to pursue limited wars.

Inchon is a masterpiece. Whatever his subsequent faults, MacArthur had an unwavering sense of the objective. He gathered the forces required and insisted that the tight timetable be adhered to at all costs. Perhaps only a general of MacArthur's stature and seniority could have brought all the threads together so quickly and secured the consent of his superiors. Under his umbrella the professional Navy and Marine staffs put the flesh on the bones of the plan he had laid down. Without the reservoir of specialist knowledge of amphibious operations held by men like Doyle and O. P. Smith, Inchon would have remained either an intellectual concept or a military catastrophe to rival Gallipoli.

CHAPTER ELEVEN

March to the South Atlantic

This has been a pimple festering in the ass of progress for two hundred years and I guess someone decided to lance it.—General Alexander Haig, US Secretary of State

T HE Falkland Islands lie 400 miles off the coast of South America, 350 miles north-east of Cape Horn. Their land mass covers 4,700 square miles—roughly the size of Sicily or the state of Connecticut. The first recorded landing on the islands was made in 1690 by a Captain John Strong from Plymouth, who named the stretch of water which separates the two islands 'Falkland Sound', after the commissioner of the Admiralty, Lord Falkland. From 1767 there was a continuous British presence on the islands, usually a Royal Marine garrison. Following the break-up the Spanish Empire in Latin America, the islands were colonized by Argentina from 1826 to 1831. However, in 1831 the Argentine governor foolishly arrested two United States merchant ships on suspicion of poaching and by way of retribution the Argentine settlement was destroyed by a party from the USS *Lexington.* British rule was restored on 2 January 1833.

The Argentine Government never abandoned its claim to the islands, which, apart from anything else, served to distract attention from domestic events at home. Occasionally the Argentines made menacing noises about the Falklands, but the discreet dispatch of naval forces and a reinforcement of the garrison usually served to contain the incident. However, in December 1981 a new *junta* came to power in Argentina led by General Leopoldo Galtieri. More right-wing than its predecessors, it seized on the 'Malvinas question' as a panacea for all its domestic ills. A successful reconquest of the islands would boost its prestige at home and throughout Latin America (except Chile) and would distract domestic attention away from the gradually worsening economic situation and the *junta*'s deplorable record on human rights. In this it was right: for a short time after the invasion the Argentine leadership was hugely popular, but this state of affairs did not last. In its thinking on the Falklands the *junta* was encouraged by the British 1982 Defence Review, in which the sale of the Royal Navy's two aircraft carriers was announced, together with the withdrawal of its ice patrol ship, HMS *Endurance*.

The Argentine invasion of the Falkland Islands on 2 April 1982 came as a complete surprise to the British public. It was true that tension had been mounting in the light of previous Argentine sabre-rattling in the South Atlantic and the presence of Argentine 'scrap merchants' on the island of South Georgia, a Falkland Islands dependency 700 miles to the east, but no one seriously believed that the Argentines would invade a group of small islands at the other end of the world. Once the immediate shock of the invasion had been digested, there was an unusual unanimity among British politicians about the response to the Argentine move. The Government announced that a task force would be dispatched promptly to the South Atlantic. In an emergency debate on the invasion in the House of Commons, politicians of all persuasions—even Michael Foot, the leader of the Labour Party and a man not known for bellicose sentiments—called for an immediate military response.

Prime Minister Margaret Thatcher was resolute in her determination to secure the return of the islands to Britain, even when it seemed that she was fighting a war on two fronts—against the Argentines on the one hand and against those in her government who favoured a less robust approach and a negotiated settlement on the other. The political determination to carry the war through to a victorious conclusion was a major factor in overcoming the considerable problems faced by the British in securing the islands' recovery. Apparently, at the beginning the campaign Mrs Thatcher realized the difficulties of what Britain was undertaking. She asked Admiral Sir John Fieldhouse for a straightforward answer as to whether Britain would succeed. Fieldhouse looked the 'Iron Lady' straight in the eye and said that success was guaranteed so long as the political support remained firm. True to her reputation, she never wavered.

This was most fortunate, for in seeking to regain the Falklands the Royal Navy faced enormous difficulties. Briefly, these encompassed the considerable distances between Great Britain and the islands, the nearness of the Argentine mainland, the approach of the austral winter and the lack of air cover and specialized amphibious support ships required for such an operation. These considerations alone would have deterred all but the most determined; indeed, there was significant opposition to the operation. Rear-Admiral John 'Sandy' Woodward, who was appointed to command the task force, listed those who opposed the operation for these very reasons:
1. The United States Navy, which considered the recapture of the Falkland Islands to be a military impossibility.

2. The Ministry of Defence in Whitehall, which generally regarded the whole idea as far too risky.

3. The Army, which considered it to be ill-advised, for lack of a proper advantage ratio in land force numbers.

4. The RAF, which, seeing little role for itself on account of the vast distances, and no chance of a navy's surviving in the face of an air force, was inclined to agree.

5. The Secretary of State for Defence, Mr (now Sir) John Nott, since success in it would probably overturn the 1981 Defence Review.

What made the operation happen was the political will to win, expressed by the Prime Minister. The political decision that the Falklands would be retaken overrode conventional military thinking and reservations.

The obstacles were huge. The Falkland Islands lie 8,000 miles from the United Kingdom. The nearest British forward base was situated on Ascension Island, which lies roughly half way between the Falklands and the UK. Never before had an amphibious operation been mounted so far from the main base. All the fuel, ammunition and other stores required by a modern military force would have to be carried these enormous distances to the forward area. To complicate matters, the Falkland Islands lie only 380 miles away from the Argentine mainland with its cluster of airfields at Rio Grande, Rio Gallegos, San Julien and Comodoro Rivadavia facing the Falklands in a crescent.

To the factor of distance was added that of bad weather. The area is not known for its benevolent climate. Storms at sea are frequent and would hamper flying operations and refuelling at sea. May would see the coming of the austral winter with its driving winds, snow and bitter cold. Operations would have be concluded before winter set in, since any sort of combat in those conditions would be impossible.

In terms of military considerations, the single most important factor affecting a British operation was the lack of organic air power for the task force. Argentina had begun to modernize its air force and naval air arm in the 1960s, largely with second-hand American equipment but also by purchase from other countries, particularly France and Israel (a surprising choice in view of the known pro-Nazi sympathies of the Argentine Government). The Navy acquired Lockheed P-2 Neptunes for long-range reconnaissance and Grumman S-2 Trackers for carrier AEW, and also the A-4B (designated A-4Q for the Argentine export model) Skyhawk. This last was a light attack aircraft capable of operating from Argentina's only carrier, the *25 de Mayo*, and able to lift a respectable weight of free-fall bombs or two Sidewinder missiles if fitted as an interceptor.

The Argentine Air Force also acquired the Skyhawk, the A-4C version, which had a bad-weather flying capability and two additional underwing hardpoints for fuel or ordnance. From the late 1960s the Americans refused to supply more modern aircraft, so the Argentines looked elsewhere. They found little joy in Britain, where all they were allowed to acquire was a dozen Canberra bombers in 1970. The French proved more willing suppliers and permitted the *Fuerza Aérea Argentina* to buy the Mach 2 Mirage fighter, Mirage IIIEA interceptor and Mirage IIIDA two-seat trainer. From Israel the Argentines acquired the Dagger.

There was no sympathetic country in the theatre which would permit Britain the use of airfield facilities: not even Chile, traditionally hostile to Argentina and friendly to Britain, would go that far. Any air power for the task force would have to be carrier-based. Fixed-wing naval aviation in the Royal Navy had effectively ended with the decision not to proceed with the construction of CVA-01 in 1967. The older fleet carriers lingered on in service until the last, HMS *Ark Royal*, was paid off in 1978. Two older carriers, *Bulwark* and *Hermes*, survived, but as commando or anti-submarine carriers with air groups composed entirely of helicopters.

The construction of the three ships of the *Invincible* class and the introduction into service of the Sea Harrier FRS.1 appeared to breathe some life into British naval aviation. However, although the Sea Harrier was a highly competent aircraft, capable of a number of roles, the lack of a dedicated fixed-wing carrier meant that the task force had no AEW aircraft such as the E-2 Hawkeye. This was to be a critical weakness.

Whatever the weaknesses of the Royal Navy, the decision had been taken and the gradual deployment of forces to the South Atlantic began. The first to head south were ships under the command of Rear-Admiral John Woodward which had just completed Exercise 'Springtrain 82' in the Mediterranean and were anticipating a rest period at Gibraltar. This was not to be. In the small hours of 2 April seven of Woodward's ships were detached from the exercise and ordered south, covertly, each ship making an individual passage to Ascension so as not to attract too much attention. This sudden decision presented some problems. None of the seven ships selected was prepared for a long deployment to the South Atlantic and thus had to be 'topped up' with fuel and supplies. Gibraltar Dockyard, run down over the years and scheduled for closure since July 1981, was ill-equipped for such a vast operation and so the deficiencies had to be made good from the supplies and, in one case, personnel of the ships heading for home. This posed some problems as there were five different types of ships involved. The *Leander* class frigates *Ariadne*, *Aurora*, *Euryalus* and *Dido* served the two 'County' class DLGs *Antrim* and *Glamorgan*, together with the two Type 42s *Glasgow* and *Coventry*; HMS *Active* supplied the Type 42 destroyer HMS *Sheffield* while her sister ship *Arrow* took whatever *Euryalus* and *Dido* had left after supplying the destroyers; and only in the case of the two Type 22s, *Battleaxe* and *Brilliant*, was the match an even one, with the latter taking everything that could be spared or detached.

The whereabouts of British submarines was a subject that greatly exercised the media. *Spartan* and *Oracle* had both been withdrawn from 'Springtrain', and after the former had taken all the latter's torpedoes she sailed for the South Atlantic on 1 April. On the same day her sister ship HMS *Splendid* slipped quietly out of Faslane, followed by the older HMS *Conqueror* on 4 April. HMS *Superb* had also been at Gibraltar, and much had been made of her departure in the media. In truth, she was heading the other way, back towards Faslane, but it did no harm to keep the Argentines guessing about the forces deployed against them.

But it was in Britain that the greatest attention was focused. On 1 April the order had been given to bring the aircraft carriers *Hermes* and *Invincible* to 48 hours' notice for sea. The assault ships *Fearless* and *Intrepid*, the latter already de-stored prior to disposal, were also ordered to be brought forward. This was no small task. *Hermes* was two weeks into a six-week refit while *Invincible*'s ship's company were on leave following exercises. That weekend saw almost herculean labours on behalf of the Naval Stores and Transport Organization to prepare the ships for sea. Food, fuel (three different kinds), clothing, spares, ammunition and a host of other items had to be found. The dockyard at Portsmouth, where the carriers were lying, witnessed scenes that had not been known since the Second World War. As well as dockyard labour, all available service manpower was employed—the Field Gun Crew, the RN Display Team, officers and ratings under training in nearby shore establishments and even the denizens of the RN Detention Quarters found themselves loading stores.

The carriers embarked their aircraft and helicopters on 2 April, 800 Naval Air Squadron in *Hermes* and 801 NAS in *Invincible*. As originally formed, the squadrons were made up of five aircraft each but by combing the United Kingdom for every serviceable Sea Harrier which could fly, including an experimental version from Boscombe Down, and by absorbing the aircraft from the training squadron, 899 NAS, a total fighter force of twenty aircraft was cobbled together. There was no problem in finding extra maintenance crews for the aircraft but there was a shortage of aircrew, so much so that two pilots who were still undergoing operational training were taken along, completing their training en route. The three helicopter squadrons arrived on 3 April. 820 NAS, composed of anti-submarine Sea King helicopters, went to *Invincible* while 826 NAS with anti-submarine Sea Kings and 846 NAS with Mk 6 'commando carrying' assault helicopters went to *Hermes*.

On Sunday 4 April the first ship sailed from Britain for the South Atlantic when, quietly and without fuss, the RMAS tug *Typhoon* slipped out of Portland. (She would also be one of the last to return, on 24 September 1982.) *Typhoon* was by no means the most glamorous unit of the task force, but she would play an essential role in the support services. On Monday 5 April movements began in earnest. From Devonport departed the two Type 21 frigates *Alacrity* and *Antelope*, but it was at Portsmouth that the media's attention was focused.

Invincible sailed the next day from Portsmouth, her departure watched by thousands lining the sea wall and by millions on television. Half an hour later *Hermes* followed her out of the harbour. The flight decks of both carriers were crammed with aircraft and helicopters which provided a bravura display of firepower but concealed the chaos reigning in the hangars below, where tons of stores were still being sorted and stowed. Other departures on 5 April, made with much less fuss, included those of the LSLs (Landing Ships Logistic) RFA *Sir Geraint* and RFA *Sir Galahad* from Devonport and RFA *Sir Lancelot* and RFA *Sir Percivale* from Marchwood. Together they carried 400 Royal Marines, most of the stores for 3 Commando Brigade (the main land force earmarked for the operation) and three Scout and nine Gazelle helicopters of the Commando Brigade's air squadron. Once at sea the LSLs were joined by the RFA oilers *Olmeda* and *Pearleaf* and the AEFS (Ammunition, Explosives, Food and Stores) ship *Resource*. Finally, on the 5th HMS *Broadsword* and HMS *Yarmouth*, which were at Gibraltar about to sail for the Suez Canal, had their orders changed and were sent instead to the South Atlantic. Of the eleven frigates and destroyers assigned to 'Corporate', only *Yarmouth* would come through the campaign unscathed.

The exodus from the ports continued. On 6 April the assault ship HMS *Fearless*, having disembarked her midshipmen under training, left Portsmouth carrying motor transport for 3 Commando Brigade and more of the brigade's air squadron's helicopters, together with three Sea King Mk 4 ASW helicopters of 846 NAS. *Fearless* and her sister ship *Intrepid* were immensely capable ships. They possessed a dock which could accommodate four 100-ton Landing Craft Utility (LCUs), each designed to carry two main battle tanks. The ships also carried four smaller Landing Craft Vehicle and Personnel (LCVPs) stowed in davits along the superstructure. 'Garage' space inside each ship allowed the embarkation of a squadron of main battle tanks and their supporting vehicles or a total of about eighty-five Land Rovers or 4-ton vehicles. A spacious flight deck allowed the operation of even the largest helicopters, while each ship could accommodate 300 troops in reasonable conditions, a number which could be doubled for short periods. This last feature would be tested to the limit, for while off Portland *Fearless* embarked Brigadier Julian Thompson and his staff. Conditions were cramped, with one officer having to commandeer a bathroom to serve as both cabin and office.

On 7 April RFA *Stromness*, a stores ship, left Portsmouth. Her departure was more remarkable than most. On 2 April she had been in dry dock in Portsmouth, a dead ship without stores or crew. Five days later she sailed fully equipped, carrying twelve months' rations for 7,500 men and 400 Marines.

The warships and their associated supply ships formed the first 'flight' of the task force. If push came to shove on the Falklands and it proved impossible to persuade the Argentines to withdraw by diplomatic means, the islands would have to be retaken by force, which would mean lifting a large body of men and their equipment 8,000 miles. It was decided that the main force sent south in the first instance would be 3 Commando Brigade, under Brigadier Julian Thompson, which consisted of 40, 42 and 45 RM Commandos (an RM Commando is slightly larger than a standard infantry battalion) and associated divisional units such as artillery, engineers, signals and medical. The Marines would be augmented by the 2nd and 3rd Battalions of the Parachute Regiment (thus leaving the 1st Battalion to enjoy the unenviable nickname of the 'Non-Combatant Battalion'), thereby creating a very potent force of troops accustomed to arduous training in difficult climates.

Thompson was alerted during the evening of 31 March when a staff officer rang his home and said simply, 'I think you should know that there is a problem on the Falkland Islands.' This was confirmed on 2 April when Thompson was called by Major-General Jeremy Moore, his immediate superior, and told, 'You know those people down south? They are going to be attacked.' At 0315 on 2 April, 3 Commando Brigade was formally ordered to be at 72 hours' notice to move.

However, assembling Thompson's forces was easier said than done. Most of the brigade staff were in Denmark, where they had just finished an exercise. 42 Commando were on leave, 40 were near Liverpool and 45 were in Scotland. The recalls were quickly issued (one unlucky officer of 42 Commando was hauled out of his wedding reception in New York) and a stream of men and vehicles headed south to Devonport. At this stage there was little planning for the operation other than the mechanics of getting the brigade to sea. One last-minute recruit for Thompson's staff was Major Ewan Southby-Tailyour, an officer who had served as commander of the RM detachment in the Falklands and who, as a keen amateur yachtsman, had charted the islands' coastlines. Southby-Tailyour had been asked by Thompson for the loan of his notes and the former readily agreed on condition that he came too. Normally, as commander of the RM landing craft section at Poole, Southby-Tailyour would have had no place in the operation, but in the mood prevailing the niceties of administrative protocol could be dispensed with and Southby-Tailyour found himself attached to Thompson's staff.

To transport the troops a large amount of shipping would have to be requisitioned. The legal side of this was taken care of by an Order in Council signed by the HM the Queen at Windsor on 4 April. In practical terms a telephone call or letter from the Marine Division of the Department of Trade to the relevant shipping company sufficed. The largest ship to be requisitioned in the first batch was the P&O liner *Canberra*, then returning from a cruise in the Mediterranean. On her way home she was hove-to off Gibraltar and boarded by a group of naval officers and constructors (posing as customs officers), who would assess the suitability of the ship as a troop carrier.

Canberra docked at Southampton on 7 April, and no sooner had the last passenger been ushered ashore then the shipwrights moved in. Two flight decks were constructed, one forward and one aft, and the ship was fitted with communications equipment compatible with that used by the Navy and fuel points to enable the ship to be replenished at sea by a tanker. In the process *Canberra* acquired the designation LPL(L)—Landing Platform Luxury (Large). The work was completed by 9 April, when, amid emotional scenes, she sailed from Southampton carrying 40 and 42 Royal Marine Commandos and 3 Para, together with associated units. Elsewhere the P&O 'ro-ro' ferry *Elk* was requisitioned to carry the Scorpion and Scimitar light tanks of the two reconnaissance troops of the Royal Horse Guards (which made up the Brigade's only armour component) and the ferry *Norland* was converted at Hull to carry 2 Para.

A hospital ship was another essential element of the task force. Although *Canberra* carried a full medical and surgical team, she could not be declared a hospital ship since was also carrying troops. Another vessel was needed, so the P&O liner *Uganda* was requisitioned. *Uganda* was on an educational cruise of the Mediterranean with several hundred schoolchildren embarked. The youngsters were hurriedly off-loaded at Naples (where they astonished the locals with a lusty rendition of 'Rule Britannia' as the ship was secured alongside the jetty) before the liner headed for Gibraltar, where she was converted and medical personnel were embarked, including nurses of the QARNNS (who were serving at sea for the first time). *Uganda* was painted in the white livery of a hospital ship and was declared as such to the ICRC. Three former survey ships, *Hecla*, *Herald* and *Hydra*, were converted to ambulance ferries and declared to the ICRC. Their role would be ferrying casualties from *Uganda* to a neutral port in Uruguay for air repatriation to the United Kingdom. Even their Wasp helicopters were painted white and had their red anti-collision lights replaced with blue 'ambulance' lights.

It was, thus, a gaggle of ships which streamed south in no particular order. The whole operation had been mounted extremely quickly. As one officer subsequently put it,

> In six days the brigade and all its stores were loaded for war and sailed. The confusion can only be imagined . . . we could have actually sailed two weeks later having trained, conducted rehearsals and loaded the ships in a more satisfactory manner—and still have landed on 21 May.

That point, valid though it undoubtedly is, ignores the political dimension. The sending of the task force was a visible demonstration of British resolve. The Argentines could not but be aware that a large and powerful battle group, backed up by nuclear submarines, was on its way south. A naval blockade would be instituted. Behind the warships was the landing force composed of units the Argentines knew had an awesome reputation.

Meanwhile Admiral Woodward was making his dispositions. On 7 April the destroyer HMS *Antrim* (Captain Brian Young RN) was ordered to proceed ahead of the main body of warships with the frigate HMS *Plymouth* (Captain David Pentreath RN) and the oiler RFA *Tidespring*, the AEFS ships *Fort Austin* having gone on ahead. On 10 April the 'Antrim Group' reached Ascension Island, where they embarked 'M' Company of 42 Royal Marine Commando, No 2 SBS and 'D' Squadron SAS Regiment, together with two Wessex Mk 5 helicopters of 845 NAS, before sailing on the 11th. On the same day the destroyers HMS *Glamorgan* (flag; Captain Michael Barrow RN), *Glasgow* (Captain Paul Hoddinott RN), *Sheffield* (Captain Sam Salt RN) and *Coventry* (Captain David Hart-Dyke RN) and the frigates HMS *Arrow* (Commander Paul Bootherstone RN) and HMS *Brilliant* (Captain John Coward RN) arrived at Ascension. Three days later, after a considerable amount of 'cross-decking' of stores and the embarkation of more stores and ammunition, the three Type 42s and *Arrow* sailed under the command of Captain Coward in HMS *Brilliant* for a position 1,200 miles south of Ascension, where they were to provide distant cover for the 'Antrim Group' and an advance screen for the carriers.

At Ascension things began to take shape. Admiral Woodward left in *Glamorgan* on 14 April and on the next day rendezvoused with HMS *Hermes* and hoisted his flag in her. The carrier was screened by HMS *Broadsword* (Captain John Canning RN), *Yarmouth* (Commander A. Morton RN) and *Alacrity* (Commander C. J. S. Craig RN). Behind and making up time was the other carrier, HMS *Invincible* (Captain J. J. Black RN), which had been delayed by a locked propeller shaft. Repairs, a difficult and massive job for a ship's engineering department to carry out without dockyard support, were effected at sea, and on their completion a 28-knot full-power trial was conducted. Further north were RFA *Olmeda*, HMS *Fearless* (Captain E. S. J. Larken RN) and the LSL group screened by HMS *Antelope* (Commander N. Tobin RN), with the troopships *Canberra* and *Norland* following.

HMS *Hermes* arrived at Ascension on the 16th, followed by HMS *Invincible* and the amphibious force, consisting of HMS *Fearless*, RFA *Stromness* and the five LSLs, on the 17th. A furious programme of cross-decking began, with stores and equipment which had been hurriedly embarked in Britain being transferred to its rightful place. Woodward hoped to sail with his carriers on the 18th, leaving the amphibious group to assemble fully and give the soldiers and Marines a chance of some live-firing ashore.

During the voyage south the preliminary stages of the operational plan to recover the Falklands had been achieved. On 16 April Woodward flew north to meet *Fearless* and attend a meeting with his Amphibious Warfare Commander, Commodore Michael Clapp, and the commander of 3 Commando Brigade, Brigadier Julian Thompson. The meeting was not a particularly harmonious one. The amphibious warfare specialists had hoped for the appointment of another officer, Rear-Admiral Derek Refell, who had both carrier and amphibious warfare experience (Woodward, a submariner, had little or no experience of either) to command the battle group: 'as a first time operational commander he [Woodward] did not, sadly, gain the confidence of his amphibious subordinates,' was the opinion of one officer on Thompson's staff who saw Woodward as totally preoccupied with the surface and sub-surface threat. In particular, the Marines felt that Woodward underestimated the likely effects of Argentine air operations.

On 17 April Admiral Sir John Fieldhouse, Commander-in-Chief Fleet, arrived at Ascension with his land forces deputy, Major-General Jeremy

Moore, to confer with Woodward, Thompson, Clapp and their respective staffs and integrate their separate ideas into a single operational plan. Fieldhouse opened the meeting by giving an outline of the diplomatic negotiations currently in progress. He had little hope of their success, and he reminded those present that, whatever the outcome of the negotiations in the UN, the Government had decided that the islands would be liberated. He then went on to give a precise statement of their aims. First a maritime exclusion zone (later known as the Total Exclusion Zone or TEZ) and then an air exclusion zone were to be established around the Falklands, then they were to plan 'to land on the islands with a view to re-establishing British administration.'

Planning to land had, of course, been at the centre of the commandos' thoughts since leaving Britain. In the voyage down to Ascension, Thompson's staff had prepared four options for Fieldhouse to study. The first was that South Georgia should be re-taken first and used as a springboard to the Falkland Islands. Secondly, the main body of the amphibious force could remain at Ascension to await reinforcements while carrying out a series of hit-and-run raids on the islands to keep the Argentines on their toes. This would allow a proper superiority to be built up and allow a thorough reconnaissance of the islands and full training. Thirdly, they could proceed south into the TEZ, remain at sea while the Argentines were softened up with selective raids and then launch the landings. This had the advantage of allowing more time to plan and build up reinforcements, but it meant that the main land force would be at sea longer while exposed to the risk of Argentine air attack. The fourth option was to launch the main landings direct from Ascension as soon as possible. This option was fraught with danger in that it allowed little opportunity for reconnaissance and training and no time to establish air or naval superiority. It was the least favoured option of them all.

In the event the decision was made for them. Fieldhouse ruled out the South Georgia option without saying why. The second and third options were ruled out by the time factor. When the assault would take place was governed by factors which could not be altered. By mid-June the austral winter would be in full force, effectively ruling out carrier operations and making life for troops committed on the ground extremely uncomfortable. Moreover, by mid-June the ships of the carrier battle group would, in Admiral Woodward's succinct phrase, 'be falling apart without proper maintenance', there being no friendly dockyard in the area where his ships could have their defects remedied. Therefore Woodward had to work backwards from mid-June:

We were obliged to make the critical assumption, there and then, that the land battle would have be over by the end of June, and preferably two weeks before that . . . On that basis, therefore, if the land forces were to be given reasonable time to do their stuff, we had to put them on the beaches by about 25 May. That would give them a month to establish the beach-head, break out, march to the likely main positions around Stanley and defeat the Argentinians on the ground.

A critical factor in Woodward's planning was the arrival of HMS *Intrepid*, sister ship to *Fearless*, which would be needed as an HQ ship if *Fearless* were to be sunk. The earliest that *Intrepid* would arrive would be 16 May.

The landing window extended from 16 May to 25 May. Inside that time we had to have most of the land forces ashore, and to be in good shape by mid-May we were to going to have to get the special forces ashore very soon.

One way or another the plan was emerging, and so Admiral Fieldhouse was able to return to London with a proposal for the Chief of the Defence Staff, Admiral of the Fleet Sir Terence Lewin, to present to the Cabinet. In essence the plan provided for a period of blockade and other operations designed to eliminate the Argentine surface and sub-surface threat, to be followed by an assault on the Falklands at a time before 24 May.

Woodward's inflexible timetable meant that the carrier battle group would have to sail from Ascension on the 18th by midday at the latest. His decision to sail without the amphibious ships was interpreted by some, particular those in 3 Commando Brigade and COMAW's staff, as being akin to saying 'I'm off to fight the war—you follow on as best you can.' However, Woodward was desperately concerned about the threat posed by Argentine submarines and ships:

The possibility of taking on the Argentine fleet and air force with a large convoy of amphibians and merchant ships requiring simultaneous protection—all wallowing along at twelve knots—had been a considerable cause of worry to me. Now we had the option to fight without one hand behind our backs, which was a good idea really.

In other words, the operational area had to be secured before the Amphibious Group was in the theatre. There seems to have been very little understanding of each other's problems among the various British commanders. The amphibious planners believed Woodward to be uncaring about their difficulties. However, they in turn showed no awareness of the wider aspects of the war they were about to engage in, other than the mechanics of getting men ashore on the beach. The problem lay in the British command structure. Overall command was vested in Admiral

Fieldhouse at his headquarters at Northwood outside London. The three theatre commanders, Woodward, Thompson and Clapp, were all of similar seniority. What was needed was a theatre commander in the South Atlantic to draw the various aspects of the operation together and allocate priorities.

After Woodward's departure, planning for the landings went on in earnest. With options 1 to 3 ruled out, the planners were forced to apply themselves to the idea of a direct assault on the Falklands from Ascension. A number of bizarre ideas were given an airing, including an Entebbe-style landing on Port Stanley airfield by the SAS followed by the swift elimination of the Argentine command. There were a number of other such options, all equally impractical.

But the discussion, however fruitless, had at least cleared the air, and planning for a more conventional end to the Argentine occupation could proceed. Thompson and Clapp had four requirements that had to be fulfilled before a landing could take place. The first of these was good intelligence concerning where the enemy was and in what strength. In the event this requirement would be 'left on the table'. No adequate intelligence about the Argentine order of battle was acquired, and when aerial reconnaissance photographs did arrive they came too late and were of such poor quality that they were of little or no use. Consequently, for the first time since the Dardanelles in 1915, an amphibious landing would be mounted with no aerial reconnaissance photographs of the enemy's dispositions. Much, therefore, would depend on the men of the SAS and SBS parties and their use of the 'mark one eyeball'.

Secondly, most of the amphibious group ships had left the United Kingdom in such a hurry that their loads had been badly stowed: they were not 'combat loaded' (shades of the Dardanelles). Stores would have to be offloaded and re-stowed so that what was required first was loaded last. Another factor was that many of the LSLs were hopelessly overloaded; some arrived at Ascension up to eighteen inches over their loading marks. The prospect of unloading a huge quantity of supplies to shore before redistributing them was unpalatable to say the least. Fortunately the arrival of the empty RFA *Sir Bedivere* at Ascension from Belize provided the opportunity to undertake the re-stowing.

Thirdly, there was a need for all the troops in the brigade to practise their skills. Each commando, battalion and battery (with the exception of 2 Para) had one day of helicopter training and a day and night's landing-craft training. They were then sent ashore for one day to fire weapons, the trip to the range including a five-mile forced march there and back. However, the value of Ascension as a training facility was very limited. One commando officer subsequently commented: 'Although being a tropical, precipitous, volcanic dustbin, it would have been difficult to find an area more dissimilar to the place to which we were actually going.'

2 Para and the Rapier SAM battery from 12 Air Defence Regiment RA arrived late and were only able to manage landing craft drill before going south. But there was more to master in the training field than how to get out of helicopter or a landing craft. How were men to disembark from *Canberra* and *Norland*, which were not configured for managing large numbers of heavily laden men? Would it be possible to carry a Scorpion or Scimitar in the bow of an LCU and use the craft as an improvised Landing Craft (Gun) which had been found so essential in suppressing enemy fire during landings in the Second World War? These and hundreds of other questions needed to be addressed.

Allied to the question of individual unit training, there was the need for a full, brigade-size rehearsal of the landings carried out at night. This was deemed a 'must', based on the all the bitter experience gained during the Second World War. But any rehearsal was impossible for a number of factors: there were no beaches at Ascension, no training areas, insufficient helicopters and landing craft to finish the re-stowing and conduct such a rehearsal, and no time.

Fourthly, but by no means least, there was the planning of a landing site. A short list of nineteen sites was drawn up, and time and time again the indefatigable Southby-Tailyour would be summoned to see Thompson and Clapp and asked for his comments on such and such a bay or such and such a beach. His experience, based on personal observation, was invaluable. Eventually five areas were selected for detailed examination by Special Forces while at the same time the idea of a landing on East Falkland was dropped. Any landing near Port Stanley would probably encounter well dug-in Argentine defensive positions, minefields and beaches covered by gunfire. The task force lacked the armoured amphibious vehicles and close-support craft required for such an operation and could not afford the casualties it would inevitably entail. Thus any site had to be out of range of gunfire from Stanley and preferably be far enough away so that any Argentine reaction would arrive after the beach-head had been consolidated. Conversely, the beach-head could not be so far away that any approach to Stanley would involve a long march with all the logistical problems that that entailed.

The site had to have gradients suitable for LCUs and Mexeflotes to beach and the terrain behind the beach had to afford good exits even though the brigade had comparatively few wheeled or tracked vehicles. The site had to be easily defended and have sufficient room to accommodate all the ammunition, supplies, fuel and other stores which the brigade would need to fight the land battle. It would also have to give good cover from the high wind which was a feature of the climate and give protection against attack by missile, from the air and by submarine.

At this stage it became clear that it was going to be impossible to achieve total air superiority over the landing site. This went against the experience gained in Norway, Crete and other centres for amphibious operations in the Second World War. Thompson addressed a letter to Northwood on the subject but was told that the operation was to go ahead and that he was 'not to worry'. The landings were to proceed whatever the outcome: in Marine terms, it was 'shit or bust'.

Eventually the nineteen sites were whittled down to three, Cow Bay/ Volunteer Bay, San Carlos and Berkeley Sound. Cow Bay/Volunteer Bay was only an option if the Argentines looked as if they wanted to surrender and a face-saving operation had to be mounted. The beaches were exposed and were uncomfortably near to Stanley. Berkeley Sound suffered from the same problems. Though not ideal, San Carlos had the best balance between military and naval factors. It was a good anchorage, with steep shores giving good protection from missile attack. Aircraft flying over the hills or round the headland would have little time to acquire their target (conversely, this meant that the AA defence ships would have to very quick in acquiring incoming aircraft). Other advantages were that the area was unguarded by the Argentines and that there were few civilians in the vicinity. The disadvantages, however, were formidable. The site was as far from Stanley as it was possible to be. The entrance to either San Carlos or Falkland Sound could be easily mined by the Argentines, and since the carriers would be operating well to the east the Sea Harriers would be very limited in their time over San Carlos in direct defence of the AOA.

Though San Carlos was only third in order of preference for a landing site, subsequent events gave it an additional advantage. On 5 May HMS *Sheffield* was struck by an air-launched Exocet missile and was subsequently abandoned. The missile threat was suddenly very real, and the steep shores of San Carlos were seen as a real asset. Furthermore, on the same day a signal arrived from Woodward to the effect that the carrier group could remain at sea only for another month before the maintenance problem became critical. In other words, something had to be done. Other factors were the transit of Falkland Sound by HMS *Alacrity* (Commander C. J. S. Craig RN), which reported no mines and no Argentinian troops around San Carlos, a fact which was confirmed by SAS reconnaissance later.

On 29 April Thompson's superior, Major-General Jeremy Moore, visited Ascension and was briefed on the choices facing the amphibious group planners. Moore returned to London with the Amphibious Group's staff's recommendations, which were presented to the Chiefs of Staff and the Cabinet for approval. The choice of San Carlos was approved by the Cabinet and signalled to Thompson on 12 May, though final approval for the operation was withheld for the moment.

While the planning was in progress the Amphibious Group had put to sea.. The five slow LSLs had sailed, escorted by HMS *Antelope*, on 1 May. *Canberra* and the main body sailed on 7 May. At this stage the amphibious planners had assumed that they would have the use of *Hermes* to land one commando on the high ground behind the beaches while *Invincible* provided CAP for the task force. They were to be rudely disabused. Woodward pointed out that he had hardly enough aircraft to defend himself let alone the AOA, and to prevent *Hermes* from launching her Sea Harriers until after the initial assault had gone in would be a risky enterprise. The decision was taken in Northwood that both carriers would be required for providing CAP. The assault on the Falklands would be a traditional one, with troops being put ashore from landing craft on a string of beaches, co-located and mutually supporting.

On 13 May Thompson briefed all unit commanders at a conference aboard *Fearless*. The die was cast. The planning of the landings and the co-operation between Thompson's and Clapp's staff had been a model of inter-service co-operation. To hark back to an earlier era of amphibious warfare, there was a 'good and perfect understanding'.

CHAPTER TWELVE

Fighting Back

I counted them all out and I counted them all back.—BBC
Correspondent Brian Hanrahan, after the first Sea Harrier attack on
Port Stanley

BY mid April the nuclear-powered fleet submarines which had hurried south from Gibraltar were off the Falklands and the first stage of the blockade could be put into action. At midnight on 12/13 April the Argentine Government was informed that henceforth its warships, and merchant ships flying the Argentine flag, navigated within 200 miles of the Falklands at their own risk. This was the Maritime Exclusion Zone (MEZ) which Admiral Fieldhouse had announced at Ascension. The Argentines responded, knowing that in the absence of any Royal Navy ships the blockade would have to be enforced by SSNs. They withdrew their surface ships that were in the area, except for light craft and a few vessels of the Argentine state shipping line, in order to publicize blockade-running operations. These last ships were tracked by the submarines but allowed to pass on the grounds that the political and diplomatic fall-out if a British submarine sank an Argentine merchant ship without warning would be unimaginable.

The next stage of the plan was the departure of the carrier battle group from Ascension. The departure was precipitated by the sighting of what was identified as a periscope 'feather' by RFA *Olmeda*. Fearing that an Argentine submarine might be in the area, Woodward had the CBG (consisting of *Hermes*, *Glamorgan*, *Broadsword*, *Alacrity* and *Yarmouth*) at sea two hours earlier than planned; *Invincible* was scheduled to leave later and catch up. The 'target' was quickly tracked by frigates and helicopters with 'dipping' sonar and it took fast evasive action for over an hour, causing most to believe that if it was a submarine it was a Soviet nuclear boat snooping at naval activity off Ascension. It was only when an RAF Nimrod reported a school of whales that the contact was formally classified as such. It would not be last time during the conflict that these creatures would cause an anti-submarine alert.

After sailing, Woodward made some refinements to his plan. The course adopted by the CBG after leaving Ascension might lead a shadower to guess that the ships were heading for Buenos Aires; moreover, if the CBG were detected on radar the ships would fire 'chaff' to make it appear as if the amphibious ships and troopships were in company. The purpose of these moves was, firstly, to persuade the Argentine high command to keep some of their Navy and Air Force assets in the north and, secondly, to make them think that the landings were taking place earlier than planned. It was hoped that the Argentine command would then commit some of its ships and aircraft to an engagement which Woodward hoped he would win and which would guarantee air and sea superiority around the Falklands.

Meanwhile the *Antrim* Group had been ploughing steadily south. On 14 April it rendezvoused with the ice-patrol ship HMS *Endurance*, which had been hiding amid the icebergs ever since the conflict began. It was a moving meeting and the men of the warships turned out to cheer the little red-and-white painted vessel. Not least among the reasons why *Endurance* was pleased to meet *Antrim* and her consorts was that the ice patrol ship was running out of fuel.

The reason *Antrim* and *Plymouth* had been sent on ahead was to recover South Georgia—hence Fieldhouse had been against the South Georgia option at Ascension. The British Government considered that South Georgia lay outside the negotiations then in progress at the UN and had decided on the island's recapture. The operation would serve as a useful demonstration of British resolve. Accordingly, Captain Young was ordered to retake the island in Operation 'Paraquet'.

The operation (which lies outside the scope of this narrative) was successful, though only just. The plan went awry when the SAS reconnaissance teams had to be hurriedly evacuated on 22 April on account of the severe weather. To complicate matters for Captain Young, he was informed of the presence of the Argentine submarine *Santa Fe* in the area and, he believed, he was detected by Argentine air reconnaissance—an Argentine Boeing 707 circled *Endurance* for some time on 24 April. Captain Young was in a quandary, for the main body of his troops, 'M' Company of 42 Commando, were 200 miles away on the RFA *Tidespring* and he could not be sure how long it would be before the Argentines came looking for his small force with a vengeance. However, the successful disabling of the *Santa Fe* by helicopters from *Antrim*, *Endurance*, *Plymouth* and *Brilliant* (the last detached by Admiral Woodward in support) on 25 April caused Young to order the assault to go ahead with what troops were available—Marines of *Antrim*'s detachment and an assortment of SBS, SAS and Royal Artillery NGS teams. Though improvised, the attack worked. That evening, after a vigorous bombardment with 4.5-inch shell-

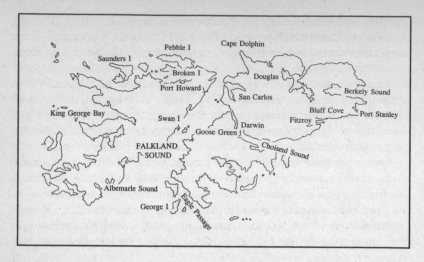

The Falkland Islands

fire from *Antrim* and *Plymouth*, the Argentines at Grytviken surrendered; those at Leith did so the next day. Captain Young sent the by now famous signal to London: 'Be pleased to inform Her Majesty that the White Ensign flies alongside the Union Jack at Grytviken.' The British had anticipated a stiff fight for South Georgia; now, as Admiral Woodward put it, it had become a matter of looking after the prisoners.

Meanwhile Woodward's carrier group was heading south. On 21 April the group was sighted by a Boeing 707 of the Argentine Air Force. It was escorted away by Sea Harriers of 800 NAS but the shadower was to become a persistent nuisance over the next few days. In order to counter the possibility that the Boeing might be directing a surface or submarine task group towards the British ships, Woodward ordered the Sea Harriers to conduct clearance searches, which were backed up by Nimrods and Victors flying from Ascension. Eventually Woodward secured approval from Northwood to change the rules of engagement so that he could have the shadower shot down. On 23 April the latter duly appeared again, but some sixth sense made the British check his course, which corresponded to a civil air route between Durban in South Africa and Rio de Janeiro. Woodward ordered 'weapons tight' just two minutes before the aircraft came into firing range and ordered a visual inspection by Sea Harrier. It was just as well, for the aircraft was a DC-10 of the Brazilian national carrier Varig. Had the aircraft been shot down, the diplomatic consequences would have destroyed whatever minimal pro-British feeling there was in Latin America. As it was, the British Government was quick to tender a formal apology for any alarm caused to the passengers, and the Brazilian press took a reasonable line in reporting the issue.

On 28 April the British Government declared that the MEZ would be replaced by a Total Exclusion Zone (TEZ) at midnight on 30 April. Henceforth any ships, civil or naval, or aircraft supporting the illegal occupation of the Falklands would be liable to attack if found within 200 miles of the islands. The timing of the declaration was intended to allow the carrier group to be in position by midnight on 30 April, but for a while it looked as if bad weather would force the date to be put back. However, the skies cleared on 28 April and, after a last replenishment 500 miles to the east of Port Stanley, the ships turned to the west and entered the TEZ on 30 April to begin a series of attritional operations against the Argentine fleet and Air Force which would precede the arrival of the Amphibious Group.

As the carriers headed into the TEZ a Vulcan bomber took off from Ascension supported by eleven Victor tankers. The Vulcan's mission was to bomb the runway at Port Stanley and thereby prevent its use by fast jets such as the Étendard and the A-4. When the Vulcan was well to the northeast of Port Stanley it came down to 300 feet to avoid detection by TPS-43 radar before climbing to the bombing height of 10,000 feet about fifty miles from the target. The load of twenty-one 1,000-pound bombs was released at 0746 in a five-second string which resulted in a line of hits about 1,000 yards long at an oblique angle of about 35 degrees to the runway. Though the mission was undoubtedly a considerable feat of airmanship, its value against the facilities at Port Stanley was minimal. Only one bomb struck the runway, which the Argentines continued to use for C-130 Hercules and light attack aircraft such as the Pucará throughout the conflict.

In any case, the Argentines had never really seriously considered basing fast attack aircraft at Port Stanley: although the runway was theoretically long enough for an Étendard or A-4 to use, it was safe for these aircraft only when dry and when there was no cross-wind—conditions virtually impossible to achieve on the Falkland Islands. Quite apart from the limitations of the runway, there was the risk, which was obvious from 1 May onwards, that any aircraft based at 'BAM Malvinas' would be a sitting target for naval gunfire. From the British perspective, the operation was a horrifically expensive way of dropping 21,000 pounds of bombs. To take the Vulcan and the eleven Victors to the Falklands and back required an inordinate amount of fuel; the Sea Harriers on the two carriers could have done the same job for far less. Cynics have said that the operation represented an attempt by the RAF to 'have a piece' of an operation that was Navy- and Marines-dominated: they may have a point.

Whatever the merits of the operation, the shooting war had now started with a vengeance. The bombing of the airfield was followed at 1015 by a PR sortie by two Sea Harriers of 801 NAS over the airfield. Shortly before 1100 on 1 May all twelve Harriers of 800 NAS took off from HMS *Hermes* for strikes on Port Stanley and the Pucará base at Goose Green. At Stanley the first four Harriers delivered nine air-burst 1,000-pound bombs and three delayed-action 1,000-pounders; moments later the second wave attacked with three 1,000-pound parachute retarded bombs and twelve cluster-bomb canisters. The Harriers were met by a large amount of AA fire, including Tigercat and Roland missiles, from the defenders, now thoroughly on the alert, but the high speed and terrain-hugging approach of the aircraft proved highly effective. Only one was damaged. At Goose Green the attack was completely successful, with one Pucará destroyed while about to take off.

Meanwhile 801 NAS were providing CAP over Stanley using two aircraft with another two ready on deck. There now began a hectic series of air-to-air engagements which effectively decided who would possess air superiority over the Falklands. At 1100, just as the *Hermes* strike was returning, the fighter controller on board *Invincible* directed the CAP on to two contacts inbound from the mainland which turned out to be Mirage IIIs. The Argentine pilots broke away on afterburners after firing missiles. Later that morning three Turbo Mentors were attacked in cloud over the north coast of East Falkland. The Argentines got away, although one had a 30mm cannon-shell hole in his cockpit as a souvenir of the encounter. Shortly afterwards the CAP was vectored on to a pair of Mirages approaching at 35,000 feet. However, the Argentine aircraft were warned by the VYCA-2 controller of the CAP's presence and they turned away after firing three missiles, hopelessly out of range.

At this stage the Argentine command was building up a fairly accurate picture of the location of the carrier battle group from observing the movements of the Harriers, and the decision to launch a major strike was taken. Accordingly, twenty-eight A-4s, six Canberras and a dozen Mirages took off (although only 28 of the 46 aircraft launched actually reached the Falklands). From mid-afternoon onwards this force began to appear on the radar screens of various ships in the task force. Two Mirages were detected by the destroyer *Glamorgan*, in company with *Arrow* and *Alacrity*, which were heading in to bombard Port Stanley. *Glamorgan* was controlling her own CAP, which was vectored on to the targets. The Mirages were sighted over San Carlos Water and engaged: one was shot down by a Sidewinder missile fired by Flight Lieutenant P. C. Barton RAF (the first air-to-air victim for a Royal Navy fighter since the Korean War) and the other was damaged by Lieutenant S. Thomas and was later shot down by 'friendly' AA fire while diverting to Port Stanley. Simultaneously a pair of Daggers from VI Air Brigade were acquired by *Hermes'* CAP. In the engagement which followed all four aircraft fired missiles and one of the Daggers, flown by *Primer Teniente* José Ardiles (a cousin of the international football player) was shot down by Flight Lieutenant A. R. Penfold RAF. Meanwhile a third force of three Daggers had flown down Falkland Sound and then headed towards Port Stanley. They appeared to be making for the CBG, but after CAP was scrambled they turned back and headed for *Glamorgan* and her consorts, now less than ten miles away.

The three ships had just completed the first leg of a bombardment of Port Stanley airfield, firing air-burst 4.5-inch shell over defensive positions and the buildings. By the time the Daggers were spotted they were too close for the ships' Seacat missile systems to be activated and all they could do was use small arms and manoeuvre. Fortunately all the bombs missed, although *Glamorgan* and *Arrow* were strafed with 20mm cannon fire, the latter ship's Seacat aimer being slightly wounded.

Of the twenty eight A-4s which were launched, only one flight achieved anything; the remainder all failed to contact either British ships or the CAP. The A-4 flight bombed and strafed one of their own ships, the *Formosa*, belonging to the state shipping company. Fortunately the bombs did not go off: they were released at too low a level and thus did not have time to arm. No cognizance was taken in the *Fuerza Aérea Argentina* command of this important operational detail.

These engagements had taken just thirteen minutes and in that time the battle for air superiority over the Falklands had been won. Three Argentine aircraft had been shot down without loss to the British, while the Sea Harrier had proved itself in combat against aircraft of theoretically far superior performance. This was a major set-back for the *Fuerza Aérea Argentina* and it demonstrated that, given the conditions in which it had to fight over the Falklands, it would always be at a disadvantage against the Sea Harriers.

There was more action to come on 1 May. HMS *Brilliant* and *Yarmouth* were hunting the Argentine submarine *San Luis* when they detected three Canberra bombers circling the ships at low altitude. One of these was subsequently shot down by the 801 NAS CAP.

Despite the air attack by the three Daggers, *Glamorgan* and the two Type 21 frigates continued with their bombardment of Port Stanley. Shore bombardment was to become an almost nightly feature of the Falklands campaign: in all, there were 63 fire support operations, in which 7,500 rounds of 4.5-inch shell were expended. Commenting on the campaign in retrospect, one Royal Artillery officer noted that

> Night after night, NGS [naval gunfire support] kept the enemy awake, made him stand-to in the freezing cold, destroyed his defences and equipment and killed or injured his comrades too foolish or slow to take cover.

Glamorgan's bombardment also served another purpose, and that was to mask the infiltration into the Falklands of the SAS and SBS parties. This was done early in the morning of 2 May by Sea King helicopters of 846 NAS, the pilots using PNG night-vision goggles.

The Vulcan and Sea Harrier attacks, together with the appearance of *Glamorgan* and the two Type 21s off the islands, had persuaded the Argentine command that invasion was imminent. Argentine naval operations in support of their forces on the Falklands were the responsibility of *Contralmirante* J. J. Lombardo. When details of the events of 1 May were known in Buenos Aires, Lombardo set his countermeasures in motion. In the event of a British landing he had divided the *Armada Republica Argentina* into four task groups, each of which had a stand-off strike capability and an oiler attached for endurance and mobility. It was intended that the four groups would launch a series of attacks on the British from different directions, rather than engage in a classic 'pincer' attack.

Task Groups 79.1 and 79.2 remained in company. This was the main strike force of the *ARA* and was built around the aircraft carrier *25 de Mayo* and her two British-designed Type 42 destroyers. These ships had been loitering off Desado, 400 miles north-west of Port Stanley, but on 1 May altered course to the east to open the battle on 2 May with a dawn Skyhawk strike, possibly co-ordinated with a Super Étendard Exocet strike, which would be followed by attacks using the surface-to-surface MM.38 Exocets carried by the destroyers *Segui* and *Comodoro Py*. The object of this operation was to eliminate the two British carriers. To the north of the carrier group was TG.79.4, consisting of three 24-knot *A.69* class corvettes each armed with a quadruple MM.38 Exocet and a 100mm gun.

The *ARA*'s real firepower lay with TG.317.8, which consisted of the 6-inch gun cruiser *General Belgrano* and two MM.38 Exocet-armed destroyers. *Belgrano* was positioned on the edge of the TEZ and could just have easily altered course towards the carrier battle group or headed for South Georgia. However, she and her consorts were not alone, for trailing astern of them and reporting their every move was the British submarine *Conqueror* (Commander C. L. Wreford-Brown RN).

The Argentine carrier group had evaded British submarine patrols but its position was readily apparent to Admiral Woodward's staff from the interception of Argentine signals and from observation of the tracks of the shadowing aircraft launched by *25 de Mayo*. Woodward felt that his rear was safe with *Conqueror* shadowing the *Belgrano* and felt able to concentrate on dealing with the Argentine air strike. The British fully expected that the *Fuerza Aérea Argentina* would put up a maximum effort to join its naval colleagues, but they were mistaken. For a variety of reasons, including poor staff work and inter-service rivalry, the *ARA* had not informed its colleagues of the attack and as a result the Southern Air Force Command had planned for only nineteen sorties against 56 flown on 1 May.

At 0325 on 2 May a Sea Harrier was scrambled to investigate a contact to the north of the carrier group. It turned out to be a Grumman S-2E Tracker from *25 de Mayo*. No interception was made, but Woodward ordered a surface search by three 801 NAS Sea Harriers. The aircraft flew out at low level to a range of 150 miles, when they 'popped up' to carry out a search using their Blue Fox radars. At 0425 Flight Lieutenant Ian Mortimer, searching the north-western sector, popped up to make his search and immediately detected a group of four or five ships. More importantly, he found himself illuminated by a number of radars, including Type 909 Sea Dart tracking radar. Since the nearest friendly Type 909 was 150 miles astern of him, the radar in question had to be on one of the two *ARA* Type 42s, *Hercules* or *Santissima Trinidad*. In fact it was the former. Mortimer had been detected by the Argentine ships, which had vectored the Tracker out of his patch. *Hercules* had been allotted the target but Mortimer broke away and dived to low level to break the radar's lock.

Woodward meanwhile had been reinforced by the five ships which had been detached for bombardment and the submarine hunt and was able to make his dispositions to meet the expected air strike well before dawn. Up-threat were the three Type 42s, *Coventry*, *Sheffield* and *Glasgow*, to act as a picket line. Behind them were *Glamorgan*, *Yarmouth*, *Alacrity* and *Arrow*, forming an anti-aircraft and anti-submarine screen to protect the two carriers and the RFAs *Olmeda* and *Resource*. Lastly, tucked in close to the two carriers were their 'goalkeepers', the two Type 22 frigates with their potent Seawolf close-range AA missile systems.

The first CAP was flown off at daylight but the attack never came. The *25 de Mayo* was readied to launch her eight Skyhawks but, unusually for those southern latitudes, the wind had dropped and there was not enough wind-over-deck to fly off a fully fuelled and armed Skyhawk. The Argentines had three choices: to launch the aircraft with sufficient fuel but no bombs, to close to a distance of 70 miles before launching, or to wait for wind. The first was pointless and the second suicidal, so all day the Argentine pilots waited for wind (the atmosphere in the aircrew briefing rooms on board the *25 de Mayo* must have been strained, to say the least) while the Sea Harrier pilots investigated transmissions from the Argentine Trackers and Neptunes and wondered where the Skyhawks were. By mid-afternoon, when it became clear that it would not be possible to launch a strike, Lombardo ordered the three separate groups to withdraw, to await a change in the weather which would permit a second attempt to be made on 3 May.

However, the position of the *Belgrano* group to the south was causing Woodward some concern. Although *Conqueror* was still in contact, her ability to stay that way might be jeopardized if the *Belgrano* chose to make a sudden turn to the north-east for an attack on the carrier group. It is important to stress at this stage that *Belgrano*, though an old ship and one barely capable of 25 knots, was viewed very seriously as a threat. Her armament consisted of fifteen 6-inch guns which fired shells weighing 130 pounds to a range of 26,000 yards, far in excess of the range of the 4.5-inch guns fitted to the British ships (whose maximum range was some 20,000 yards) while her 4-inch armour belt made her impervious to a hit from an Exocet, the only stand-off strike weapon on the Royal Navy's surface inventory. Only an air strike (which was unlikely for fear of heavy losses) or a submarine torpedo could do the job.

If the *Belgrano* did make a sudden turn to the north-east, then she would pass over the Burdwood Bank, an area where the South American and African tectonic plates meet. To the south of the Burdwood Bank the water depth is in excess of 10,000 feet but over the bank it shoals to as little as 150 feet while the contours of the bank are very uneven and marked with underwater pinnacles and cliffs. It would be very easy for *Belgrano* to shake off the *Conqueror* if she passed over the bank. If contact were lost, then the submarine would have to head round the bank and seek to re-acquire the cruiser, which all the time would be heading straight for the carrier group.

Woodward's concern was very real. Not long before the Falklands crisis blew up, in his flagship HMS *Glamorgan* in an exercise in the Persian Gulf, he had penetrated the defences of an American carrier task group and 'sunk' the USS *Coral Sea*. The prospect that Captain Hector Bonzo in the *Belgrano* might be planning a repeat performance was constantly on his mind. Accordingly Woodward decided that one of the Argentine pincers should be removed. As neither of the other two British submarines, *Spartan* and *Splendid*, were in contact with the other two *ARA* task groups, it had to be the *Belgrano*.

It was not, however, a simple matter of ordering *Conqueror* to dispatch the cruiser. For one thing, she was outside the TEZ and therefore immune from attack according to the rules of engagement (ROE) then in force. Secondly, command of the submarines involved in 'Corporate' had not been delegated to Woodward but was being exercised from the headquarters at Northwood. What Woodward had to do was to persuade London to change the ROE and order *Conqueror* to sink the cruiser.

Nevertheless, rather than follow the correct procedure of requesting a change in the ROE, Woodward simply ordered *Conqueror* to attack at 0745Z. The signal was read in London with some consternation and taken off the satellite so that it never actually reached the submarine. At the same time Woodward's staff were briefing their colleagues at Northwood on the reason for the request. The request went up the chain to the Prime Minister, who was meeting with other members of the War Cabinet. Mrs Thatcher, on the advice of Admiral Lord Lewin, the Chief of the Defence Staff, acceded to Woodward's request and at 1330 (mid-morning off the Falklands) the appropriate signal was transmitted to HMS *Conqueror*.

Conqueror, however, was having problems receiving the signal owing to a faulty radio mast. The correct procedure would have been for her to break away from *Belgrano* and, at a safe distance, hung around at slow speed with masts raised while trying to re-access the satellite. But the danger of losing *Belgrano* was very real, and Wreford-Brown stayed with the cruiser all afternoon while his technicians tried to fix the mast. Eventually, at 1730, *Conqueror* was able to pop up, access the satellite and receive the clear text of the War Cabinet's decision.

Wreford-Brown now set up his attack with considerable deliberation. *Conqueror* closed to a position 1,400 yards off the *Belgrano*'s port bow and fired three Mk VIII** torpedoes. The Mk VIII** was a totally unsophisticated weapon and had been the mainstay of British submarines' armament throughout and since the Second World War. Its virtue lay in its tremendous warhead of 750 pounds of torpex—far larger than anything carried by more modern guided weapons.

The first torpedo struck the *Belgrano* right forward between the bow and the forward 6-inch gun turret and the second exploded under the after superstructure; the third hit the destroyer *Bouchard* but did not explode. *Belgrano* had been dawdling along at 10 knots and was not at any state of readiness, and fifteen minutes later she rolled over on to her port side and sank by the bows with the loss of 321 of her crew.

The sinking of this old cruiser had consequences out of all proportion to the actual deed. The main Argentine task group headed by the *25 de Mayo* (which, perversely, had been unable to operate her aircraft on 3 May because of too much wind) was withdrawn to shallow waters near the Argentine mainland where the big SSNs could not operate. There they remained for the rest of the war, no threat to either the CBG or the Amphibious Group.

In a sense, by the evening of 2 May Woodward had (though he would have barely known it) established some of the requirements for the successful landings on the Falklands. The Argentine Navy had been sent back to its bases, while in air-to-air combat the Sea Harriers of 800 and 801 Naval Air Squadrons, though not having established air superiority by any means, had at least shown that the *Fuerza Aérea Argentina* could not attack the CBG with impunity.

Between 2 May and the eventual landings on 21 May Woodward established what one author has referred to as a 'bad-weather blockade' of the islands. By day the CBG would retire well east of the Falklands, protected by a screen of radar pickets, before closing the islands at night for more NGS operations and/or the infiltration of special forces parties. The aim of these operations was to wear the Argentines down. As always, the unalterable maintenance deadlines of the CBG dictated what could be achieved. As Woodward put it,

> For a start, *Hermes* herself had locked her port shaft while seeing to a lube oil problem. *Invincible* reported trouble with the leading edges of 820 Squadron's helicopter rotor blades. *Glamorgan* reported a 992 radar problem which we certainly did not need. Then *Glasgow* checked in with a 965 radar problem with short pulse and target identification difficulties. This is just terrific, I thought. We're on half power in the flagship, the helicopters are falling apart, *Glamorgan* can't see straight and *Glasgow* can't shoot straight.

Bad weather or defects regardless, the campaign of attrition against the Argentine forces had to go on. It was not without loss on both sides.

On 3 May Lynx helicopters from *Coventry* and *Glasgow*, armed with the new Sea Skua air-to-surface missile, were vectored on to two surface targets which had fired on a Sea King Mk 4 of 846 NAS shortly after 0130. An unidentified ship, probably an *A.69* class corvette, was sunk by Sea Skua missiles from *Coventry*'s Lynx while *Glasgow*'s helicopter damaged the patrol vessel *Alferez Sobral*. On 4 May a Vulcan bomber attacked Port Stanley airfield. The bombs 'missed the runway completely' (Woodward's comment on this) but greatly discomfited the airfield's defenders.

On 5 May the Argentine Navy struck back and in the now well-publicized air attack hit the destroyer HMS *Sheffield* with an AM.38 Exocet missile.

Although the missile's warhead did not explode, the fires resulting from the explosion of the missile's fuel proved impossible to control and *Sheffield* had to be abandoned; she subsequently foundered on 10 May while under tow. On 6 May two Sea Harriers of 801 NAS collided in fog and both pilots were killed.

On 9 May the end came for an Argentine trawler, the *Narwhal*, which had been hanging around the task force for some days in a suspicious manner. Woodward believed that she was acting as an intelligence-gathering vessel and ordered that she be stopped. After being strafed by two Sea Harriers she was boarded by the SBS and found to contain one worried Argentine lieutenant-commander and an array of very sophisticated communications equipment. On the same day HMS *Coventry* proved the efficiency of the long-range Sea Dart SAM system by shooting down two A-4 Skyhawks (although these 'kills' were not confirmed until after the war) and an Argentine Puma helicopter.

By this stage Woodward needed to know the extent, if any, of Argentine minelaying in Falkland Sound which divided East and West Falkland. A British SSN had already observed minelaying to the east of Port Stanley, and Woodward feared that the Argentines might have extended their activities in this respect. Since there no minesweepers attached to the CBG, the only way to check for mines was to send a ship in and steam up and down the Sound. It had to be a ship which Woodward to could replace quickly—which ruled out sending any of the Type 22 or Type 42 ships—and in the end the choice fell on the Type 21 frigate HMS *Alacrity*.

Commander C. L. Craig knew what was expected of him and realized that it meant the potential loss of his ship, but the voyage up Falkland Sound from south to north was anything but a furtive search for mines. *Alacrity* proceeded up the sound making a good deal of noise and firing starshell over the settlement at Fox Bay to keep the defenders on their toes before obtaining a solid radar contact, which was engaged by the frigate's 4.5-inch Mk VIII gun. The ship, the Argentine freighter *Isla los Estados*, was carrying 325,000 litres of avgas and exploded with a very satisfactory column of flame. *Alacrity* proceeded up the Sound to the northern end, where she cast about, constantly widening the known safe area. Then she withdrew to where HMS *Arrow* was waiting for her. At this stage both ships were attacked by the Argentine submarine *San Luis*, under the command of *Capitan de Fregata* F. M. Azueta. Azueta's fire control computer was 'down' and he only fired one wire-guided SST-4 torpedo, using ranges and bearings obtained from his sonar (he did not bother to use his periscope). The torpedo was successfully decoyed by a noise-maker towed by *Arrow*.

Woodward kept up the pressure on the Argentine defenders by day and night. By day a Type 22 frigate and a Type 42 destroyer would operate off the islands. With their combination of Sea Dart SAMs for dealing with high-level, long-range air attacks and Seawolf for point defence, it was adjudged that the 'Type 64' combination (as it became known) would be able to defend itself against air attack while making life uncomfortable for those ashore. The combination of *Coventry* and *Broadsword* had already worked; now, on 12 May, *Brilliant* and *Glasgow* were to be stationed off the islands. On this occasion both ships were lucky to escape, for the Argentine command was determined to stop the bombardments which were causing such havoc ashore. In the first attack by four A-4 Skyhawks, *Brilliant*'s Seawolf missiles shot down three of the attackers after both *Glasgow*'s weapons systems, Sea Dart and 4.5-inch gun, had malfunctioned. Morale was high when a second group of A-4s was detected. These four flew in very fast and kept close formation so that *Brilliant*'s Seawolf fire control computer could not distinguish one from the other and consequently shut down. The ships had no defence other than manoeuvring (to place themselves beam-on to their assailants) and extemporized small arms on the upper deck. These scored hits on at least one aircraft but could not stop the attack. One bomb bounced over *Brilliant* but the other struck *Glasgow* and went right through the ship, exiting on the other side without exploding. The raid succeeded in bringing about a temporary halt to daytime bombardments since Woodward now had only one undamaged Type 42, HMS *Coventry*, left in his command and reinforcements, HMS *Exeter* and *Cardiff*, were some days away from joining the CBG. Night bombardments by the Type 21s and the two 'County' class DLGs would, however, continue.

On 14 May the SAS raided an Argentine airfield on Pebble Island and destroyed six Pucarás, four Turbo Mentors and a Short Skyvan in what was practically a textbook special forces operation. On 16 May Sea Harriers sank two Argentine ships in Falkland Sound, the *Rio Carcarena* at Port King on the east side of the Sound and the *Bahía Buen Sucesso* in Fox Bay.

May 17 was Argentine Navy Day and in the CBG there were confident expectations that the occasion would be marked by another Exocet attack of the kind which had been so successful against *Sheffield*. These expectations were fulfilled. The YC2YA radar operators had been building up an analysis of where the British carriers were by looking at British helicopter and Harrier movements. This information was passed to the mainland for an Exocet operation to be organized, and on the 17th two Étendards were dispatched to where the *ARA* believed the carriers would be. However, the

British were one step ahead, for Woodward's staff had considered this possibility and the carriers were never where the Argentines thought they would be. Consequently, when the two Étendards 'popped up' for a radar sweep they found an empty horizon. Fearing interception from the CAP, the Étendards turned for home without selecting a further target.

During the evening of 17 May *Invincible*, screened by *Broadsword*, was detached from the CBG and headed west at great speed. When west of the Falklands the carrier increased speed until she surpassed anything achieved on trials. Then a heavily laden Sea King Mk 4 of 846 NAS took off from her flight deck. The helicopter was found near Punta Arenas in Chile two days later, the crew having given themselves up to the Chilean authorities. Their excuse was that they had been on a reconnaissance of Tierra del Fuego and had become lost in bad weather. This fooled nobody, and speculation about the real nature of the operation was rife. John Witherow, the defence correspondent of *The Times*, who was on board *Invincible* at the time, believed that the helicopter was landing special forces and, if so, given the helicopter's launch point well to the west of the Falklands, it meant that they were being put ashore in Argentina, probably to observe aircraft movements and give advance warning of raids. By dawn on 18 May *Invincible* was back inside the TEZ. Later that day the CBG rendezvoused with the ships of the Amphibious Group. Thirty-two ships steaming in formation was a stirring sight, and one not seen since the end of the Second World War

The three-week blockade phase had succeeded in achieving two major objectives. First, following the loss of the *Belgrano*, the surface ships of the ARA remained in coastal waters, blockaded by SSNs, and were effectively eliminated as a serious threat: Woodward's fears of an Argentine surface group getting in amongst the slow amphibious ships could be laid aside. Secondly, the blockade had been made effective. The Falklands were cut off from the Argentine mainland and the Argentine occupiers were therefore denied reinforcement other than by what could be flown in on the nightly C-130 runs. There were other achievements too. Nightly NGS bombardments, in which over 1,500 rounds of 4.5-inch shell had been expended, had done a good deal of material damage and a great deal more to morale. Air strikes from the Harriers and the Vulcans had delivered over fifty-one tons of ordnance on to the islands, although in the case of the Vulcan strikes their effectiveness was marginal. Special forces were ashore on the islands (and possibly elsewhere) and the Argentine defenders had not succeeded in locating any of them (although they were aware of their presence). The special forces were already sending back useful information about potential landing sites and the nature and strength of the Argentine defences. The general level of awareness and alertness of the defenders was not high, and this gave cause for optimism.

On the other hand, the British had been unable to lure the *Fuerza Aérea Argentina* out to wear down its numbers: despite the loss of ten of the 51 jets which had reached the islands, it could still put up thirty-eight A-4s, two dozen Daggers and six Canberras for strikes on the Falklands as well as the seven naval A-4s disembarked from the *25 de Mayo*. This was a sizeable force which, if properly briefed and co-ordinated, could inflict significant damage. Then there was the ability of the Exocet-armed Étendards to sink ships from a great distance and the lack of any AEW capability in the CBG. Although the Argentines were believed to have only five Exocet missiles, the prospect of a successful attack on a carrier was to influence the deployment of the CBG throughout the campaign: henceforth it would always lurk well to the east of the islands, to force the Étendards to operate at their maximum range without refuelling.

CHAPTER THIRTEEN

Ashore on the Falklands

At that moment, exactly 45 minutes late and after 8,000 miles and seven weeks of planning, we landed to repossess that which had been so cruelly and obscenely taken from us.—Major Ewan Southby-Tailyour

O N 13 May the unit commanders assembled on board *Fearless* for their briefing. Each had received the brigade operational orders (all 47 pages of them) twenty-four hours earlier and each had received a general briefing to familiarize himself with Thompson's intentions. Despite the preparation there was absolute silence in the room when, after preliminary briefings on the Argentine defenders and the disposition of friendly forces, Thompson announced his intention to 'conduct a silent night landing by landing craft so that by first light the brigade would have secured the high ground overlooking Port San Carlos, San Carlos Settlement and Ajax Bay.' The landing plan was simple—if anything that required landing 3,000 men and their equipment at night on a potentially hostile shore could be called simple.

The operation was to take place in three phases. In phase 1, 40 and 45 Commando were to go ashore at night by landing craft on 'Blue Beach One' and 'Red Beach One' respectively, to secure San Carlos settlement and Ajax Bay (42 Commando were to remain afloat as brigade reserve and were required to be at 30 minutes' notice to land): 40 Commando were to secure San Carlos and then establish a defensive position on the reverse slopes of the mountains behind it; and 45 Commando were to secure the Ajax Bay complex and then establish a defensive position on the reverse slopes of the high ground covering the bay. The landing craft would then return and land 2 and 3 Para: 2 Para would land on 'Blue Beach Two' and then clear forward to Sussex Mountain while 3 Para, on 'Green Beach One', were to secure Port San Carlos settlement and then establish themselves on the reverse slopes of Settlement Rocks and Windy Gap, to secure Sussex Mountain and Port San Carlos. Phase 3, to begin at first light, was to use helicopters to move artillery and the important Rapier anti-aircraft missiles ashore. The briefing was long and complex and covered every subject from naval gunfire support to the burial of the dead. Finally Thompson impressed on all present the necessity of achieving the units' objectives regardless of the opposition.

The plan had to be modified after intelligence was received from special forces on the Falklands to the effect that the Argentines were established in company strength on Fanning Head, overlooking the entrance to San Carlos Water. Both Clapp and Thompson were extremely worried about this new development. First, should the Argentines position heavy infantry support weapons such as 105mm recoilless rifles on Fanning Head, they could sink a landing craft; after all, the Royal Marines garrison on South Georgia had nearly disposed of the *A.69* corvette *Granville* with such a weapon, so there was no reason why the Argentines should be any less inventive. It was also reported that the Argentine mobile reserve, which had last been observed at Fitzroy, had now moved to Darwin, a good deal closer to San Carlos.

Clapp wanted the 'Fanning Head Mob', as they became known, taken out or, at the very least, kept occupied during the landings. The solution lay in landing a twenty-five man SBS section armed with twelve 7.62 GPMGs near Fanning Head on the night of 20 April to attack the Argentine positions from the east. A further refinement was to include a fluent Spanish-speaking officer in the team to invite the Argentines to surrender in the face of superior forces. If this worked, it would be a good indicator of the morale and commitment of the Argentine troops.

Thompson was more concerned about the location of the Argentine mobile reserve. If the Argentine command so much as had a suspicion of the landing, they could quickly move troops on to Sussex Mountain, which commanded views over three of the four beaches. Thompson was so concerned about this threat that he revised the landing plan. The landing of 2 Para was brought forward from phase 2 to phase 1: now 2 Para would land slightly ahead of, but alongside, 40 Commando, and 45 Commando would land in phase 2. Otherwise the plan remained unchanged. Having made the changes, Thompson had to visit the five battalion commanders and brief them: Lieutenant-Colonel H. Jones of 2 Para in *Norland*; Lieutenant-Colonel A. F. Whitehead of 45 Commando in *Stromness*; and Lieutenant-Colonels Malcolm Hunt (40 Commando), Nick Vaux (42 Commando) and Hew Pike (3 Para), all on board *Canberra*.

While the planning went on, training on the troopships was remorseless. Decks echoed to the pounding of feet and there was continual small-arms firing over the stern. Captain I. R. Gardiner of 45 Commando recalled that

On *Canberra* one could run for miles unimpeded; she was also very comfortable, and even in bad weather training was not seriously interrupted. On the LSLs, however, space was severely limited and, in any kind of weather at all, the commonest form of physical exercise was the famous guardrail dash!

Training covered all subjects, including first aid. The Medical Officer of 2 Para, Captain S. Hughes RAMC, had some experience of the Israeli Army's practice of each man carrying a bag of intravenous fluid. Many of his medical orderlies were trained to set up an IV line, but, in case a 'Tom' (as a paratrooper was affectionately known) was stranded out in the open, each man was taught the technique of rectal infusion. Practice in this highly effective survival technique was conducted with some hilarity

It was not all work, however. The crossing of the Equator was marked with all the usual ceremony. King Neptune and his court came aboard, and those who had not 'crossed the line' were subjected to the traditional indignities; the CO of 29 Commando Regiment RA was charged with failing to have arranged Easter leave for the regiment!

The day of the landings had been set for 21 May. Now there remained a considerable amount of 'cross-decking' (the transfer of men and equipment between ships) to ensure that the supporting units (artillery, armour, air defence, etc) were in the same ship as their parent unit. This exercise required careful planning, to ensure that the helicopters required were not 'double-booked'.

Just as the staff had finished the cross-decking plan, everything had to change on receipt of orders from Northwood. The planners in London were concerned about possible casualties from air attack and they considered that having three battalions in *Canberra* was too risky. Thompson's and Clapp's staffs had already looked at this and found it impractical to undertake the cross-decking of 1,000 men without a secure anchorage. However, Northwood had decreed otherwise and the Amphibious Group staff now had to work out which units to move, and how, without wrecking the plan. In the end it was decided to send 40 Commando to *Fearless* and 3 Para to *Intrepid*. The prevailing sea state in the South Atlantic appeared to rule out transfer by landing craft and a helicopter transfer would take forever and be highly expensive on fuel—and, in any case, the helicopters were already booked for the cross-decking of the supporting arms. The only alternative was for *Fearless* and *Intrepid* to steam either side of *Canberra* and move the men one by one using a light jackstay transfer. In the meantime the executive officers in the two assault ships were left to ponder where to accommodate and how to feed an additional 500 men each.

Fortunately the weather on 19 May proved moderate and Captain Jeremy Larken of *Fearless* suggested using the landing craft after all. The weather held all day, so the LCUs could shift the two battalions, 1,000 men going to *Fearless* and 750 to *Intrepid*. The troops had to leave *Canberra* via ports in her side and make a leap into the LCU which at one moment might be level with them and the next ten feet below them. The operation went ahead without incident except for one Marine who fell between *Canberra* and the LCU and who was rescued wet but unharmed.

On 20 May the Amphibious Group left the CBG and turned west at 1415, heading for San Carlos. The weather which had been so favourable for the cross-decking on 19 May now turned against them. Clapp had planned for the fleet to steam boldly towards Stanley in the hope that they would be seen, either by an Argentine aircraft or by a submarine, and reported as heading for Stanley. The ploy required clear skies; instead there was rain and heavy cloud cover. Then, on the night of 20/21 May, when all the commanders prayed for thick weather to mask their approach to San Carlos, the skies cleared and there was a brilliant moon.

The commandos and paratroopers were embarked in *Canberra, Fearless, Intrepid, Norland* and *Stromness* and enduring varying degrees of discomfort. Things were no better for their supporting units, the gunners of 29 Commando Regiment RA, the sappers of 59 Independent Commando Squadron, the pilots and ground crew of the Commando Brigade Air Squadron and 656 Squadron AAC, 16 Field Ambulance RAMC, and the gunners of 'T' Battery, 12 Air Defence Regiment RA, who were embarked, also in varying degrees of discomfort, in the *Europic Ferry* and the LSLs *Sir Galahad, Sir Geraint, Sir Lancelot, Sir Tristram* and *Sir Percivale*. The force headed west at 12 knots, screened by *Antrim, Broadsword, Brilliant, Plymouth, Yarmouth, Argonaut, Ardent* and the RFA *Fort Austin*.

At 1600 'Darken Ship' was ordered and *Antrim* and *Ardent* went ahead. At 1900 *Antrim* flew off Marines of 3 SBS, who were going to deal with the 'Fanning Head Mob'. By 2300 the Marines and an NGS team had been landed and their passage had been totally undetected by the Argentines. Meanwhile the main body of the Amphibious Force was forming into three groups, *Intrepid* and *Fearless* in the lead, followed by *Canberra, Norland* and *Stromness*, with *Europic Ferry* and the LSLs bringing up the rear. The first two waves were spaced to arrive 45 minutes apart but the LSLs were not due to arrive until four hours after the second wave. In the meantime HMS *Ardent* had made the passage into Falkland Sound and had taken up position for a diversionary bombardment of Darwin in support of an SAS raid. The SAS troopers were flown in by PNG Sea Kings of 846 NAS.

Shortly after 2215 *Antrim* entered Falkland Sound, closely followed by *Yarmouth*, which was carrying out an anti-submarine sweep supported by two Sea Kings of 826 NAS. The two vessels established a patrol line between the North West Islands and Poke Point on West Falkland to cover the first two waves of assault ships. At 2245 *Fearless* and *Intrepid* entered Falkland Sound, passing close under Jersey Point opposite Fanning Head. Only when they were well inside the sound did the two LPDs turn north and close East Falkland to anchor west of Chancho Point. The second wave followed shortly afterwards. *Fort Austin* anchored inshore between Chancho Point and Cat Island while *Canberra*, *Norland* and *Stromness* anchored in a line off the entrance to San Carlos inlet. HMS *Plymouth*, the oldest ship in the force, took up a position from where her twin 4.5-inch guns could cover Port San Carlos to the east and the broader and longer San Carlos Water running south-south-east. The whole operation was accomplished without reaction from the Argentine look-outs on Fanning Head and Mount Rosalie on West Falkland. They had failed to see or hear the passage of eleven ships (one of which was one of the world's largest liners), had failed to hear the clatter of helicopters flying around and had not noticed the unmistakable noise of ships anchoring less than two miles from their positions.

The calm was rudely shattered at 0052 when HMS *Antrim* fired the first ranging shots against the 'Fanning Head Mob' and then began to fire carefully and systematically on the instructions of the NGS team ashore. In just over thirty minutes, 268 4.5-inch shells, each weighing 56 pounds, were poured on to the Argentine position. When the bombardment lifted the SBS team stormed the position, where they found twelve dead and nine wounded and dazed survivors. Thompson's fears about the 'Fanning Head Mob' had been proved right. Among the equipment found was a 105mm recoilless rifle, several 81mm mortars and modern night viewing equipment. If the 'Mob' had been half awake, they could have inflicted severe damage on the assault ships coming to anchor south of Fanning Head.

While *Antrim* was firing on Fanning Head, *Intrepid*'s LCUs were moving over to *Norland* to embark 2 Para. Delays were inevitable, for the paratroopers had not had as much time at Ascension as the other troops to practise landing-craft skills. Meanwhile the Marines of 40 Commando were boarding their LCUs in the red-lit tank deck of HMS *Fearless*. In the event 2 Para were nearly an hour late boarding, and the delay was eating into the time allotted for them to reach their objective. At one stage Southby-Tailyour, who was now in charge of landing-craft operations, considered going ahead with 40 Commando and leaving the paratroopers to manage as best they could, but this was vetoed on the grounds that it would take too long to communicate the necessary changes in orders and would inevitably cause more confusion than anything else. In the end it was decided to press on with three out of four of *Intrepid*'s LCUs, leaving 'Tango 4' to follow on behind, and continue with all four of *Fearless*'s LCUs carrying 40 Commando.

Thus, sixty-five minutes late, the seven LCUs crossed the start line and headed at full speed for the beach. On the run-in to the beach Southby-Tailyour, who was in the leading LCU from *Intrepid*, was concerned at the absence of the recognition signals from the SBS to indicate that the beach was safe. However, he went ahead and, after warning Lieutenant-Colonel H. Jones that 'any men on the beach taking no action will be SBS', put the LCUs ashore and broke radio silence with the traditional code-word 'putty', to indicate a successful landing (although for one reason or another this signal was not received in *Fearless* and it was to be another 45 minutes before Thompson knew that his troops were ashore). To the left of 2 Para, 40 Commando were going ashore as planned.

No opposition was encountered on either beach, and while the paratroopers fanned out and made their way up Sussex Mountain, 40 Commando 'liberated' San Carlos settlement and, after making their presence known to the residents, ran up the Union Jack. From Sussex Mountain the paratroopers were able to look down and cover the approach of the nearest Argentine infantry units at Darwin (who were at that time on the receiving end of a diversionary attack by 'D' Squadron of the SAS). Much further away, at Stanley, the Argentine main force was under the impression that the landing was to take place there, their beliefs strengthened by a massive starshell and high-explosive display from HMS *Glamorgan*.

Now came phase 2 of the landings. The LCUs from *Intrepid* went to *Stromness* to collect 45 Commando (picking up the third company from *Intrepid* on the way) while craft from *Fearless* collected 3 Para from *Intrepid*. Once embarkation was complete, the second flight set off, the Marines for Ajax Bay and the paratroopers for Port San Carlos. This landing, too, went ahead without a hitch, although the first of *Fearless*'s LCUs grounded on a ledge short of the shore. Ordering the other three LCUs to hold off and find alternative sites to land, Southby-Tailyour called in the four shallow-draught LCVPs and 'cross-decked' the paratroopers. The makeshift operation went very smoothly and soon the paras were fanning out eastwards.

As 3 Para moved into Port San Carlos they made the only contact with the Argentine forces that day. Some forty Argentine soldiers had arrived in Port San Carlos the previous day. On being engaged by the paratroopers, they fled and were pursued out to the limit of 3 Para's exploitation. Major H. M. Osborne subsequently described 3 Para's landing:

At 0930 on 21 May I threaded my way down to the bowels of HMS *Intrepid*, just one of the many helmeted and heavily laden figures as the whole battalion clambered through an endless maze of bulkhead doors. As we boarded the landing craft, mortar rounds and grenades were thrust into our hands, and as the landing craft emerged we realized that it was broad daylight. We had been briefed for a night attack: war was living up to its expectations.

Soldiers stood in the landing craft with all their kit on and many of them refused to kneel or rest, having spent ages getting their loads properly adjusted. Ammunition loads varied from 50 pounds for a rifleman up to 80–100 pounds for signallers and 84mm mortar men.

Thirty minutes after loading we approached Port San Carlos Bay. B Coy, who were already ashore, appeared like ants swarming across the flat ground at the head of the beach. There was no firing; the landing was unopposed.

'A' Coy pushed through 'B' Coy and into Port San Carlos settlement. 'B' Coy held the beach-head, and my own company, 'C' Coy, climbed to the 600-foot ring contour of Settlement Rocks, our home for the next five days.

It was at this stage that the Commando Brigade suffered its only casualties on 21 May. As soon as there was enough light, the Sea Kings of 846 NAS began the movement of equipment ashore. One such lift, part of a Rapier missile battery, was escorted by two Gazelle gunships of 3 Commando Brigade Air Squadron. The Gazelles noticed movement up the San Carlos river and went to investigate. These troops were the Argentines whom 3 Para had just evicted. Unfortunately the paratroopers possessed no means of contacting the Gazelles and the helicopters were shot down, the Argentines firing on the aircrew in the water. Only one of the four NCOs survived. The Argentines escaped and were able to get a message to Stanley about the landings. Major-General Menendez, the Argentine 'governor' of the Falklands, did not know in what strength the British had landed, but his staff had already informed *Fuerza Aérea Sud* on the mainland that help was needed and by 0830 a strike of Daggers was on its way.

Once the troops were ashore, the ships of the Amphibious Group prepared to move into San Carlos Water. *Canberra* moved just after 0530, but, too big to enter San Carlos, she anchored three miles south-east of Fanning Head. She was followed by *Norland* and *Stromness*, which anchored at 0630. By now the third wave, the LSLs, were rounding Chancho Point, keeping to the timetable although the landings were running some-what behind schedule. In fact *Sir Percivale* (Captain A. F. Pitt RFA) overtook 45 Commando in their LCUs and after anchoring off Ajax Bay turned so that the 40mm Bofors on the forecastle could lay down supporting fire on the beach if required—the largest Landing Ship Gun in the history

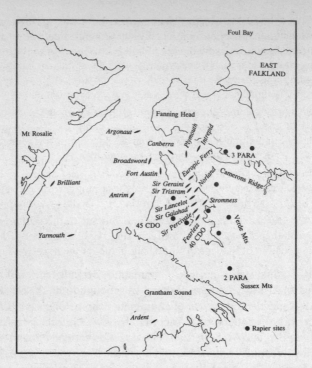

San Carlos Water, 21 May 1982

of amphibious warfare! *Fearless*, with 3 Commando Brigade's staff still on board, and *Intrepid* weighed anchor at 0715 and, followed by *Europic Ferry*, entered San Carlos shortly afterwards. *Fearless* took up a position between Ajax Bay and San Carlos settlement while *Intrepid* anchored at the entrance to Port San Carlos at the other end of the line of LSLs.

As it became lighter, those ashore and on the ships could see more of their surroundings. San Carlos Water extends for five miles from Doctor's Head to the head of the inlet. The width of the inlet is about a mile, with deep water close inshore as far up as the northern shore of Ajax Bay. The only flattish areas of land and beaches free of kelp are around the settlement and refrigeration plant at Ajax Bay, both at the foot of steep slopes which close into the water's edge at the northern end. The ridges which enclose the arm of the sea, Campito to the west and the Verde Mountains to the east, rise to over 650 feet, and the 500-foot contour lines on the maps are never more than three miles apart. There were only two avenues of approach for aircraft carrying out a low-level strike. One was the 1½-mile opening between Fanning Head and Chancho Point, but this would give an attacker only two miles—fifteen seconds if travelling at 550mph—to complete his turn, select a target and line up for the attack. The other approach was from the southeast, along the north side of Sussex Mountain. Pilots would be able to see ships in Ajax Bay from a distance of only six miles.

Within San Carlos, work now began on unloading the thousands of tons of equipment and stores. Ashore, the main supply dump was established at the disused refrigeration plant at Ajax Bay, the Brigade Maintenance Area (BMA). The LCUs and LCVPs, released from their troop-carrying duties, were joined by Mexeflotes, large motorized rafts manned by men of Port Regiment, Royal Corps of Transport. The Mexeflote crews endured an uncomfortable existence, without any form of shelter from the elements or air attack, but shifted huge quantities of stores direct from the ships to the beach. Staff Sergeant Boultby describes life on a Mexeflote:

We had only been in San Carlos an hour before we received our first air raid. It was then that we realized how many men can climb a rope ladder at once. We then endured a further three air raids during the building of our raft. At one stage we were alongside RFA *Stromness* when we were attacked by Argentine aircraft. As they flew between us and RFA *Fort Grange*, four 1,000-pound bombs were dropped. We completed loading and started on our way, and were just passing HMS *Broadsword* when the last wave came in using rockets to attack *Broadsword*. So there we were, surrounded by a raft load of Rapier missiles, grenades and other ammunition. Under these circumstances one is tempted to place one's head between one's knees and kiss one's rear goodbye.

Seven Sea King Mk 4 helicopters from 846 NAS were available for load-lifting, supported by a control unit embarked in *Fearless*. In the nine hours of daylight on 21 May they picked up 288 loads, totalling over 220 tons, and 520 men and delivered these to twenty-one different sites. Lighter loads were carried by the Wessex Mk 5 helicopters of 845 NAS, which could operate from the midships flight decks of the LSLs as well as the large stern platform. One Wessex Mk 5 and one Sea King Mk 4 were allocated for casevac duties. The Wessex was for overland work and had a medical team embarked, while the Sea King brought casualties from ships to *Canberra*, where surgical teams were embarked.

The most important elements to be air-lifted off were the 105mm light guns of 29 Commando Regiment RA and the complete Rapier SAM battery. Great things were expected from Rapier, but the officers of 12 Air Defence Regiment were unsure how the delicate electronics would react after six weeks in a salt-laden atmosphere on the heaving, vibrating tank deck of an LSL. Their fears were justified: Rapier would require some time before all the 'gremlins' in the system were ironed out. Sorting out the problems was not helped by the fact that the REME technicians had been landed at Ascension on the grounds that they would not be immediately required!

In mid-morning Thompson decided that 42 Commando, held in *Canberra* as brigade reserve, were to go ashore, after it became clear that, if *Canberra* were hit, casualties among the Commando would be very heavy. Furthermore, after 3 Para had reported contact with the enemy, Thompson felt that their sector of the beach-head could do with reinforcement.

At 0723 HMS *Ardent* began a bombardment of Goose Green, where the SAS had observed Pucará aircraft preparing to take off. The little frigate opened fire at a range of 22,000 yards and throughout the morning delivered over 150 rounds of 4.5-inch shell in support of the SAS. Although she destroyed one Pucará about to take off, she did not close the field and four pairs of these unpleasant aircraft took off, although one was later shot down by the SAS with a Stinger heat-seeking missile. At the same time two Harrier GR.3s of No 1 Squadron RAF struck at an Argentine helicopter base on Mount Kent, destroying two Pumas and a Chinook and thus reducing the Argentines' capacity to move troops to San Carlos by air.

However, the Argentine reaction was not slow in coming. The first air attack of the day came when a Macchi MB.339 armed trainer streaked across San Carlos Water and strafed HMS *Argonaut* with rocket- and cannon-fire before making off. This was the first attack in a five-day battle for air supremacy over the beach-head so that large-scale operations could be conducted outside the air defence umbrella. There had not been such a battle since the air war over Okinawa in the spring of 1945. The cost to the British was three ships sunk and 77 casualties, nearly all of them officers and men of the Royal Navy. On the other hand, many Argentine aircraft were destroyed, and, although the British never established total air superiority, the Argentine air forces were so whittled down that they failed to pose a major threat to the campaign.

CAP was operating from the two aircraft carriers from 0635. For the rest of the day there was always one pair of Sea Harriers either on, or within five minutes' flying time of, the CAP stations. Controlled by HMS *Antrim*, the Sea Harriers flew in racetrack patterns to the west of Grantham Sound and to the north of Pebble Island so as to be able to intercept any attacks coming from the south-west or north-west. However, the limitations of the aircraft's Blue Fox radar system over land meant that the pilots were very much dependent on their own eyesight for detection and too often could react only after the Argentines had delivered an attack. The lack of airborne early warning placed the Royal Navy, and the land forces they were protecting, at a critical disadvantage.

Shortly after 0900 *Ardent* was attacked by two Pucarás, which were driven off with 4.5-inch gunfire and Seacat missiles. The first major air attack came shortly after 0930 when three Daggers of VI Brigade came round Mount Rosalie and through the gap between Fanning Head and Chancho Point. One was shot down by a Seacat from HMS *Plymouth* (this venerable and much derided SAM enjoying a new lease of life and proving remarkably effective), the second strafed HMS *Broadsword* while the third attacked *Antrim* and left a 1,000-pound bomb lodged, unexploded, deep inside the ship.

Ten minutes later a second flight of Daggers arrived and concentrated on the damaged *Antrim*, which was making her way into San Carlos to gain the protection of HMS *Broadsword*'s Seawolf system. The destroyer was strafed once again, but one of the Daggers was shot down by *Broadsword*'s Seawolf. At 1045 two Pucarás made another attempt on HMS *Ardent* and were driven off. In a second attack, one was shot down by CAP from 800 NAS but the other clipped the frigate's Type 992 radar aerial as it came in from dead ahead. The radar continued to function, displaying a perfectly adequate, though tilted, picture of events.

At 1330 six A-4B Skyhawks from V Air Brigade swept in from the open sea and attacked the first ship they saw, the frigate *Argonaut* in her position under Fanning Head. To those watching it seemed as if the frigate disappeared under a welter of bomb splashes and cannon-fire. Ironically, those bombs that missed exploded while the two that hit the ship penetrated inside but failed to go off. *Argonaut* was left without power and drifting on to the cliffs at Fanning Head. She would have undoubtedly gone aground had it not been for the cool-headedness of the OOW, Sub-Lieutenant P. T. Morgan RN, who ran forward and released the anchor manually. Eventually *Argonaut* was towed to safety by a motley collection of landing craft.

The attack by the A-4B Skyhawks had masked the approach of a flight of ARA A-4Q Skyhawks of the 3rd Fighter Attack Squadron, which caught *Ardent* out in the exposed waters of Falkland Sound. Of nine 500-pound retarded bombs dropped, three hit the ship, two exploding in the hangar; the third, which failed to explode, landed in the after auxiliary machinery room. While her damage control parties fought to master the fires, *Ardent* began to retire up the Sound to gain the protection of the ships at San Carlos. While she was undergoing her ordeal the CAP from 801 NAS wiped out an entire section of Daggers.

After the third had been shot down the CAP saw three white-painted Skyhawks heading down Falkland Sound toward a burning frigate. They were too far out of range to engage, but the 800 Squadron CAP just coming over the islands were warned. These were a second flight of A-4Qs led by *Capitan de Corbeta* A. J. Philippi. All three aircraft went straight for *Ardent* from astern, opposed only by one 20mm Oerlikon and a number of GPMGs, and all three scored hits with 500-pound bombs. Two of the three Skyhawks were later shot down by the 800 NAS CAP. However, it was the end of the war for the gallant *Ardent*. After receiving advice from his heads of department, Commander West decided that his ship could not be saved and ordered his crew to transfer to the *Yarmouth*. At 1455 West was the last man to leave the ship, which was abandoned at 1505. Twenty-four of her crew had been killed and 30 injured. The last air attack of the day was at 1415 by five A-4Bs which did no damage, the aircraft making good their escape.

No account of the first day's air raids can come near to describing the atmosphere at San Carlos that morning. The attacks happened extremely quickly, and missile-aimers and gunners had only a matter of seconds to fire as the aircraft flashed past at close range. The excellent camouflage of the Argentine aircraft, particularly the A-4s, made them very difficult targets to hit. Once the raids were in progress, the amount of noise was incredible, with the roar of the aircraft being drowned by the sound of hundreds of rifle-calibre machine guns opening up together with the heavier, rhythmic thumping of 40mm Bofors and the occasional *whoosh* of a SAM. Then, almost as quickly as they had begun, the raids were over. Lieutenant-Colonel Nick Vaux of 42 Commando found himself sheltering under a table in *Canberra*'s meridian room with a journalist from *The Sunday Times* and discussing the relative merits of being fired on by the IRA in Belfast and enduring the attentions of the Argentine air forces. On balance, Vaux preferred the IRA.

The Royal Navy had not seen air attacks of such intensity since the Pacific campaign in May 1945. Only two of the seven escorts, *Plymouth* and *Yarmouth*, had escaped damage, and of the rest only *Broadsword* was capable of steaming and fighting. *Antrim* and *Argonaut* had been spared only because the bombs aimed at them were released so close that they had not had time to arm their fuzes. Yet, if the Royal Navy had been shocked by the violence of the day's events, the picture from the Argentine side was less than rosy. Two aircraft had been lost to SAMs and eight had been claimed by the CAP. Though the skill and courage of the Sea Harrier pilots is beyond praise, some credit is due to HMS *Brilliant*, which took over fighter control after *Antrim* was damaged. By chance, *Brilliant*'s first lieutenant, Lieutenant-Commander Hulme RN, was an experienced fighter direction officer and was able to use a radar system which had not been designed for fighter control to set up three successful interceptions on inbound raids and a fourth which avenged the attack on *Ardent*.

For all their courage the Argentine pilots had not interfered substantially with the landings. The *Armada Republica Argentina's* effort was modest, but all six of its sorties got through at the cost of half the force. Although landing craft, Mexeflote and helicopter movements were halted during the raids, the steady flow of men and material from ship to shore continued throughout the day. The pilots had attacked the first ships they saw, usually the exposed frigates, and almost ignored the assault and stores ships, although it must be said that the pilots probably ignored *Canberra* because they believed that, with her white livery, she was a hospital ship. Even though they were incorrect, all credit is due to them for their restraint in this respect.

Aircraft losses were also serious. Apart from the ten aircraft shot down, many more were damaged by 7.62mm machine-gun fire, which was not enough to shoot down a plane but sufficient to wreck its sensitive electronics or navigation equipment and keep it grounded. Moreover, the Argentines had no bottomless pit of aircraft and spares. Total losses since the beginning of the war had so far reduced the inventory to fourteen out of eighteen A-4Cs, thirty-two out of thirty-six A-4Bs and twenty-six out of thirty-three Daggers. The *Armada Republica Argentina* had lost three of its A-4Qs but still had all four airworthy Super Étendards, although these aircraft were reserved for Exocet strikes only. With a UN arms embargo in place, there was no hope of replacing these losses nor of obtaining spare parts. Neither the modest striking rate nor the heavy losses of 21 May could be sustained.

The air attacks on 21 May convinced Clapp that *Canberra* could not be left in San Carlos overnight. She would have to leave. *Antrim* would go with her, since without her Seaslug SAM system she was more of liability in San Carlos and would be useful as an anti-submarine/anti-surface escort in the TRALA (Tug Repair and Logistic Area) being established outside the TEZ.

Canberra's move created major turmoil for the planners since the liner was to be used as a floating hospital (though not declared as such to the Red Cross) where casualties would be treated before being sent on to the hospital ship *Uganda* operating in her Red Cross 'box'. Now the field dressing station and the paratroop clearing team would have hurriedly to disembark, complete with all their kit, and set up in highly unsuitable surroundings in the refrigeration plant in the BMA right next to brigade HQ. It was not the best position for a dressing station, given that the surgeons would need to use bright lights at night, but there was no alternative. Consideration was given to marking the building with prominent red crosses, but this idea was rejected since the BMA's ammunition stores were located too close to the building and this would contravene the Geneva Convention. In any case, as it was pointed out with some apprehension, Argentina was not actually a signatory to the Geneva Convention and was therefore under no obligation to respect its provisions.

To the surprise of all, 22 May passed peacefully, with only the appearance of two Skyhawks at 1610 to disturb the unloading operation. The Skyhawks roared over Fanning Head and disappeared without a shot being fired at them, possibly because two of the RAF's Harrier GR.3s were in the area and the plot was 'confused'. Unloading the storeships proceeded frantically, everything that could fly or float being pressed into service. The move of the Rapier battery was completed and by noon three of the four sections were operational. A strong CAP was maintained all day—indeed, more sorties were flown on 22 May than on any other day during the operation—but the Argentine aircraft were grounded by bad weather. However, the 800 NAS CAP did score one significant success when it drove the Coast Guard vessel *Rio Iguazu*, carrying two 105mm howitzers to Goose Green, ashore.

Early in the morning of the 23rd *Stromness*, *Norland* and *Europic Ferry* entered San Carlos, having topped up with stores from *Elk* and *Resource* at the edge of the TEZ throughout the 22nd. Most importantly, *Stromness* was carrying steel planking to form a forward operating base for Sea Harriers and the GR.3s. Once the site was established, the Wessex and Chinook helicopters embarked in *Atlantic Conveyor* could be flown ashore.

At 1240 *Antelope*'s Lynx saw four A-4 Skyhawks coming up Falkland Sound. The helicopter tried to warn the ships in the AOA but by then the strike had split up and was attacking from the north and east. Two of the four were turned away by the barrage of 4.5-inch, 40mm and 20mm gunfire, not to mention the vast quantity of 7.62 ammunition and Seacat, Rapier and Blowpipe missiles. It was a barrage to daunt even the boldest pilot. The other two aircraft came in and went for the *Antelope*. The first dropped a 1,000-pound bomb which lodged, unexploded, near the petty officers' mess before clipping the HF/DF aerial. The aircraft was then blown out of the sky by a simultaneous hit from a Rapier and a Seawolf. The second Skyhawk also went for the *Antelope* and succeeded in putting another 1,000-pound bomb, which also failed to explode, in an auxiliary machinery space forward. The frigate was damaged but could still fight and move.

There were three more raids that day, one by three A-4Qs and two by Daggers. All the aircraft returned safely without scoring any hits, except for

Above: Live firing at Ascension on an improvised range. In this photograph an 81mm mortar team goes through its paces. (IWM FKD.385)
Below: A Sea King helicopter in the hover over *Canberra*'s midships flight deck during the voyage south. (MoD)

Left: A Samson armoured recovery vehicle in one of HMS *Fearless*'s LCUs at Ascension. This particular LCU, *F4*, was bombed and sunk by Argentine aircraft on 8 June 1982. (IWM FKD.391)

Above: Lieutenant-Commander Nigel ('Sharkey') Ward, commanding officer of 801 Naval Air Squadron in HMS *Invincible*. 801 NAS was one of two Sea Harrier units deployed to the Falklands. (MoD)

Below: LCUs from HMS *Fearless* (which is seen in the background) engaged in cross-decking operations on 20 May 1982, before the landings took place. (IWM FKD.392)

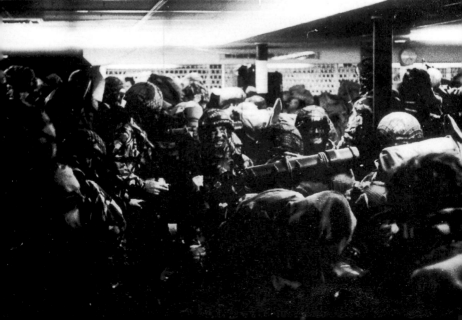

Left, upper: An unidentified Type 21 frigate in lumpy seas in the South Atlantic. The Type 21s were the most versatile of all the warships in the task force. (MoD)

Left, lower: Heavily laden paratroopers of the 3rd Battalion the Parachute Regiment wait in a mess deck on board the *Intrepid* before embarking in their landing craft, 21 May 1982. (MoD)

Above: Paratroopers disembark from their LCVPs on the shores of the Falkland Islands, 21 May 1982. (MoD)

Right: 'Digging in' ashore at San Carlos. In the background is a Volvo Snotrak. (IWM FKD.400)

Above: HMS *Argonaut* wreathed in smoke after being attacked by six Skyhawks of V Air Brigade on 21 May 1982. (MoD)
Below: An Argentine Dagger overflies RFA *Sir Bedivere*. The ship survived a bomb which bounced off the head of her big crane and passed through a bulkhead forward without exploding. (IWM FKD.183)
Right, upper: The Operations Room of the carrier *Invincible*. In the darkened room, lit only by the glow from the radar screens, sailors spent long hours managing and directing the air battle. (MoD)
Right, lower: An Argentine Dagger is just visible between the masts of HMS *Fearless* in San Carlos Water. The stern-down attitude of the assault ship is explained by the fact that her dock is flooded to enable her to operate landing craft. (MoD)

Left, top: HMS *Yarmouth* alongside the stricken HMS *Ardent* on 21 May 1982. While *Ardent*'s ship's company, clad in orange 'once-only' survival suits, move forward to clamber down on to *Yarmouth*'s flight deck, members of *Yarmouth*'s crew play fire hoses on to *Ardent*'s side to keep the ship cool. (IWM FKD.140)

Left, centre: A Rapier SAM position above San Carlos Water, looking over to Chancho Point. The Rapier system was not operational until 22 May, having suffered during the voyage south. (IWM FKD.168)

Left, bottom: An armoured bulldozer of the Commando Logistic Regiment approaching an LCU at San Carlos to unload more supplies for the Commando Brigade ashore. (IWM FKD.402)

Right, top: The Brigade Maintenance Area at Ajax Bay—a very congested site comprising HQ, stores, administration, field hospital and PoW cage. (IWM FKD.93)

Right, centre: The wreck of HMS *Antelope* photographed in the morning of 24 May, her back broken by the explosion of a 1,000-pound bomb and her Seacat magazine. Shortly after this photograph was taken the second 1,000-pound bomb exploded and the frigate sank by the stern. At San Carlos the Royal Navy faced air attacks on a scale which had not been experienced since the Second World War. (IWM FKD.71)

Right, bottom: The *Atlantic Conveyor*, derelict and on fire on 26 May 1982, the day after the Exocet attack. (IWM FKD.217)

Left, upper: A Wessex 5 helicopter on the smouldering deck of the *Atlantic Conveyor*. Three Chinooks and six Wessexes were lost with the ship, and their absence had a significant effect on the conduct of the land operations. (IWM FKD.149)

Left, lower: The burial at San Carlos of the dead of 2 Para killed in the battle for Goose Green. Sixteen officers and men of the battalion lost their lives in this action. (MoD)

Above: The *Canberra* and the *Queen Elizabeth II* at South Georgia on 27 May. Over 3,000 men of 5 Infantry Brigade and supporting units, together with 250 tons of stores, were transferred to the *Canberra* in less than twenty-four hours. (IWM FKD.928)

Below: Guardsmen of 5 Infantry Brigade come ashore at San Carlos on 2 June 1982. (MoD)

Left: RFA *Sir Galahad* burning at Bluff Cove on 8 June as a result of the Argentine air attack. (MoD)

Right: A wounded soldier is brought ashore at Bluff Cove following the bombing of the *Sir Galahad*. (MoD)

Below: The mountainous terrain barring the final advance on Port Stanley. Mount Tumbledown is on the left, taken by the Scots Guards during the night of 13/14 June, and Mount William is on the right. The assault on the latter was allocated to the 1/7th Gurkha Rifles, but the Argentine surrender meant that the operation did not take place. (MoD)

Left, upper: British troops advance towards Stanley in foul weather. The need to conclude operations before the onset of winter was a driving force throughout the campaign.
Left, lower: Guns of 29 Commando Regiment RA firing on Argentine positions around Stanley. (MoD)
Right, top: A dead Argentine soldier on the mountains around Stanley. The Argentines occupied positions of great natural strength which, in some cases, they defended stubbornly. (MoD)
Right, centre: Major-General Jeremy Moore with jubilant Falkland Islanders after the signing of the surrender on 14 June 1982. (MoD)
Right, bottom: Guardsmen of 7 Platoon, 'G' Company, 2nd Battalion Scots Guards hear the news of the surrender. (IWM FKD.314)

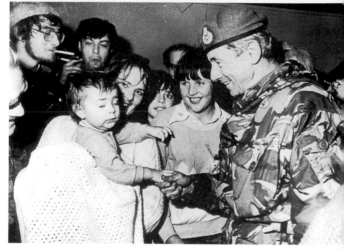

Above: Defeat: Argentine prisoners under Royal Marine guard. Over 11,000 Argentine combatants were returned to their country. (IWM FKD.164)
Below: Victory. The *Canberra* returns to Southampton on 11 July 1982, her decks packed with commandos.

one Dagger of the second strike which was shot down by the 800 NAS CAP just after 1405. This brought the number of the VI Brigade pilots killed to seven in twenty-one sorties—a 33 per cent casualty rate.

The struggle to save *Antelope* went on throughout the afternoon. Her ship's company were mustered on the forecastle and the flight deck while two Army bomb disposal specialists, assisted by two of *Antelope*'s senior engineers, tackled the bomb in the frigate's air-conditioning unit. After a defuzing charge was fired, the bomb itself exploded, killing one of the disposal team. Fires broke out across the width of the ship and throughout three decks. At 1820 she was abandoned. Within ten minutes of the last man leaving the ship, the ready-use Seacat SAM magazine exploded, followed shortly after that by the main Seacat and torpedo magazines. The silhouette of the frigate against the explosion was captured by Press Association photographer Martin Cleaver and remains one of the indelible images of the war. *Antelope* burned throughout the night and, after another major explosion—possibly caused by the other 1,000-pound—bomb, broke her back and sank.

The 24th would see another major effort by the *Fuerza Aérea Argentina*, with nine Skyhawks from V and IV Brigades and eight Daggers from VI Brigade. The attacks developed from 0945 onwards and lasted until after 1045. In a very hectic hour the LSL *Sir Lancelot* was hit by two 1,000-pound bombs; these failed to explode, but the ship had to be evacuated. Her consorts *Sir Galahad* and *Sir Bedivere* were also damaged, the former by another 1,000-pound bomb which failed to explode and the latter by a glancing blow from a 1,000-pound bomb which struck her bridge and then fell into the sea, where it did explode. All three ships suffered damage from strafing runs, and *Sir Galahad* and *Sir Lancelot* would be out of action for some days while they were made safe. However, the Argentine losses continued to mount: three Daggers from a four-aircraft flight were shot down by 800 NAS CAP.

The Argentines had enjoyed a favourable opportunity to inflict massive damage of the ships in the AOA but their most significant failure lay in not attacking *Fearless*, the Brigade and Amphibious HQ ship lying immobile and conspicuous at the head of San Carlos Water. In fact the AA barrage put up by the *Fearless* suited her name entirely, for it was so intense that the Argentine pilots preferred to fly around her and take their chances with the Rapiers (which they considered relatively easy to avoid) and lighter weapons beyond. Nevertheless, VI Brigade had lost three of the eight Daggers deployed, bringing the total loss to ten in 27 sorties. Given that many other aircraft were damaged, or even written off on account of AA damage, the Daggers were a fast-wasting asset and it was doubtful if VI Brigade could mount another operation before the end of the month.

May 25 was Argentina's National Day, and both the Amphibious Group and the CBG were aware that it would bring an all-out effort on behalf of both the *Armada Republica Argentina* and the *Fuerza Aérea Argentina* and everyone was correspondingly on the alert. (The Argentines subsequently denied that anything special was arranged for this day, and this is borne out by the low number of sorties flown in comparison to previous days.) Consequently, when at 0200 knocking noises were heard on the hulls of RFA *Resource* and *Fort Austin*, frogmen were called and the hulls of all ships in the AOA were inspected. As a precaution, all the storeships were moved over to the eastern side, further away from the BMA but affording more protection from air attack.

The defence dispositions were much the same, with the two LPDs at each end of San Carlos Water and protection provided by four frigates, *Antelope*, *Yarmouth*, *Plymouth* and *Argonaut*. To the north of Pebble Island were *Broadsword* and *Coventry* in their highly exposed 'missile trap' position, designed to break up Argentine raids using *Coventry*'s Sea Dart system while *Broadsword* covered both ships with Seawolf.

The first raid was detected by *Coventry* shortly after 0830 when four A-4Bs of V Air Brigade were tracked orbiting over West Falkland. A well-aimed Sea Dart accounted for one of the aircraft and the other three broke away without pressing their attacks. The next attack came in just after 1050 and was again detected by Coventry. However, hers was not the only radar about, for the VYC2A detachment at Port Stanley warned the Daggers that the CAP had been vectored on to them and they too broke away and returned to the mainland.

At 1130 a number of A-4Cs entered San Carlos Water from the southeast. One was brought down by a Seacat fired by *Yarmouth* and another three were shot down by Rapiers. Warships and stores ships were completely unscathed, the redisposition proving extremely successful. While the three surviving Skyhawks headed for the mainland, *Coventry* took one of them out.

The Argentine command were now well aware of *Coventry*'s activities and voices could be heard saying that they would 'get that Type 42'. A strike of four A-4Bs of V Air Brigade took off and split into pairs. They were detected by *Coventry* but their easterly heading indicated that they were making for San Carlos. However, the aircraft suddenly changed course and headed inland over West Falkland. The CAP from 800 NAS was in position and stood a good chance of interception but was called off as it entered the 'envelope' of *Coventry*'s Sea Dart. At this critical moment the Sea Dart failed and *Broadsword*'s Seawolf failed to acquire the targets. It was an exact repetition of the *Brilliant/Glasgow* scenario thirteen days earlier. The two ships had nothing to defend them but small-arms fire. Fortunately, of the four 1,000-pound bombs dropped, three missed and the fourth hit the water and bounced up through Broadsword's flight deck without exploding but wrecking a Lynx helicopter.

No sooner had the aircraft passed than the second pair were detected coming in from Pebble Island. The CAP was called as *Broadsword*'s Seawolf was tracking the aircraft perfectly. At the critical moment, however, *Coventry* fouled *Broadsword*'s range and once again both ships were left with nothing but rifle fire. This time three of the four bombs hit *Coventry* and exploded deep inside her hull. In fifteen minutes the destroyer rolled over and sank with the loss of nineteen of her crew.

Out to sea the CBG was much further to the east than usual. Woodward's carriers were covering the *Atlantic Conveyor* before she made a night-time dash into San Carlos to unload her stores. In addition to five Chinook and six Wessex helicopters, *Atlantic Conveyor* was carrying four complete tented camps capable of supporting 4,500 men together with their associated cooking, laundry and sanitary facilities, runway tracking for the STOVL field at Port San Carlos, a portable refuelling system and many hundreds of helicopter spare parts. Not the least important part of her cargo was 76 tons of cluster bomb units.

The CBG was short of escorts and the Type 42 HMS *Exeter* (Captain Hugh Balfour RN) was the only picket. *Brilliant* and *Alacrity* were 'goalkeeping' for *Hermes* and *Invincible* respectively and *Glamorgan* and *Ambuscade* were screening *Atlantic Conveyor*; in the same area were two of the LSLs, *Sir Bedivere* and *Sir Percivale*. At 1536 *Exeter* detected the distinctive transmissions of an Agave radar, indicating that Super Étendards were out and about, and issued a general threat warning. Two minutes later a missile launch was detected and all ships began firing chaff. Two Exocets flew through *Ambuscade*'s chaff pattern but, on emerging the other side, their radar seekers locked on to the largest target in front of them—*Atlantic Conveyor*. Captain Ian North, the ship's master, frantically tried to turn his vessel so that the missiles would strike her stern with its massive loading ramp, but she moved too slowly and both Exocets ploughed into her port quarter. Huge fires swept the ship and rapidly got out of control. Shortly after 1615 the ship's drenching CO_2 fire-fighting system was activated but failed to stem the flames. As the fire moved nearer and nearer the 76 tons of CBUs, Captain North, in conjunction with Captain Nick Layard RN (the senior naval officer on board), took the decision to abandon ship. Twelve of her crew were killed, including Captain North. *Atlantic Conveyor* floated, burning furiously, until the next day, when a vast explosion blew her bows off and she sank. Although the Argentines had failed to do any damage in the AOA, they had marked their country's national day in spectacular fashion. A valuable stores ship had been sunk, together with a troublesome destroyer.

Ashore at San Carlos, Brigadier Thompson was making the final adjustments to his plans for the advance. Thompson had planned to send 2 Para to Goose Green but decided against it on the grounds that all effort must be directed against Port Stanley. He was holding his evening conference at around 1800 when the news of the loss of the *Atlantic Conveyor* arrived. He had been depending on the extra Wessex and Chinook helicopters to move his brigade forward; now fuel supplies and ammunition would be competing for scarce helicopter assets, delaying the build-up in the forward area. More importantly, as one dismayed staff officer said on leaving the brigade CP, 'We'll have to bloody well walk.'

CHAPTER FOURTEEN

White Flags over Stanley

All this crap about being educated from birth about the Malvinas. If they were that committed, why didn't they fight for it?—Major Chris Keeble, 2nd Battalion, The Parachute Regiment.

WHILE the Navy were engaged in the battle for air supremacy, the Marines and paratroopers of 3 Commando Brigade were establishing themselves ashore. To the Navy, the establishment of the beach-head seemed painfully slow. Woodward complained in his diary:

> What the hell are they doing? Digging bloody holes? Cleaning their little rifles? Looking at maps? Waiting for their nutty rations? My ships have unloaded five thousand tons of kit for five and half thousand troops—that's nearly a ton each! What more do they want?

Later he confessed to writing: 'They've been here for five days and done f*** all!' His irritation was understandable: while the brigade was establishing itself, it was Woodward's ships which were being bombed and sunk. Moreover, the tyranny of the timetable was such that by mid-June the Royal Navy would be out of the war. Every day the brigade remained at San Carlos brought that day nearer.

Thompson, however, was governed by his own considerations. He needed to build up sufficient munitions and equipment ashore to sustain his advance. He was also waiting for the arrival of reinforcements in the shape of 5 Infantry Brigade commanded by Brigadier Tony Wilson. The brigade comprised the 2nd Battalion the Scots Guards, the 1st Battalion the Welsh Guards, the 1/7th Duke of Edinburgh's Own Gurkha Rifles and supporting units. It had sailed from Southampton on board the Cunard liner *Queen Elizabeth II* on 12 May together with Major-General Jeremy Moore who, once ashore on the islands, would assume divisional command of 3 Commando and 5 Infantry Brigade as Commander Land Forces Falkland Islands (CLFFI). In Moore's directive to Thompson of 12 May, he indicated that he expected to be in the Falklands by D+7, whereafter he would land 5 Brigade and 'develop operations for the complete repossession of the Falkland Islands'. Unfortunately, during the voyage south Thompson could not liaise with Moore in *Queen Elizabeth II* because their communications fits were incompatible. Both could talk to London, but not to each other.

One other aspect of Moore's directive was that Thompson should 'establish moral and physical domination over the enemy'. While pondering on the best way to do this, Thompson seized on the idea of sending 2 Para to clear out the Argentine garrison in Goose Green, but he was forced to cancel this on 24 May when bad weather meant that it would be impossible to fly-in any of the 105mm light guns necessary for support. Moreover, the loss of the *Atlantic Conveyor* changed all that.

In the evening of 26 May—the day after the sinking of the *Atlantic Conveyor*—Thompson was summoned to the satellite terminal at Ajax Bay to speak directly to Major-General Richard Trant at Northwood. Trant's orders were unequivocal: the brigade had to move, even if that meant marching to Stanley on foot. Thompson had favoured waiting until 5 Brigade arrived, but, as he later put it, 'people at the back end were restless'. Indeed they were, and not just for military reasons: there were rumours of yet another peace initiative at the United Nations, one that Britain might be forced to accept and one which would leave the Argentines in Stanley and the British at San Carlos. As Thompson remarked,

> It had become quite clear to 3 Commando Brigade that, apart from the wholehearted support from the Royal Navy, the Brigade was on its own: no assistance or support of any kind would be forthcoming from anyone, either close at hand or at home.

So Thompson drew up his orders. 42 Commando were to reinforce 'D' Squadron of the SAS, who had established themselves on Mount Kent. This was easier said than done. Because of bad weather it was not until the night of 29/30 May that the SAS had secured the heights of Mount Kent and the Tactical HQ of 42 Commando, 'K' Company and the Mortar Troop, together with three of 29 Commando Regiment's 105mm light guns, could be flown in. Even so, the weather took a hand in events and, despite some skilful flying in appalling conditions, the helicopters returned to San Carlos with their passengers. The move was eventually made during the night of 30/31 May, though not without incident: as the helicopters were approaching, an Argentine patrol wandered into the area and had to be dealt with by the SAS. It was an unnerving moment for the pilots, who could see the tracer fire crossing the LZ. Nevertheless, by dawn on 31 May Lieutenant-Colonel Nick Vaux stood on the summit of Mount Kent with Lieutenant-Colonel Mike Rose of the SAS and surveyed the town of Stanley below them. It was a triumphant moment, made even more so because it was evident that the

Argentine defenders on Mount Kent had simply cleared off when the Marines arrived, leaving food, weapons and ammunition behind them, and because, with the three light guns established, Vaux could order the first direct fire mission against Argentine positions around the town.

Meanwhile 45 Commando and 3 Para were to march to Douglas and Teal Inlet respectively. The Marines left Port San Carlos on 27 May and reached their objective at 1300 the next day, having spent an uncomfortable night in the open. The Argentines had fled from the area two days earlier, but not before they had subjected the local inhabitants to a number of indignities. The Commando dug in while their rucksacks and rations were flown forward. In the event, the Marines devised a fighting order so that they would not be dependent on helicopter lift for their rations.

3 Para had also reached their objective. They had set off after 45 Commando and arrived at Teal Inlet at 1100 on 28 May. They were joined by their mortar platoon, which had been 'lifted' across country in two tractors and trailers. Both 45 Commando and 3 Para were then ordered to move to Estancia House. 3 Para would get there first, having started from Teal Inlet, so Thompson planned to push 45 Commando through 3 Para and on to Long Island Mount. This was achieved, and both units were in their new positions by the night of 31 May.

This is a very dry account of the movement—the 'yomp', in Marine terms—of 3 Commando Brigade. It was a stupendous feat of endurance by all involved. Corporal J. A. Steeles of 3 Para recalls the 'Tab' to Mount Estancia:

> I look at my section. The oldest is 21 the youngest 18, some are already starting to suffer with the cold and wet, one or two have been complaining of sore feet. I brief them quickly and explain that at least you keep warm on the march. Again, we joke about marching all the way to Stanley and set off as Point Section. The going does not disappoint us. The ground is a permanent bog, very soon boots are soaking wet and at the first stop to check maps we change loads. On we plod. We have been on the march for nearly five hours and we meet up with the CO and RSM at a river crossing. We ford across and everyone is amazed to find that the RSM seems to have dry feet—he obviously walked across, is the general opinion. We stop and make a brew, it's getting dark and still no sign of the fence line we hope to use as a navigational aid. We set off again. It's dark now and men are continually stumbling and falling. A mist has come down and a steady drizzle is falling. It's becoming harder to keep control.

After spending a night in the open with no cover, 3 Para set off again in the morning:

All too soon we are marching again. We are no longer Point and it is a case of 'follow my leader' for hour after hour. All that matters now is to reach Teal. All my section are still with me and as darkness closes in we meet up with Special Forces just outside Teal Settlement, who inform us that the enemy have bugged out. We had made it, but at a price: three of my section cannot continue due to the state of their feet; the story is the same throughout the battalion.

Lastly, what of 2 Para (40 Commando were left at San Carlos to guard the BMA)? Thompson had ordered Jones to revive the plan for an attack on Goose Green. Enemy opposition was estimated as three infantry companies together with support troops. Just before 2 Para were about to launch their attack, the BBC graciously announced details of the brigade's movements, to the fury of all and of Jones in particular. On 28 May there was the last low-level raid on the BMA. This time the Skyhawks went for the refrigeration complex. Three 400kg bombs hit the dressing station, fortunately without exploding, but those that did explode struck the ammunition stocks waiting to be lifted to 2 Para. These had to be replaced quickly and the Commando Logistic Regiment had their work cut out for them.

The attack on Goose Green was to be in two phases. By night 2 Para would take the heights overlooking the settlement before moving down in daylight, when it would be easier to distinguish civilians. The battalion began the attack in companies from a start line by a sea inlet at Camilla Creek. 'B' Company took the west flank towards Boca House but soon ran into stiff opposition. Meanwhile 'A' Company headed for Darwin Hill and also met opposition. By dawn both companies were well short of their objectives and there could be no air support because of low cloud. However, HMS *Arrow*, assigned to provide NGS, stayed long after she should have withdrawn to continue to batter the Argentine positions with remorseless 4.5-inch gunfire. At this stage Lieutenant-Colonel Jones went forward to encourage 'A' company and in doing so was killed; his action showed the real meaning of the word 'leadership' in the Marine and paratroop units.

By morning 'A' Company were atop Darwin and 'B' had taken Boca House, with assistance from 'D' and Support Companies. The battalion's second-in-command, Major Chris Keeble, had now taken command and ordered a three-pronged attack on the airstrip, Goose Green and the area south of the settlement. However, as the paratroopers came down the slopes they ran into intense concentrations of small-arms, machine-gun, artillery, mortar and 20mm AA (used in the ground role) fire coming from the Argentine positions. Little or no cover was available and the Argentine positions were beyond the range of anything in Keeble's armoury except the three 105mm guns, which were now almost out of ammunition. Then, at 1525, three Harriers came in, expertly guided by the NGFO (who was also trained as an FAC) and silenced the Argentines with a well co-ordinated CBU attack which broke the will of the defenders.

Keeble proposed to offer the Argentines an opportunity to surrender, and on 29 May two Argentine PoWs were sent in under a flag of truce with an ultimatum that unless there was a surrender the Argentines would have to 'take the inevitable consequences'. At 0940 Keeble informed Thompson that he had agreed a dignified surrender with the Argentine commander, Air Commodore Pedroza. The Argentines marched out on to a playing field, where they piled their arms and sang their national anthem before going into captivity. What amazed the British was the sheer number of men they had captured—1,100, together with four 105mm pack howitzers, two 35mm AA guns, six 120mm mortars and two Pucarás. British casualties were twenty dead and forty wounded. It was the most remarkable action fought by a British battalion since the Second World War.

The battle was to have a profound affect on the rest of the campaign. It opened up the southern route to Stanley, and since the Argentine command always believed that the final assault would come from the south, it kept them thinking that way and thus distracted them from the assault mounted by 3 Commando Brigade from the north and west. More than anything else, it told the Argentine command of the determination and fighting skills of the British infantry.

By 4 June the Commando Brigade, less 40 Commando at San Carlos, was established in a ring around Stanley, with brigade HQ now situated at Teal Inlet. 5 Infantry Brigade, under the command of Brigadier Tony Wilson, were now arriving in the Falklands. For political reasons it was decided not to send the *Queen Elizabeth II* into San Carlos but instead to South Georgia, where 5 Brigade would 'cross-deck' to *Canberra* and *Norland* before going to San Carlos (thus giving rise to a memorable banner produced by 42 Commando for their homecoming: '*Canberra* cruises where *QE2* refuses'). General Moore and his staff came ahead in HMS *Fearless*.

5 Brigade came ashore at San Carlos on 2 June and occupied defensive positions vacated by the paratroops and commandos who had gone forward. Colonel Malcolm Hunt of 40 Commando pressed to be allowed to go forward to join the rest of his brigade but General Moore would not agree—much to the former's chagrin. Moore realized that the Argentines still had the capacity to launch an attack on the BMA and wanted a unit for its defence who were tough and familiar with the terrain. In the meantime Brigadier Wilson was figuring out how to move his brigade forward to

comply with the orders from Moore that he should advance along the southern route to Stanley via Goose Green. It was not easy because, for a number of reasons, 5 Brigade had come south without any dedicated logistics regiment. Consequently the Commando Logistics Regiment which would normally have supported two battalions, together with support troops, in a brigade now found itself supporting seven infantry battalions and a greatly enlarged number of ancillary units.

Wilson was fortunate that luck intervened. He sent a patrol from 'B' Company of 2 Para to visit Swan Inlet. From there the company commander telephoned the settlement at Bluff Cove and confirmed that there were no Argentines present. In a quick move 'A' Company and a mortar detachment were flown in that evening, 4 June, by the only Chinook to have survived the sinking of *Atlantic Conveyor*; the rest of the battalion was flown in the next day. (Legend has it that the Chinook's loadmaster protested that two many paratroopers were being carried, only to be hauled off the tailgate by the RSM who said, 'That's one less!')

The move to Fitzroy was audacious, and reported in the British press as such, with Wilson himself getting the credit for the famous telephone call. Wilson later justified the move:

> I thought it was now or never, because they [the Argentines] could come back during the night. I decided that unless I took that chance, I might end up fighting for Fitzroy and Bluff Cove, and only a fool would fight for something he could have for nothing.

Wilson, sometimes criticized for this move, was right. The longer his brigade (through no fault of its own) loitered at San Carlos, the more jeopardized was the position of the Marines and paratroops in the mountains around Stanley since their southern flank was open. The problem was that there were insufficient logistic resources to sustain such an operation. There were now five areas in the Falklands which had to be protected, each having its own special requirements: the Carrier Battle Group, in the eastern sector of the TEZ; the TRALA, the mobile home for damaged warships and merchantmen awaiting convoy into San Carlos; San Carlos itself, the main land force base and harbour, where nightly convoys of *matériel* were discharged; Teal Inlet, the new advanced base for 3 Commando Brigade; and Fitzroy/Bluff Cove, the new forward base for 5 Brigade.

The priorities were conflicting and there was no clear way as to how they should be resolved. The military ashore needed time to build up supplies and consolidate, while at sea the tyranny of the maintenance chart drawn up at Ascension was making itself felt. As Woodward confided to his diary,

. . . the battle group was now well on its way to falling apart, aside from the losses, we were coping with daily breakdowns in equipment and, as the land forces prepared for the breakdown from Carlos, we faced an almost overwhelming workload.

The Guardsmen could walk from San Carlos to Fitzroy but that would take days and, given the experience of 3 Commando Brigade, result in numerous casualties from exhaustion, trench foot and other non-battle causes. It was felt by the Marines—and General Moore was a Marine—that the Guards were not up to a strenuous march across difficult country. On the other hand, to go by sea from San Carlos to Fitzroy would take five hours and Wilson would have his troops in position in a much shorter time and in a much better state.

Eventually it was decided that the two battalions of Guardsmen should go by sea. An LPD would take them by night to a dropping-off position and they would then be taken to Bluff Cove by LCU. The Scots Guards would go first, during the night of 6 June. *Intrepid* would go as far as Lively Island, south of the Choiseul Sound—but no further. It was known that the Argentines had land-based Exocet missiles, and London would not accept the loss of one of the LPDs. From Lively Island, the Guardsmen would be taken in all four of *Intrepid*'s LCUs to Bluff Cove. Southby-Tailyour, whose job it would be to command the landing craft, was not sold on the idea and felt that the LPD should go in further, but he was overruled.

At 0430 on 6 June the four LCUs undocked and headed around Lively Island. As they left the island's shelter the weather worsened and the Guardsmen were all quickly soaked to the skin. En route they were suddenly illuminated by starshell. This had been fired by the destroyer HMS *Cardiff* (Captain M. Harris RN) ,which was combining a bombardment of Wireless Ridge and Sapper Hill with a missile-trap patrol. *Cardiff* was not aware of *Intrepid*'s movements and had illuminated the target prior to opening fire. Fortunately the LCUs were recognized and sent on their way, although Southby-Tailyour was furious that the exchange of signals between him and the destroyer, by light, may well have given his position away to any watching Argentine ashore. Eventually, after seven miserable hours in a bucketing landing craft, the Guardsmen were unloaded at Bluff Cove.

Now it was the turn of the Welsh Guards, although Commodore Clapp felt that *Cardiff*'s interception had compromised the plan: any Argentine half awake in an OP would have seen the starshell and may even have seen the LCUs. The plan was for *Fearless* to embark the Welsh Guards and rendezvous with *Intrepid*'s four LCUs south of Elephant Island. *Fearless* would sail with just two of her LCUs, leaving the other two to continue unloading at San Carlos. At the rendezvous *Fearless* would retract her own two (pre-loaded) LCUs and then embark two of *Intrepid*'s, load these quickly with men and retract them. She would then bring in the two empty *Intrepid* LCUs, shut her stern gate and head back to San Carlos before light. The plan went awry when *Intrepid*'s four LCUs became dispersed at Bluff owing to bad weather on 7 June and could not be contacted. They did not reappear in time for the rendezvous with *Fearless*. Rather than take the entire battalion back to San Carlos, *Fearless* dispatched two companies in her own LCUs and the ship then returned to San Carlos with the remainder. Colonel J. Ricketts of the Welsh Guards was not particularly happy with this arrangement but was assured that the rest of his battalion would be brought in the next night.

At San Carlos the remaining Guardsmen of a rifle company and support company were transferred to RFA *Sir Galahad* to join 16 Field Ambulance and a Rapier Troop. The Rapier troop and field ambulance were destined for Fitzroy, which was being established as 5 Brigade's forward maintenance area, whereas the Guardsmen needed to get to Bluff Cove. It was decided that the Guardsmen would be 'dropped off' at Bluff Cove en route. Embarkation went ahead very slowly, and it was not until 2200 that *Sir Galahad* sailed, with a Sea King of 825 NAS embarked, to begin the offload at first light.

At this stage it should be remembered that there was some concern about the wisdom of sending *Sir Galahad* into Fitzroy/Bluff Cove in daylight. The area was overlooked by Argentine OPs, and although the bad weather over the previous few days had kept Argentine aircraft grounded, that state of affairs could not be guaranteed. Most importantly for the Argentine pilots, and of concern for COMAW and his staff, Bluff Cove/Fitzroy was not a protected anchorage like San Carlos: attacking pilots would have plenty of time to make their approach from whatever direction suited the situation. However, the decision was not taken lightly: *Sir Galahad* was the only empty LSL at San Carlos, and, following the use of *Fearless/Intrepid* during the nights of 6 and 7 June, CinC Fleet at Northwood had banned the use of the LPDs in the forward area—it was just too risky. COMAW was faced with conflicting priorities: the Rapier Troop, Field Ambulance and Welsh Guards were required at Bluff Cove/Fitzroy. The only practical way they could get there was by sea, despite all the risks of repeating an operation for the third time, and the only asset available was *Sir Galahad*.

Sir Galahad's arrival at Fitzroy caused some consternation, for the unloading of *Sir Tristram*, which had arrived the previous day with some of 5 Brigade's equipment, was not complete. The shores at Fitzroy were unsuitable for beaching, and only one LCU (of the two which had taken the Welsh Guards from *Fearless* on 5 June) and a Mexeflote—both partially loaded with ammunition—were available since *Intrepid*'s four LCUs were required back at San Carlos. COMAW's staff had assumed, quite correctly, that *Sir Tristram* would have been already unloaded and that two LCUs, one Mexeflote and a Sea King were more than sufficient to unload *Sir Galahad*. They were not to know that the unloading of *Sir Tristram* had taken far longer than expected because she had been overloaded at San Carlos and that one of the two LCUs had been sent back to Darwin to collect 5 Brigade headquarters' vehicles.

The indefatigable Southby-Tailyour was on board *Sir Tristram* and crossed over to *Sir Galahad* to attempt to offer his specialist advice. In an impromptu conference on the LSL's stern ramp, he advised the Guardsmen that they should disembark as soon as possible; then they could either march to Bluff Cove, which was only seven miles away (although the Guardsmen believed it to be further, as they did not know that the bridge at the head of Port Fitzroy had been repaired), or they could wait at Fitzroy until dark, when they would be taken round to Bluff Cove by LCUs. Above all, it was paramount that they should get off the LSL because of the threat of air attack. One Guardsman remembers watching the 'conference' from *Sir Galahad*'s upper deck:

> A Marine officer came across and started discussing with our own officers about getting us off. Our officers weren't having any of it. We'd been buggered about ever since landing and we were fed up.

Once again, there were conflicting priorities. The Guardsmen wanted to get ashore at Bluff Cove: they felt that their battalion was dangerously exposed ashore since only two rifle companies had been deployed. Moreover, since arriving in the Falklands they had been treated like the Duke of York's 'ten thousand men' and were understandably aggrieved. They had not seen a single air attack since they arrived in San Carlos and had different perceptions of the air threat from the Marines, who had seen what the Argentines were capable of. They also had great faith in Rapier and underestimated the length of time it would take to land and deploy the missile launchers. One way or another, they did not share Southby-Tailyour's estimate of the danger if they stayed on the ship.

The discussion on *Sir Galahad*'s ramp became heated and ended with the Guardsmen ignoring Southby-Tailyour's advice and refusing to land for a variety of reasons; most of these are explained above, but, in addition, they would not put infantry in an LCU or Mexeflote which was loaded with ammunition (which was rather strange in view of the fact that *Sir Galahad* was virtually a floating bomb). Southby-Tailyour went ashore to 5 Brigade's HQ and succeeded in convincing the staff of the urgency of the situation. At first the staff refused to believe that there were any Guardsmen on *Sir Galahad*, believing that all had disembarked from *Fearless* the previous evening. However, when orders to disembark were issued by Brigade, they were countermanded by the CO of 16 Field Ambulance, who wanted the LCU to finish offloading his unit. Thus it was not until the afternoon that the LCU was available to move the Welsh Guards. Unfortunately, when it did arrive, its ramp was found to be defective, so while the Guardsmen began the long laborious descent down rope ladders over the LSL's side their equipment was lowered down by crane.

Elsewhere 8 June was proving to be the liveliest day since the invasion. *Hermes* had had to withdraw from the TEZ because of an urgent need to clean her boilers; the ship had steamed over 20,000 miles without a refit and her engineers were taking bets as to which boiler would break down first. Consequently, the 801 Squadron CAP was having to make greater use of the STOVL strip at San Carlos, now named HMS *Sheathbill*. Unfortunately the strip was put out of use when an RAF Harrier GR.3 crashed on take-off after suffering a sudden loss of power.

At 1258 HMS *Plymouth* was about to begin a bombardment of Mount Rosalie when five aircraft, Daggers, were sighted. They came in fast, at low level, firing their machine guns before releasing their bombs. *Plymouth* was struck by four 500-pound bombs, each of which failed to explode. However, the attack was a serious one: the ship was badly on fire and a depth charge on the flight deck had exploded, blowing a hole in it. As the Daggers were retiring, pursued by the CAP, five A-4s came round the southern coast of East Falkland and, on passing Bluff Cove, just as they were about to turn away, they sighted the masts of the LSLs.

To this day there is no evidence as to whether this strike was directly vectored in by an Argentine OP. That the Argentines knew of these operations is undeniable, but after the war Commodore Clapp stood at one of the Argentine OPs with powerful binoculars and noted that it would only be possible to see the trucks of the LSLs' masts. It is more likely that the Argentines knew of British activity in the area from the increase in signal traffic which inevitably accompanied the establishment of 5 Brigade's headquarters.

Whatever the circumstances, as the five Skyhawks came in, the LSLs barely had time to warn their 'passengers' let alone bring their 40mm guns into action. At 1315 *Sir Tristram* was hit by two 500-pound bombs which failed to explode and missed by a third which did explode and tore her stern ramp off. *Sir Galahad* was the more badly damaged, hit by three 500-pound bombs. Both ships caught fire immediately, *Sir Galahad* so seriously that her master, Captain P. J. G. Roberts RFA, ordered her immediate abandonment. The explosions and fire resulting from the bombs were quickly followed by secondary explosions from the ammunition and ordnance on board. Fire-fighting efforts were to no avail, and at 1415 Captain Roberts was the last to leave the ship. *Sir Tristram* was also abandoned, as all the superstructure aft of the bridge was burned out, but, fortunately, her ammunition was not affected.

Casualties amounted to 50 men killed or missing and 57 wounded, many horribly burned. (This was the number of wounded evacuated to *Uganda*; the number treated at Ajax Bay and returned to their unit was much greater). The majority were from the Welsh Guards—39 killed and 28 wounded. The television pictures of the shocked and burned survivors coming ashore are still the most searing images of the Falklands War. That there were not more casualties was due to the superb flying skills of the helicopter pilots, who plucked survivors from the ships, despite the intermittent explosions, rescued them from the water or used the downdraught from their rotors to blow the life rafts away. The casualties went to the field hospital at Ajax Bay, which was already dealing with the wounded from HMS *Plymouth*.

Surgeon-Commander Jolly was in charge at Ajax Bay:

Slowly things degenerate into a nightmare. As night creeps over the horizon, load after load of helicopter casualties begin to arrive at Ajax Bay. Each patient seems worse than the last, until soon the triage and resuscitation areas are completely choked . . . I race down to Log[istic] HQ and get on the radio to Division. We ask them, urgently, to prepare a list of ships that can take up to a hundred lightly injured. The number staggers the duty officer.

Mercifully, at about 150 the numbers begin to slow. With ten from *Plymouth*, that means 160 injured, standing or lying around in the building. The teams get to work on the more afflicted as the runner comes up with the news that *Fearless*, *Intrepid* and *Atlantic Causeway* are waiting to receive two dozen each.

The Welsh Guardsmen are stoical and cheery as we break the news to them. Standing near the doorway, blowing on their tattered and painful hands to keep them cool, many are pathetic sights. The skin hangs from the fingers like thin white rags, their faces are blistered and raw, their hair singed short. The bad news of another half an hour in an LCU before they can be treated is simply and willingly accepted. Each man seems to know of someone else in the building more seriously injured than himself, and all would rather see him treated first. Its heartbreaking to turn nearly 70 young men away from the casualty department door they have paid so much to reach, but there is no other way.

The *ARA*'s last victim on 8 June was one of *Fearless*'s LCUs which had gone on ahead from Bluff Cove to Darwin to collect the HQ vehicles of 5 Brigade. Her only armament was a single machine gun, which was no defence against the four A-4Bs of V Air Brigade which attacked her on the return journey. It may seem to have been unwise to send the LCU on such a long trip unescorted, but her coxswain, Colour Sergeant Brian Johnstone, also knew that 5 Brigade needed their HQ vehicles so that Wilson could exercise proper control and communications (and it was, after all, communications problems that were the cause of the losses on 8 June). It was a calculated risk, taken by a professional, which in this case went tragically wrong.

In human terms, and for the Welsh Guards as a regiment, the events at Bluff Cove were a disaster. The loss of *Sir Galahad* (she was eventually sunk as a war grave) and the damage to *Sir Tristram* rank as the episode in the Falklands War which people now most readily recall. There was, however, no one person to blame for what happened, only a series of inter-related circumstances which tragically came together to leave the two LSLs at the mercy of the Skyhawks.

In the wider context of the war, however, the incident was not one to check the British campaign. General Moore still had six infantry battalions, together with two-thirds of the Welsh Guards (reinforced by two companies of 40 Commando). His artillery was intact and the ammunition supply was building up satisfactorily, albeit slowly. The loss of two LSLs was serious, but three were still immediately available to meet the short-term needs of the land force. Most importantly, the move of 5 Brigade, however haphazardly it had been carried out, had put it across the southern approaches to Port Stanley.

The move of 5 Brigade to Fitzroy/Bluff Cove was the last major amphibious operation of the Falklands War. With the two brigades positioned round Stanley like a vice, the end was in sight for the Argentine defenders. There had been a number of plans discussed for the capture of Stanley. 5 Brigade planners favoured a sharp thrust on a narrow front to split the Argentine defences. On the other hand, 3 Commando Brigade planners favoured a methodical seizure of the high ground around Stanley; this was the plan that was chosen. The build-up for the attack took time: the relative ease with which 42 Commando had captured Mount Kent fooled nobody, and all available intelligence suggested that the Argentines were deployed in strength. Although the interrogation of prisoners had shown that morale in the Argentine forces was low, they still had the terrain on their side and, as Captain Iain Gardiner of 45 Commando pointed out, 'Even if only one man was prepared to sit behind a machine gun in a well-prepared defensive position, he was still going to be pretty dangerous.'

The attack took place in two phases. During the night of 11/12 June the units of 3 Commando Brigade would go first: 3 Para would seize Mount Longdon, 45 Commando would attack Two Sisters and 42 Commando would seize Goat Ridge and Mount Harriet. 2 Para were to remain in the rear as brigade reserve. The objectives were duly secured, though not without hard fighting, particularly on Mount Longdon. All three battalions were supported by warships, which provided constant NGS. The destroyer *Glamorgan* was supporting 45 Commando when, just after 0230, a fast-moving radar contact was detected. At first the contact was identified as a shell from the one of the Argentine 155mm howitzers, but after it continued beyond gun range and was actually sighted by HMS *Avenger* it was identified as an Exocet. The destroyer immediately increased speed and fired Seacat missiles to deflect it. This last-ditch manoeuvre actually worked, for the missile was turned upwards and struck the edge of the deck on the port side near the hangar rather than the ship's side. The hangar and the helicopter were devastated: nine men were killed, four missing and fourteen injured. However, *Glamorgan* could still steam and her 4.5-inch guns and Exocet were working, and, declining an invitation to shelter under the Rapier umbrella at Fitzroy, she returned to the CBG at 18 knots.

The Marines and paratroopers were all secure at their objectives by 0800 on 12 June. Throughout the day they had to suffer unpleasant harassing artillery- and mortar-fire from Argentine defenders. During the day the helicopters were busy moving the guns of 29 Commando Regiment to new sites as well as the eternal ammunition supply. The gunners had fired 3,000 rounds in support of 3 Commando Brigade and this had to be replaced before phase 2.

Phase 2 involved the Scots Guards, who were tasked to capture Mount Tumbledown, the 1/7th Gurkhas, who were to take Mount William, and 2 Para (assigned to 3 Commando Brigade for this operation), who were to secure Wireless Ridge. The assault was scheduled for the night of 12/13 June but was put back twenty-four hours to allow more time to replenish ammunition supplies and to allow further reconnaissance of Mount Tumbledown.

June 13 saw the last major Argentine air raid. Seven A-4Bs of V Air Brigade came in over East Falkland from the south east. Whether by accident or design, given the Argentines' claims that they made the attack on the basis of their analysis of radio traffic, the area they chose to attack at the base of Mount Kent was the site of 3 Commando Brigade's tactical HQ at the exact time that General Thompson was having an 'O-Group' meeting at which General Moore was present. Few of the 500-pound bombs exploded, but the attack was too close for comfort and the HQ was hurriedly shifted. The brigade helicopter area was also attacked and a Scout and a Gazelle were damaged. It was fitting that the last daylight raid of the war should have been by V Air Brigade. The Skyhawk pilots were individually courageous and, despite the age of their aircraft, had been responsible for most of the naval losses inflicted by the *Fuerza Aérea Argentina—Coventry*, *Antelope*, *Sir Galahad* and LCU *F4*—as well as damaging *Argonaut*, *Glasgow*, *Broadsword*, two LSLs and the Ajax Bay BMA. They had lost ten aircraft and nine pilots.

At approximately 2200 on 13 June the British launched their offensive. Tumbledown was strongly held by Argentine Marines of the 5th Marine Battalion, which was well-led and well-equipped and had a lower than usual ratio of conscripts to regulars in its ranks. The Scots Guards were supported by HMS *Active*, which fired 220 rounds of 4.5-inch HE in support. However, the Argentine Marines were not easily dislodged. They outnumbered their attackers and from 0100 to 0400 on 14 June halted their advance. *Active* was joined by *Avenger*, and the two frigates poured an impressive weight of fire on to the Mountain, but the ships had to depart before dawn. The fighting on Tumbledown was fierce, hand-to-hand combat (one sniper was removed by a 66mm rocket fired at a range of six yards), and it was only with the coming of dawn and the approach of the 1/7th Gurkhas, who had taken Mount William, that the Argentine defence was broken.

Meanwhile 2 Para had taken Wireless Ridge but had exceeded their objective and streamed down on to the racecourse at Stanley, capturing the Argentines' main ammunition supply. The momentum of the assault continued, with two companies of 40 Commando being flown on to Sapper Hill in the only opposed helicopter assault of the campaign. But no sooner had the first helicopter set down than the order to cease fire was given. The Argentines were negotiating: their will had been broken by the night battles of 13/14 June and the war was over. General Menendez signed an unconditional surrender on 14 June.

CHAPTER FIFTEEN

Get STUFT!

The logistic chain was one of the wonders of the modern world. We destroyed an air force, captured an army, and caused the downfall of a dictator while we were eating fillet steak and fresh fruit which had travelled 8,000 miles.—Captain L. E. Middleton RN, HMS Hermes

THE campaign in the South Atlantic depended on a long supply line stretching all the way back to the United Kingdom. This was the weak link in the campaign and constituted the Argentines' greatest missed opportunity. Had they attempted to interdict the shipping passing between Ascension and the Falkland Islands, forcing the Royal Navy to convoy merchant ships all the way, then things might have gone very differently. Ascension Island, with its valuable airfield, was also spectacularly vulnerable to assault by special forces.

To begin with, the Royal Navy had nowhere near the maritime carrying capacity required to support the CBG and the land forces. The shortfall had to be made up by requisitioning ships from trade: the full amount of shipping which the Navy required was far from obvious. It was not a matter of simply selecting merchant ships at random and requisitioning them: a good deal of preparation was called for. Modern merchant ships are designed for maximum economy of operation in their chosen field—passenger ferries. This meant that they had little flexibility for other roles. Thus, for example, a cross-channel ferry could carry a large number of personnel and might seem ideal for use as a troopship. However, such a ship would not have the endurance to go to the South Atlantic, would not have sufficient fresh water and would probably not be strong enough to withstand the rough weather found in those southerly latitudes. In the end three qualities were required of any ship about to be requisitioned—range, endurance and seakeeping. A special committee was set up at the Board of Trade, the TUFT (Taken up from Trade) Committee, which not only had to select the ships but deal with 1,001 other questions which inevitably arose. What about insurance against normal marine risks with ships being sent to an area where these could be much greater? Should merchant ships be armed? What about foreign crews working in British-flag ships? What about the Naval Discipline Act?

Should crews receive a special bonus? There were many others. Inevitably farce intervened early in the campaign when a copy of *Jane's Merchant Ships* had to be found in a hurry on a Saturday. The only bookshop which could supply one was in Surrey, and the poor shopkeeper was kept in his shop by the police until the men from the ministry arrived to collect it!

The legal machinery was quickly put in progress. Using powers dating back to the time of Richard I and the Third Crusade, the Government acquired the right to requisition British-flag shipping 'in defence of the Realm and Sovereign Territories'. Special powers were required in order to protect British shipowners from legal action if the requisitioning of their ships meant breaking an existing contract. It would be fair to say, though, that the powers were used sensitively, with due regard for the shipowners' and managers' commercial interests.

The first types of ship that were required were troopships to lift 3 Commando Brigade and associated units. There were only a few large liners in the British merchant fleet, and because of the terrible weather expected 'down south' the choice quickly narrowed to the 44,807grt *Canberra*, owned by P&O. From the same company the 5,463grt 'roll-on, roll-off' ferry *Elk* was taken up, to transport the supporting arms and the war maintenance reserve. Additionally the ferry *Norland* was taken up when 3 Commando Brigade was augmented by the two paratroop battalions, together with the *Europic Ferry*, another 'ro-ro' ship. Subsequently the flagship of the British merchant fleet, the liner *Queen Elizabeth II*, was taken up to lift the troops of 5 Brigade, while three more car ferries, the *Nordic Ferry*, *Baltic Ferry* and *St Edmund*, were taken up to carry the brigade's logistic and support troops. For the long term maintenance of the garrison on the Falklands, the Union Steam Ship Company's *Rangatira* was taken up as a troopship and later 'doubled' as an accommodation ship.

The modifications which the troopships required were fairly basic. Each had the more luxurious passenger fittings boarded over or removed altogether. Fortunately, the large number of cabins in the two liners and in *Norland* meant that there was no need to fit extra bunks, although this was necessary on the car ferries where some rather stygian messdecks were constructed. Each was fitted with communications equipment so that the ships could 'talk' to their naval escorts, although a significant omission from the *Queen Elizabeth II*'s communications fit was the facility for General Moore to talk directly to General Thompson at San Carlos. Each ship was also fitted with refuelling-at-sea (RAS) points to enable fuel and water to be transferred while under way. The most significant modifications were the fitting of flight decks to enable the ships to operate helicopters. The speed at which the work had to be done meant that the flight decks were constructed very quickly. Design work was limited and consisted of putting enough metal to support the loaded weight of the required helicopter in parts of the ship strong enough to take the weight. *Canberra*'s design was, literally, worked out on the back of an envelope and the requirements telephoned through to Vosper Thorneycroft at Southampton so that work on the panels could begin. Swimming pools were found to be the best places, as the ships' structure was already strengthened in these areas to take the weight of 70–100 tons of water. Because of the extra weight of the flight decks high up in the ship, additional fuel ballast had to be taken on board to compensate and aerials had to be re-run to allow clear paths of approach for pilots. In all, seventeen ships were fitted with flight decks, which varied from those capable of taking the 46,000-pound Chinook to those able to handle only the smaller 5,500-pound Wasp.

The search for troopships was nothing compared to the search for tankers. No country in South America would offer bunkering facilities to the Royal Navy. The South Africans might have done, if asked, but this would have risked alienating much of the Third World at a time when Britain needed every vote possible at the UN. The nearest friendly bunkering facilities were at Freetown at Sierra Leone, 4,100 miles north of the Falklands. There was therefore an urgent need for tankers to supply not only the diesel fuel for the gas turbines of the modern warships but FFO (furnace fuel oil) for the older warships, aviation fuel for the Harriers and helicopters and the wide variety of fuels required by the merchant ships. There would also be a need for fresh water in quantity. Eventually fifteen tankers were taken up to supplement fourteen tankers of the Royal Fleet Auxiliary.

The tanker support came in four categories. First there were the base storage tankers at Ascension, which topped up ships heading home and proceeding to the Falklands. Then there were the auxiliary support tankers, which plied between the United Kingdom and the forward area, where they would transfer their cargo to the third group, the convoy escort oilers (which could either be requisitioned vessels or tankers of the RFA), which operated in the TRALA and refuelled the warships and other ships in the TEZ. Lastly there was the one water carrier, the *Fort Toronto*, which was required to supply the fresh-water needs of the task force (since many ships possessed neither distillers nor reverse-osmosis plants) and to supply fresh water ashore in the Falklands in the event of the Argentines' wrecking the local supply or it being damaged in the fighting.

The story of the tankers is a special one and deserves a book all of its own. The civilian tankers, with their white painted superstructures, stood out as massive targets among the grey ships of the CBG. They had to refuel ships in conditions which had previously been thought impossible. The *British Dart*, for example, had to make her first RAS at 0400 at 14 knots in foul weather, with seas washing over her decks while zig-zagging on account of the submarine threat and in a total black-out. Evolutions such as this called for seamanship of the highest order. On one occasion an RAS had to be aborted because the fuel in the pump had frozen solid in the cold. Icebergs were another hazard, particularly for those tankers which went as far south as South Georgia. The longest ever RAS was conducted between the *British Tamar* and RFA *Plumleaf*, in which 18,000 tons of fuel was transferred in 52 hours and 40 minutes of continuous refuelling, in winds reaching force 8, so that both ships had to turn down-wind during the operation.

Yet at no time did any ship in the CBG or Amphibious Group go short of fuel, nor was any operation ever modified or cancelled because of a lack of fuel. As in previous conflicts, the tankers, being the most travelled of the merchant ships, performed a wide variety of services—ferrying survivors back to Ascension, carrying mail and, not least, providing hot water and bathing facilities at Port Stanley after the fighting for hundreds of tired and filthy soldiers.

The most substantial conversions were the four aircraft ferries. It was essential, given the Argentine superiority in aircraft numbers, that the CBG have a mobile reserve of aircraft and helicopters. Between them the two carriers could only carry twenty Sea Harriers and 33 helicopters, and even that number was far in excess of their standard operating levels in peacetime. Not only were additional aircraft needed to replace battle losses, but aircraft and helicopters requiring major overhaul would have to be sent elsewhere to clear the carriers' decks for new arrivals. In addition, the land forces' appetite for helicopters was insatiable, and aircraft ferries were the only means of moving these helicopters down to the Falklands.

Four ships were taken up for use in this role, Cunard's 14,946grt *Atlantic Conveyor* and *Atlantic Causeway*, Sea Containers' 11,445grt *Contender Bezant* and the Harrison Line's 27,867grt *Astronomer*. All were container ships, and all except the *Astronomer* had a 'ro-ro' capability. Their conversions were all basically similar, although as each ship was taken up refinements and lessons learned from the previous job were incorporated. Thus *Atlantic Conveyor*'s conversion, the first, and completed in eleven days, was the most rudimentary while the *Astronomer*'s, done last, was the most sophisticated and, in fact, formed the basis for an Anglo-American trial on the usefulness of this sort of ship, the 'Arapaho' Project, which was sadly abandoned a couple of years after the conflict.

Each ship was given the minimum facilities to allow it to operate aircraft. The container decks became flight decks and were painted with non-slip paint, marked off with 'spots' and fitted with glide path indicators, deck landing lights and floodlights. One problem was that the flight decks had to be made 'smooth', and this meant the removal of upwards of 500 container 'tie-down' bolts per ship. 'Walls' of containers were constructed to protect aircraft carried on deck, and on the *Astronomer* these formed the hangar since this ship did not have between-decks cargo-carrying space. The containers also doubled as workshop spaces, and maintainers commented on the stability of the ships and how easy they were to work in compared to the wildly gyrating small frigates. Stowage was constructed for avgas and also the liquid oxygen required by the Harrier pilots' breathing apparatus. All this equipment meant more men—upwards of 100 a ship. Extra accommodation therefore had to be constructed, together with parallel improvements to galleys, bakeries, laundries and sick-bay facilities.

The ships also carried stores; the two Cunard ships carried 3,000 tons in addition to their aircraft. It was an incredibly difficult task loading these items since the headroom between decks was only 5 feet 5 inches and many loads had to be re-palleted before they could be stowed. The *Contender Bezant* carried several thousand of the ready-to-eat 'Compo' ration packs. All four menus were carried but unfortunately were loaded in alphabetical order by type, and invariably the desired menu containing the chicken *suprême* was right at the back!

Of the four ships, only the *Atlantic Conveyor* and *Atlantic Causeway* were involved in the conflict, the former being sunk together with her valuable cargo on 25 May. Her sister ship carried twenty Wessex Mk 5 helicopters and eight Sea Kings, together with a vast amount of stores. On 31 May she disembarked her helicopters in San Carlos and then began shuttling to and from the TA and the TRALA, where she was used as a welcome refuelling stop for helicopters. Eventually she sailed for home on 12 July, having experienced 4,000 helicopter landings and refuelled aircraft on more than 500 occasions. The *Contender Bezant* carried nine helicopters and three Harriers and joined the CBG on 14 June, the day the war ended. Her flight deck, more restricted than that of any of the other ships, made flight operations challenging to say the least. Her after cargo ramp could be used for the discharge of cargo by helicopter, though the rotor draught from the large Chinook helicopters was sufficient to set the ship swinging about her anchor cable. She carried out over 800 deck landings before sailing for the United Kingdom on July 14. The last ship, the *Astronomer*, sailed for the Falklands on 7 June and was thus en route when the Argentines surrendered.

However, as there was no formal cessation of hostilities, she still took full wartime precautions. She carried thirteen helicopters, and after offloading these at Stanley on 27 June she became part of the RN MARTSU (Mobile Aircraft Repair, Transport and Salvage Unit), maintaining Wessex helicopters. Her crew were relieved in mid-September and the ship remained 'down south' for another tour.

The four aircraft ferries were the most complex of the conversions. They were not perfect, and plenty of snags were encountered during their operation. But in the final analysis it is not what went wrong so much as what went right that mattered. They performed a task which could not have been done otherwise. In no sense were they substitute aircraft carriers, but in bringing aircraft to the fleet and the land forces and forming a mobile reserve which could maintain them, they were superb.

Then there were five dry cargo ships, *Laertes*, *Lycaon*, *Saxonia*, *Geestport* and *Avelona Star*. The first two carried substantial quantities of ammunition in addition to dry goods, while the last three, which were refrigerated cargo ships, carried food and other perishable stores. All five ships experienced considerable difficulties in performing a role which had never been envisaged for them. Transferring goods at sea in rough weather called for outstanding seamanship, with the ships rolling as much as 40 degrees. A sixth ship, the *Tor Caledonia*, was also taken up for dry stores but her load included 350 Rapier missiles; not surprisingly, she embarked a Blowpipe missile detachment at Ascension.

A large number of other ships were also required: a dispatch vessel (British Telecom's *Iris*); a minesweeper support ship; five trawlers converted to act as minesweepers (which also played a vital but unsung role in supporting the SBS and SAS in their various activities); a minehunter support ship; a mooring vessel, required for laying out moorings at South Georgia, an anchorage where the holding ground was poor and which was swept by sudden, violent winds; three tugs, which were maids-of-all-work; and two repair ships.

Perhaps more than any of the STUFT conversions, the repair ships *Stena Inspector* and *Stena Seaspread* impressed the Navy with their versatility. Both ships were designed to support the offshore oil industry. Most remarkable of all was their dynamic positioning system, which enabled them to remain within three metres of a given position in winds of up to force 9. The navigator of HMS *Endurance* was absolutely confounded when, on ordering the *Stena Seaspread* to 'let go anchor', the master simply engaged the dynamic positioning. This facility was also used when transferring stores: the ship could be held within 20 feet of the receiving ship while *Stena*

Seaspread's crane did the rest. It was difficult to convince naval officers that this was a safe procedure for their thin-skinned frigates, but they soon gained confidence once the repair ship's capabilities were known.

The *Stena Seaspread* was the first to be requisitioned, on 10 April, and she sailed on the 16th. She was in the thick of things from the beginning, and after a stand-off at South Georgia to resurrect the old whaling station she proceeded to join the CBG. Her first 'customer' was HMS *Brilliant*, damaged on 21 May. Thereafter *Glasgow*, *Arrow*, *Sir Lancelot*, *Plymouth*, *Glamorgan* and *Broadsword* all benefited from her unique capabilities. The *Stena Seaspread* even managed a number of 'firsts', notably fitting a new propeller to HMS *Avenger* and changing one of HMS *Southampton*'s Tyne gas turbines while at anchor in a blizzard. In all, she dealt with eleven warships which had received battle damage, twenty-four warships, merchant ships and RFAs with routine defects and four captured enemy vessels. No finer tribute to her services could be found than when HMS *Plymouth* pulled away after being restored to 85 per cent operational efficiency after the bombing on 8 June. As the frigate gathered way, her ship's company spontaneously lined the guardrails to cheer those who restored her seaworthiness. The other repair ship, *Stena Inspector*, was requisitioned on 25 May and arrived in-theatre after the war was over. However, she proved no less versatile than her predecessor, changing the Type 1099 radar aerial for HMS *Birmingham* in a 35-knot wind—a job which the dockyard said could only be done in a flat calm.

It was a strange and sudden transition for the officers and men of the Merchant Navy who found themselves participating in Operation 'Corporate'. Many had done no ocean navigation for years and needed refresher courses; others, like the liners' navigators, were used to having their programmes arranged years in advance and were now having to alter their plans daily. They had to embark strange naval liaison parties and cope with peculiar procedures and manoeuvres. Their whole working lives were upended at a stroke. As always, the Merchant Navy rose to the challenge, and the reconquest of the Falklands is as much their story as it is that of the fighting services.

Ascension Island, conveniently situated midway between Great Britain and the Falklands, provided a valuable intermediate base. *Matériel* could be flown there from the United Kingdom and then loaded on ships heading south, or flown south from the island for air-dropping at sea to the ship concerned. Once Stanley had fallen, Ascension became the final fuelling point for RAF aircraft engaged in the long haul south. A Royal Navy commander was appointed to take charge at Ascension and told briefly to 'go out there and make things work. Good luck!' The officer found himself running a tri-service organization where individual service priorities sometimes conflicted with the common aim. Nevertheless, Ascension fulfilled its role brilliantly as a 'halfway house', much to the amusement of the two resident USAF officers (Ascension was nominally leased to the United States, though the facilities were mothballed and the 10,000-foot runway was administered by Pan American Airways), who remained constantly amazed by the British ability to improvise. Space precludes a detailed account of events, but the island's role was essential to the success of the campaign.

South of Ascension, ships proceeded independently to the TRALA as a moving box of ocean in which merchant ships were held until either their stores could be transferred to another ship or they were brought into AOA by convoy. The TRALA was ably managed by HMS *Antrim* after her experiences in San Carlos on 21 May. Convoys would depart from the TRALA every evening for the AOA so as to make the passage, where the ships were most vulnerable to air attack, by night. Likewise, the outward-bound convoy would leave the AOA in the evening so as to be out of range of Argentine aircraft by day. Both convoys would be escorted. Thus on 2 June the inbound convoy, consisting of the *Stromness*, *Nordic Ferry*, *Blue Rover* and *Sir Tristram*, were detached from the CBG at 1330 (somewhat earlier than usual, thanks to dense fog) and were escorted by HMS *Brilliant* and *Avenger*. The *Baltic Ferry* and *Atlantic Causeway* formed the outward convoy together with the *Stena Seaspread*. The escorts were *Minerva* and *Yarmouth*. *Minerva* would turn back once the convoy was out of the danger, but *Yarmouth* would carry on to the TRALA for a maintenance period.

The convoy schedules were complicated and had to be combined with the requirements for one or two ships to be available for shore bombardment duty, AA guardship duties at San Carlos and the defence of the CBG, not to mention the support of special forces and covering ships heading for Teal Inlet (3 Commando Brigade) and Darwin (5 Brigade). No wonder Woodward complained that his frigates 'were all over the bloody place'.

There is no doubt that the continual need to keep the frigates fuelled and supplied with provisions constituted a tremendous drain on the ships' companies, who were already spending long periods of time closed up at their action stations and who were engaged in operations nearly every evening. The commanding officer of one frigate recalled

> Sprinting inshore at dusk, evading minefield and shore-battery fire whilst working the gunline, before making a rapid return to ensure being under friendly air cover before first light. But there was no respite upon re-join.

Instead there was the sapping go-round of resupply. First find your tanker, slot, connect, refuel, whilst conducting evasive steering to a darkened guide. Disconnect, find your stores and ammo ship, then the same routine as you took on 4.5-inch shells and, perhaps, provisions. Bone-weary sailors cursed and yearned for the appearance of the ubiquitous Sea King with its swift and labour-saving VERTREP. In sum, myself and my people found the entire business of logistics wearying and preoccupying like no other. And that includes fighting the enemy.

One other aspect of the logistics chain was the direct supply by air from Ascension using RAF Hercules aircraft which would parachute the supplies into the sea. Naturally, this method could only be used for essential and fairly light items or spare parts. Mail and 'human freight' were also delivered in this fashion.

This long and extended supply line went unmolested by the Argentines, save on 29 May when the tanker *British Wye* was attacked by an *Armada Republica Argentina* Hercules aircraft which rolled eight 500-pound bombs by hand out of the cargo hold from a height of 150 feet. Four fell into the sea, three exploded alongside, causing minor damage, and one hit the ship and bounced off. However, many ships reported being shadowed. On 8 June the *ARA* attempted the same trick against the tanker *Hercules*, of Liberian registry and totally unconnected with the task force. On this occasion one bomb did explode, and the ship was later scuttled in deep water. The threat posed by Argentine aircraft to the supply line was taken seriously, and ships were routed as far as possible on courses that would take them out of range of possible molestation.

But the threat never materialized into a serious effort against the supply line. Had the Argentines chosen to go for the merchant ships en route rather than the AOA, this would have had the most serious consequences for the operation. But they did not, and, while they held back, the oil, diesel, ammunition, fillet steak and fresh fruit kept coming.

CHAPTER SIXTEEN

A Good and Perfect Understanding

Surprise, violence and speed are the essence of all amphibious landings.—Winston Churchill

WINSTON Churchill's summary of amphibious warfare is essentially correct. The three most important factors are surprise, overwhelming firepower and speed in attaining the objective, and all three feature to greater or lesser extent in the campaigns described in this book. At Quebec, Wolfe achieved surprise by choosing a route to the city which Montcalm thought was impassable. Having chosen his route, he moved quickly to establish his forces on the Plains of Abraham and made Montcalm give battle, despite the latter's 'paper' superiority in numbers. At Gallipoli, it is true that surprise was lost once the British withdrew after the failure of the attack on 18 March. However, they still retained some element of surprise as the Turks could not know when and where the attack was coming.

The real problem at Cape Helles on 25 April was that the plan, worked out in minute detail, proved too inflexible to be adapted to the circumstances. It would have been better for the main force to have switched to the 'Y', 'X' and 'S' Beaches once it was known that the main landings on 'W' and 'V' Beaches were opposed. The Turks would then have been outflanked and forced to retreat. Not only was the plan inflexible, but Hamilton took such a detached view of the situation that he left the conduct of the operation entirely to his subordinates, despite his having seen the unopposed landings on 'Y' and 'X' Beaches.

It is always tempting to ponder that 'what ifs' of history, and in this connection it is interesting to consider what would have happened had the Anzacs gone ashore at Helles and the 29th Division gone ashore north of Gaba Tepe. The training and discipline of the 29th might have enabled them to cope better in the rough country inland from 'Z' Beach, while the individualism and panache of the Anzacs might have been better used on the uncontested flank landings at Helles. We shall never know. At Suvla Bay surprise was achieved and nearly two divisions were put ashore with minimal losses. However, speed and violence were most noticeably lacking. The campaign would have gone the other way had Stopford and Hammersley kept their men moving throughout 8 August while the Turkish reinforcements were still on the march.

The historian Trevor Wilson concludes that 'the events of 25 April bore witness to what an invading force must suffer when improvisation has been substituted for preparation and no calculation has been made of its needs in manpower and firepower.'[1] This is true, but it is also somewhat simplistic. The Gallipoli campaign was as much lost in London as it was on the cruel hills of the peninsula. From the beginning there were those who opposed the campaign and saw that Hamilton received neither the men nor the right commanders to achieve success. The appointment of Stopford is so ludicrous as to be beyond belief. This was a tragedy, for the Gallipoli campaign is a perfect example of how an amphibious landing can alter the course of the war. Had the campaign succeeded, then Turkey would have been out of the war, the Balkans would have been opened to attack from the east and a direct juncture would have been effected between the Anglo-French forces and the Russians. Hamilton had the strategic vision to see all this, but he failed to persuade his superiors. For the want of a few experienced divisions (in January 1916 the British Army had 34 infantry divisions in France—surely one or two could have been spared?) and capable commanders, these aims were unfulfilled. Yet Gallipoli saw much of interest in the development of amphibious warfare techniques, which were to come to fruition only in the Second World War. Specialized landing craft, dedicated bombardment ships, air spotting for naval gunfire, artificial harbours—all these and many other aspects of amphibious warfare now taken for granted were first experimented with at Gallipoli.

Inchon, in the words of the historian David Rees, was a 'twentieth century Cannae, ever to be studied.' Surely there is no better example of the application of surprise, violence and speed. Whatever the subsequent course of the Korean War—and its lacklustre end has tended to hide the brilliance of the planning and execution of the landing—Inchon remains the perfect amphibious operation in that it succeeded totally in its objectives.

The 1982 Falklands War was an operation which succeeded against all the rules. In a subsequent programme on the Falklands War, Major-General Julian Thompson said that 'luck should not be a factor in the planning of war'. He is right, but in 1982 the British went to war propelled by a political directive to do so and trusting in their own professionalism (and luck) to carry the day. Two factors make the Falklands stand out from the other campaigns in this book. First, before the landings the British had to attain local air and sea superiority so that their amphibious ships could pass freely. Secondly—and there is a similarity to Quebec here—the British commanders were working against a tight schedule. The austral winter was coming, which would close down operations; more importantly, with no base in the theatre, ships were experiencing serious mechanical difficulties which needed the facilities of a dockyard. Thus operations had to be concluded before the weather broke and the ships' multiple mechanical defects forced them back to the United Kingdom.

The Falklands campaign proved that conventional military operations which depend on the traditional virtue of surprise are still viable in these days of electronic warfare and intelligence-gathering. Moreover, it confirmed the value of the helicopter as an assault transport. Instead of securing the beach and then bringing in the guns by sea, helicopters were able to fly-in the artillery behind the troops, making for a quicker and more effective seizure of the beach-head. The helicopter has revolutionized amphibious warfare, and it will continue to influence its evolution.

However, the factors of surprise, speed and violence are not enough on their own. A fourth factor, and possibly the most critical, is that 'good and perfect understanding' between the military and naval commanders. This relationship, exemplified by Wolfe and Saunders, Doyle and Smith and Thompson and Clapp, lies at the heart of the success of an amphibious operation.

Note to Chapter 16
1. Wilson, Trevor, *The Myriad Faces of War*, Bodley Head (1985).

Appendices

APPENDIX 1
MEDITERRANEAN EXPEDITIONARY FORCE ORDER OF BATTLE, AUGUST 1915

Commander in Chief: General Sir Ian Hamilton GCB
Chief of the General Staff: Major-General W. P. Braithwaite CB
Deputy Adjutant General: Brigadier-General E. M. Woodward
Deputy Quartermaster General: Major-General G. F. Ellison (from 07/08/15: General S. H. Winter)

VIII CORPS
GOC: Lieutenant-General Sir F. J. Davies KCB

29th Division (Major-General H. de B. de Lisle CB)

86th Brigade
2nd Royal Fusiliers; 1st Lancashire Fusiliers; 1st Royal Munster Fusiliers; 1st Royal Dublin Fusiliers

87th Brigade
2nd South Wales Borderers; 1st King's Own Scottish Borderers; 1st Royal Inniskilling Fusiliers; 1st The Border Regiment

88th Brigade
4th Worcestershire Regiment; 2nd Hampshire Regiment; 1st Essex Regiment; 1/5th Royal Scots

Divisional Troops
XV Brigade, Royal Horse Artillery; XVII Brigade, Royal Field Artillery; CXLVII Brigade, Royal Field Artillery; 460th (Howitzer) Battery, Royal Field Artillery; 90th Heavy Battery, Royal Garrison Artillery; 14th Siege Battery, Royal Garrison Artillery; 1/2nd London, 1/2nd Lowland and 1/1st West Riding Field Companies, Royal Engineers; Divisional Cyclist Company

42nd (East Lancs) Division (Major-General W. Douglas CB)

125th Brigade
1/5th, 1/6th, 1/7th and 1/8th Lancashire Fusiliers

126th Brigade
1/4th and 1/5th East Lancashire Regiment; 1/9th and 1/10th Manchester Regiment

127th Brigade
1/5th , 1/6th , 1/7th and 1/8th Manchester Regiment

Divisional Troops
1/1st, 1/2nd and 1/3rd East Lancs Brigades, Royal Field Artillery; 1/4th East Lancs (Howitzer) Brigade, Royal Field Artillery; 1/1st East Lancs, 1/2nd East Lancs and 1/2nd West Lancs Field Companies, Royal Engineers

52nd (Lowland) Division (Major-General G. G. A. Egerton CB)

155th Brigade
1/4th and 1/5th Royal Scots Fusiliers; 1/4th and 1/5th King's Own Scottish Borderers

156th Brigade
1/4th and 1/7th Royal Scots; 1/7th and 1/8th Scottish Rifles

157th Brigade
1/5th , 1/6th and 1/7th Highland Light Infantry; 1/5th Argyll & Sutherland Highlanders

Divisional Troops
1/2nd Lowland Brigade, Royal Field Artillery; 1/4th (Howitzer) Brigade, Royal Field Artillery; 2/1st and 2/2nd Lowland Field Companies, Royal Engineers; Divisional Cyclist Company

The Royal Naval Division (Major-General A. Paris CB)

1st Brigade
Drake Battalion; Nelson Battalion; Hawke Battalion; Hood Battalion

2nd Brigade
No 1 and No 2 Battalions, Royal Marine Light Infantry; Howe Battalion; Anson Battalion

Divisional Troops
1st, 2nd and 3rd Field Companies, Royal Engineers; Divisional Cyclist Company

IX CORPS

GOC: Lieutenant-General the Hon. Sir F. W. Stopford KCMG
Brig-Gen, General Staff: Brigadier-General H. L. Reed VC

Corps Troops
4th (Highland) Mountain Artillery Brigade (Argyllshire and Ross & Cromarty Batteries)

10th (Irish) Division (Lieutenant-General Sir B. T. Mahon KCVO)

29th Brigade
10th Hampshire Regiment; 6th Royal Irish Rifles; 5th Connaught Rangers; 6th Leinster
Regiment

30th Brigade
6th and 7th Royal Munster Fusiliers; 6th and 7th Royal Dublin Fusiliers

31st Brigade
5th and 6th Royal Inniskilling Fusiliers; 5th and 6th Royal Irish Fusiliers

Divisional Troops
5 Royal Irish Regiment (Pioneers); LIV, LV, LVI and LVII (Howitzer) Brigades, Royal
Field Artillery; 65th, 66th and 85th Field Companies, Royal Engineers; Divisional Cyclist
Company

11th (Northern) Division (Major-General F. Hammersley)

32nd Brigade
9th West Yorkshire Regiment; 6th Yorkshire Regiment; 8th West Riding Regiment; 6th
York & Lancaster Regiment

33rd Brigade
6th Lincolnshire Regiment; 6th The Border Regiment; 7th Staffordshire Regiment; 9th
Sherwood Foresters

34th Brigade
8th Northumberland Fusiliers; 9th Lancashire Fusiliers; 5th Dorsetshire Regiment; 11th
Manchester Regiment

Divisional Troops
6th East Yorkshire Regiment (Pioneers); LVIII, LIX and LX Brigades, Royal Field
Artillery; 67th, 68th and 86th Field Companies, Royal Engineers; Divisional Cyclist
Company

13th (Western) Division—temporarily attached to Australian & New Zealand Army Corps (Major-General F. C. Shaw CB)

38th Brigade
6th King's Own Regiment; 6th East Lancashire Regiment; 6th South Lancashire Regiment; 6th Loyal North Lancashire Regiment

39th Brigade
9th Royal Warwickshire Regiment; 7th Gloucester Regiment; 9th Worcestershire Regiment; 7th North Staffordshire Regiment

40th Brigade
4th South Wales Borderers; 8th Royal Welch Fusiliers; 8th Cheshire Regiment; 5th Wiltshire Regiment

Divisional Troops
8th Welch Regiment (Pioneers); LXVI, LXVII, LXVIII and LXIX (Howitzer) Brigades, Royal Field Artillery; 71st, 72nd and 88th Field Companies, Royal Engineers; Divisional Cyclist Company

53rd (Welsh) Division (Major-General the Hon. E. Lindley)

158th Brigade
1/5th, 1/6th and 1/7th Royal Welch Fusiliers; 1/1st Herefordshire Regiment

159th Brigade
1/4th and 1/7th Cheshire Regiment; 1/4th and 1/5th Welch Regiment

160th Brigade
2/4th Queen's (Royal West Surrey Regiment); 1/4th Royal Sussex Regiment; 2/4th Royal West Kent Regiment; 2/10th Middlesex Regiment

Divisional Troops
1/1st Welch and 2/1st Cheshire Field Companies, Royal Engineers; Divisional Cyclist Company

54th (East Anglian) Division (Major-General F. S. Inglefield CB)

161st Brigade
1/4th, 1/5th, 1/6th and 1/7th Essex Regiment

162nd Brigade
1/10th and 1/11th London Regiment; 1/5th Befordshire Regiment; 1/4th Northamptonshire Regiment

163rd Brigade
1/4th and 1/5th Norfolk Regiment; 1/5th Suffolk Regiment; 1/8th Hampshire Regiment

Divisional Troops
1/2nd and 2/1st East Anglian Field Companies, Royal Engineers; Divisional Cyclist Company

2nd Mounted Division (Major-General W. E. Peyton CB)

1st (South Midland) Brigade
1/1st Warwickshire Yeomanry; 1/1st Royal Gloucestershire Hussars; 1/1st Worcestershire Yeomanry

2nd (South Midland) Brigade
1/1st Royal Bucks Hussars; 1/1st Dorset Yeomanry, 1/1st Berkshire Yeomanry

3rd (Notts & Derbys) Brigade
1/1st Sherwood Rangers; 1/1st South Notts Hussars; 1/1st Derbyshire Yeomanry

4th (London) Brigade
1/1st and 1/3rd Country of London Yeomanry; 1/1st City of London Yeomanry

5th Brigade
1/1st Hertfordshire Yeomanry; 1/2nd County of London Yeomanry (Westminster Dragoons)

AUSTRALIAN & NEW ZEALAND ARMY CORPS
GOC: Lieutenant-General Sir William Birdwood KCSI
Brig-Gen, General Staff: Brigadier-General A. Skeen

GHQ Troops

20th Brigade, Royal Garrison Artillery
10th, 15th and 91st Heavy Batteries, RGA; 24th Brigade, RGA; 17th, 42nd and 43rd Siege Batteries, RGA

Armoured Car Division (Royal Naval Air Service)

3, 4, 9, 10, 11 and 12 Squadrons

1st Australian Division (Major-General H. B. Walker DSO)

1st Australian Brigade
1st, 2nd, 3rd and 4th (New South Wales) Battalions

2nd Australian Brigade
5th, 6th, 7th and 8th (Victoria) Battalions

3rd Australian Brigade
9th (Queensland), 10th (South Australia), 11th (Western Australia) and 12th (South and Western Australia and Tasmania) Battalions

Divisional Troops
I (NSW), II (Victoria) and III (Queensland, Western Australia and Tasmania) Field Artillery Brigades; 1st, 2nd and 3rd Field Companies, Australian Engineers; 4th (Victoria) Light Horse Regiment

New Zealand & Australian Division (Major-General Sir A. J. Godley KCMG)

New Zealand Brigade
Auckland, Canterbury, Wellington and Otago Battalions

4th Australian Brigade
13th (NSW), 14th (Victoria), 15th (Queensland and Tasmania) and 16th (South and Western Australia) Battalions; New Zealand Mounted Rifles Brigade (Dismounted); Auckland, Wellington and Canterbury Regiments of Mounted Rifles

1st Australian Light Horse Brigade (Dismounted)
1st (NSW), 2nd (Queensland) and 3rd (South Australia and Tasmania) Regiments

29th Indian Infantry Brigade
14th Sikhs; 1/5th, 1/6th and 2/10th Gurkha Rifles

Divisional Troops
Maori Detachment; I and II New Zealand Field Artillery Brigades; 1st and 2nd Field Companies, NZ-Engineers; NZ Field Troop Engineers; Otago Mounted Rifles (Dismounted)

2nd Australian Division (Major-General J. G. Legge)

5th Australian Brigade
17th, 18th, 19th and 20th (NSW) Battalions

6th Australian Brigade
21st, 22nd, 23rd and 24th (Victoria) Battalions

7th Australian Brigade
25th and 26th (Queensland) Battalions; 27th (South Australia) and 28th (Western Australia) Battalions

Divisional Troops

4th and 5th Field Companies, Australian Engineers; 13th (Victoria) Light Horse Regiment

Corps Troops
2nd Australian Light Horse Brigade
5th (Queensland), 6th (NSW) and 7th (NSW) Regiments

3rd Australian Light Horse Brigade
8th and 9th (Victoria) and 10th (Western Australia) Regiments

7th Indian Mountain Artillery Brigade

APPENDIX 2
UNITED NATIONS FORCES' ORDER OF BATTLE FOR OPERATION 'CHROMITE': THE LANDINGS AT INCHON, 15 SEPTEMBER 1950

JOINT TASK FORCE 7
(Vice-Admiral A. D. Struble USN)

(1) Naval Groups

Task Force 90: Attack Group (Rear-Admiral J. H. Doyle USN)

TG	Designation	Composition	Remarks
90.00	Flagship Element	2 AGC flagships	
90.01	Tactical Air Control Element	Tactical Air Squadron 1	
90.02	Naval Beach Group	HQ Beach Group, UDT, Beachmasters, etc	
90.03	Control Element	3 APD	
		1 amp control vessel	
90.04	Admin Element	1 hospital ship	
	Service Unit	12 LSUs	
90.04.2	Repair & Salvage Unit	3 ocean tugs	
		2 repair ships	
		3 LSDs	
		1 harbour tug	
90.1	Advance Attack Group		
90.11	Transport Element	1 LSD	Wolmi-Do Attack Force 3 LSUs embarked

90.11.1	Transport Unit	3 fast transports	
90.2	Transport Group	5 assault transports	Lift for 1st Marine Division
		8 assault cargo ships	
		1 transport	
		2 LSDs	
90.3	Tractor Group	47 LSTs	
		1 LSM	
90.4	Transport Div 14	3 assault transports	Lift for 7th Regimental Combat Team USMC and Marine Air Group
		3 assault cargo ships	
		2 LSDs	
90.5	Air Support Group		
90.51	CVE Element	2 CVEs	Marine Corps aircraft
90.52	CVE Screen	4 destroyers	
90.6	Gunfire Support Group		
90.61	Cruiser Element	2 heavy cruisers	
		2 light cruisers	British
90.62	Destroyer Element		
90.62.3	Fire Support Unit 2	3 destroyers	
90.62.3	Fire Support Unit 3	3 destroyers	
90.63	LSM(R) Element		
90.7	Screening and Protective Group	2 destroyers	
		8 frigates	
		7 minesweepers	
90.8	Second Echelon Movement Group	7 transports	
		12 freighters	Lift for 7th Infantry Division and X Corps troops
90.9	Third Echelon Movement Group	3 transports	Lift for 7th Infantry Division and X Corps troops
		13 freighters	

Task Force 91: Blockade and Covering Force (Rear-Admiral W. G. Andrews)

91.1	Northern Group		
91.11	Carrier Element	1 CVE	British
91.12	Support Element	1 light cruiser	British
91.13	Screen Element	5 destroyers	3 British, 2 Australian

91.14	Coastal Element	RoK vessels	Plus 1 destroyer on loan from TG.91.13
91.2	Southern Group		
91.21	Escort Element	3 destroyers	Canadian
91.22	Coastal Element	RoK vessels	Plus 1 destroyer on loan from TG.91.21

Republic of Korea (RoK) Forces (Commander M. J. Luosey USN)

4 submarine-chasers
11 motor minesweepers

Task Force 77 (Rear-Admiral E. C. Ewen USN)
Maintain air supremacy in objective area; provide air cover and support for assault landings

77	Fast Carrier Group	3 carriers
77.1	Support Group	2 light cruisers
77.2	Screen Group	14 destroyers

Task Force 79 – Service Squadron 3 (Captain B. L. Austin USN)
Provide refuelling, re-ammunitioning and repair facilities in the objective area

79.1	Mobile Logistic Service Group	2 oilers
		1 ammunition ship
		1 store ship
79.2	Objective Area Logistic Group	1 oiler
		1 cargo ship
		1 assault cargo carrier
		3 light cargo ships
79.3	Logistic Support Group	2 destroyers
		2 repair ships
		2 tankers
		2 assault cargo ships
		1 store ship
79.4	Salvage & Maintenance Group	1 ocean tug
		1 repair tug

Task Force 99—Patrol and Reconnaissance (Rear-Admiral G. R. Henderson)
Long range reconnaissance and air patrols covering whole area of operations

99		3 seaplane tenders
99.1	Search & Reconnaissance Group	
99.11		Patrol Squadron 6

| 99.12 | | No 88 Squadron RAF |
| 99.13 | | No 209 Squadron RAF |

99.2	Patrol & Escort Group	
99.21		Patrol Squadron 42
99.22		Patrol Squadron 47

(II) Military Groups

Task Force 92.1—1st US Marine Division (Major-General O. P. Smith USMC)

92.1	Assault Landing Force, 1st Marine Division	
92.10	HQ Signals, Medical Ordnance, MT etc	
92.11	1st Marine Regiment	3 battalions
92.12	5th Marine Regiment	3 battalions
92.12.3	3/5th Marines	Assigned to Wolmi-Do attack force
92.13	17th RoK Infantry Regiment	3 battalions
92.14	Artillery Group, 11th Marines	
92.15	Shore Party	Beach parties, engineers, etc
92.16	Amphibian Group, LVTs	
92.017	Tank Battalion	
92.18	Vehicle Maintenance Unit	
92.19	Engineers	

Task Force 92.2—Follow-Up Troops (Major-General E. A. Almond US Army)

| 92.1 | 7th Infantry Division X Corps Troops | |

APPENDIX 3
BRITISH LAND FORCES COMMITTED TO THE RECOVERY OF THE FALKLAND ISLANDS, OPERATION 'CORPORATE'

3 Commando Brigade Royal Marines (Brigadier Julian Thompson)
40 Commando, Royal Marines
42 Commando, Royal Marines
45 Commando, Royal Marines
29 (Commando) Regiment, Royal Artillery

148 (Commando) Field Observation Battery, Royal Artillery
59 Independent Commando Squadron, Royal Engineers
Commando Logistic Regiment, Royal Engineers
3 Commando Brigade HQ & Signals Squadron, Royal Marines
3 Commando Brigade Air Squadron
1 Raiding Squadron, Royal Marines
2, 4 and 6 Sections, Special Boat Squadron, Royal Marines
Mountain & Arctic Warfare Cadre, Royal Marines
845 and 846 Naval Air Squadrons, Fleet Air Arm
'Y' Troop, Royal Marine Signals
SATCOM Detachment, Royal Signals
49 Explosive Device Squadron, Royal Engineers
Surgical Support Team, Royal Navy
Commando Forces Band, Royal Marines
Commando Forces News Team

Army Units attached to 3 Commando Brigade for 'Corporate'
2nd Battalion The Parachute Regiment
3rd Battalion The Parachute Regiment
Medium Recce Troop, 'B' Squadron, Blues and Royals
'T' Battery, 12 Air Defence Regiment, Royal Artillery
FOO Parties, 4 Field Regiment, Royal Artillery
RLD, 30 Signals Regiment, Royal Corps of Signals
Section, 19 Field Ambulance, Royal Army Medical Corps.

5 Infantry Brigade (Brigadier Tony Wilson)
2nd Battalion The Scots Guards
1st Battalion The Welsh Guards
1st Battalion, 7th Gurkha Rifles
4 Field Regiment, Royal Artillery
2 Ttroops of 32 Guided Weapons Regiment, Royal Artillery
FOO Parties, 49 Field Regiment, Royal Artillery
Royal School of Artillery Support Regiment
36 Engineer Regiment, Royal Engineers
9 Parachute Squadron, Royal Engineers
Detachment from 2 Port Control Regiment, Royal Engineers
656 Squadron, Army Air Corps
407 Transport Troop, Royal Corps of Transport
Elements of 17 Port Regiment, Royal Corps of Transport
16 Field Ambulance, Royal Army Medical Corps
81 Ordnance Company, Royal Army Ordnance Corps
Laundry/Bakery Detachment, 9 Ordnance Battalion, Royal Army Ordnance Corps
Elements of 421 EOD Company, Royal Army Ordnance Corps/Royal Engineers
10 Forward Workshop, REME
160 Provost Company, Royal Military Police
6 Field Cash Office, Royal Army Pay Corps
PR Detachment

Force Troops
Army Elements HQ, LFFI
12 Air Defence Regiment, Royal Artillery
21 Air Defence Battery, 27 Field Regiment, Royal Artillery
11 Squadron, 38 Engineer Regiment, Royal Engineers
EOD Detachment, 33 Engineer Regiment, Royal Engineers
Elements Military Work Force, Royal Pioneer Corps
Detachment, 11 Ordnance Battalion, Royal Army Ordnance Corps
Detachments from 14 and 30 Signals Regiments, Royal Corps of Signals
'D' Squadron plus other elements, 22 SAS Regiment
172 Intelligence and Security Section, Intelligence Corps
Elements Joint Helicopter Servicing Unit, RAF
29 Movement Regiment RE/RCT

Troops on Ascension Island
Elements of 22 and 38 Engineer Regiments, RE
Elements of Mil Works Force, RPC
Detachment 2 PC Regiment, RE
Detachment 30 Signals Regiment, RSigs
47 Air Despatch Squadron, RCT
Detachment 4 Petrol Depot, RAOC
Miscellaneous RAOC, AAC, RAF Regiment

Select Bibliography

BOOKS

Admiralty, *British Commonwealth Naval Operations in Korea 1950–1953* (1967)

Appleman, Lt. Col. R. E., *South to the Natkong—North to the Yalu*, US Government Printing Office (1961)

Aspinall-Oglander, Brig. Gen. C. F., *History of the Great War: Military Operations, Gallipoli*, 2 vols, Heinemann (1929 and 1932)

Bartlett, Lt. Col. A., (ed.), *Amphibious Warfare*, USNI (1984)

Blair, C., *The Forgotten War: America in Korea, 1950–53*, Times Books

Brown, J. D., *The Royal Navy and the Falklands War*, Leo Cooper (1987)

Bush, Capt. E. W., *Gallipoli*, George Allen & Unwin (1975)

Buxton, Ian, *Big Gun Monitors*, USNI (1984)

Cagle, Cdr. M. W., *The Sea War in Korea*, USNI (1957)

Corbett, Sir Julian, *History of the Great War Based on Official Documents: Naval Operations*, Vol. II, Longmans, Green (1921)

———, *England in the Seven Years' War*, 2 vols, Greenhill Books (1992)

Davis, B., *Marine! The Life of Chesty Puller*, Little, Brown (1962)

Ethell, J., and Price, A., *Air War South Atlantic*, Sidgwick & Jackson (1983)

Evans, M., *Amphibious Operations: The Projection of Seapower Ashore*, Brasseys (1990)

Field, J. A., *History of US Naval Operations: Korea*, US Government Printing Office (1962)

Gillam, Maj. J., *Gallipoli Diary*, Unwin & Co (1919)

Grove, Eric, *Vanguard to Trident: British Naval Policy since World War 2*, Bodley Head (1987)

Halpern, Paul, *The Naval War in the Mediterranean*, Allen & Unwin (1987)

Hamilton, Gen. Sir Ian, *Gallipoli Diary*, Edward Arnold (1920)

Hastings, Max, *The Korean War*, Michael Joseph (1985)

Hastings, Max, and Jenkins, Simon, *The Battle for the Falklands*, Michael Joseph (1983)

Heinl, R. D., *Victory at High Tide: The Inchon Seoul Campaign*, Leo Cooper (1972)

James, Robert Rhodes, *Gallipoli*, Batsford (1965)

Jolly, R., *The Red and Green Life Machine*, Century (1983)

Laughton, J. K. (ed.), *Letters and Papers of Charles Lord Barham*, Vol. 38, Navy Records Society (1910)

MacArthur, Gen. of the Army D., *Reminiscences*, McGraw Hill (1964)

MacIntire, John, *A Military Treatise on the Discipline of the Marine Forces, when at Sea, Together with Short Instructions for Detachments Sent to Attack on Shore* (1763)

Middlebrook, M., *The Fight for the Malvinas*, Viking Books (1989)

Montoss, Lynn, and Canzona, Capt. N. A., *The Inchon Seoul Operation. Vol. II: US Marine Operations in Korea*, US Government Printing Office (1955)

Moorehead, Alan, *Gallipoli*, Hamish Hamilton (1956)

Rees, D., *Korea: The Limited War*, St Martin's Press (1964)

Southby-Tailyour, E., *Reasons in Writing: A Commando's View of the Falklands War*, Leo Cooper (1993).

Steel, N., *The Battlefields of Gallipoli*, Leo Cooper (1989)

Steel, N., and Hart, P., *Defeat at Gallipoli*, Macmillan (1994)

Still, John, *A Prisoner in Turkey*, Bodley Head (1924)

Thompson, J., *No Picnic*, Leo Cooper (1985)

Vaux, N., *March to the South Atlantic*, Buchan & Enright (1986)

Villar, Robert, *Merchant Ships at War: The Falklands Experience*, Conway Maritime Press (1984)

Ward, Cdr. N., *A Maverick at War: Sea Harrier over the Falklands*, Leo Cooper (1992)

Warner, Philip, *With Wolfe to Quebec*, Phoebus (1974)

Woodward, Admiral Sir John, *One Hundred Days: The Memoirs of the Falklands Battle Group Commander*, HarperCollins (1992)

JOURNALS

The Globe & Laurel; *The Naval Review*; US Naval Institute *Proceedings*

Index

Cassell Military Classics are available from all good bookshops
or from:

Cassell C.S.
Book Service By Post
PO Box 29, Douglas I-O-M
IM99 1BQ
telephone: 01624 675137, fax: 01624 670923

040-964-01